SETTING PARENTS FREE

*How to give your kids what they need,
and where to run when you drop the ball.*

DR. JOHN L. COX

Printed in the United States of America

Cover art © 2019 John Cox

ISBN: 978-0-578-58575-8

LifeStory Publishing
109 North State Street
Jackson, Mississippi 39202
601-594-0018

Spirituality. Devotional. Instructional. Family. Children.

To Callie, Katherine, and Bonney,
who taught me I could be a lousy parent,
and then loved me anyway.

One day when our kids were small, they caught a ride home from soccer practice with a friend's mom. As they got in her car, the mom confessed that this was her husband's car and that it had a five-speed transmission. As she ground the gears and jerked into traffic the mom said, "Sorry—I'm not very good at this." One of my daughters replied, "Well, are you good enough?"

Acknowledgements

The first person I want to thank is Dr. Bruce Narramore. Bruce started Rosemead School of Psychology in 1968 while still a young man. He was my Major Professor, favorite teacher, and introduced me to the world of doing depth therapy. Bruce was also the first person who taught me about teaching parents about parenting. When he spoke at venues around Los Angeles, he would sometimes let me tag along in order to learn. Bruce wrote some fantastic parenting books during that season, such as *Help, I'm a Parent, Parenting with Love and Limits,* and *Why Children Misbehave.* My considering myself someone who could speak to parents began with his teaching. Thank you, Bruce, for the countless people who continue to give into the lives of others because of you. There's no way to fathom the impact that Rosemead and its graduates have had on our country and across the world. I hope this book will further honor your vision. *Il miglior fabbro.*

I also want to express my gratitude to the late Dr. Phil Sutherland. Phil's wisdom, humor, humility, and acute knowledge of the soul made him one of the best therapists in Los Angeles. I am grateful to have been a deep recipient of his heart.

There is no way to overestimate the power and ministry of Janie Pillow. She was my therapist and mentor as I moved back to Mississippi. Not only did she help me find my core grounding as a man and a professional, she taught me ways of thinking about therapy and growth that were initially so far above my head that I could barely grasp them. So much of my heart that you will read in this book, as well as my understanding of human growth, was given to me by her. She is a reflection of her Savior, and a mighty tool for the Kingdom of God. And no one loves and cares for children like she.

Joe Maxwell is the locomotive that has enabled this book to be published. A lifelong friend and a master writer and publisher, he has helped bring my heart and thoughts to reality—and kept my writing at least between the white lines.

I want to thank Leigh Lucas, my office manager, for her patient listening ear as this book evolved, as well as her feedback as a "test subject" parent, and for just being a really wise person.

Of course, I thank my own parents. Not only did they lovingly raise my siblings and me, but I have watched them continue to grow as people, becoming wiser, freer, and more loving. They also paid for my education.

No parenting book would be complete without my humbly kissing the ring of my loyal, patient co-parent Norma. Part of the fun of writing this book has been remembering together the cockamamie things that our kids did, as well as the joys, sacrifices, and conflicts that we experienced while trying to help them become "strong loving women who could live in the 21st-century." I think we did Good Enough, Babe.

Preface

I am a clinical psychologist, and I basically do what you think I would do. I have a couch and a pipe and a sweater—I do therapy all day long. Mostly with adults—you know, depression, anxiety, marital problems, etc. That's my job.

Then we had kids. There's an old quote that says something like, "I used to have three theories and no children, now I have three children and no theories." (Now, Norma and I are empty nesters. In other words, we have no children and three student loans!) So these days, I'm like that classic definition of a "parenting expert"—someone who has just gotten too old to remember how hard it was.

Anyway, since I've always been primarily a therapist to adults, my interest in how to parent originally emerged out of personal survival, not professional interest. All of a sudden, we had kids and I was surrounded by these little grub worms. I didn't know what I was doing.

So I said, "Come on, Cox, you're a shrink—Figure it out!"

Subsequently, with the help of a smart wife and three children who gave me a lot of material, I found myself learning about parenting. My kids, of course, always found it profoundly amusing that I was later considered a "parenting expert." I mean, can you imagine? I asked them once as they got older if they would like to attend one of my parenting conferences. They replied, "No Dad, we don't want to ruin your reputation."

Soon I was doing more therapy work with kids at the office, and then actually speaking on the topic. Over time, however, my office work with kids became more and more focused on working with the *parents* rather than the children. I found that if I could get a couple of parents on my "treatment team," we could do more in the life of a child than countless play therapy sessions. And more and more I began to love teaching parents.

As years went on, I began thinking about writing a book. I asked psychologist Henry Cloud once for his thoughts about writing. I'd known him and John Townsend from our Rosemead School connections in California.

Henry told me, "First off, John, don't write a book if you want to make money." I asked him if he was telling me this from Pelican Hill golf course in Orange County (to which he responded in an appropriately sneering manner). He went on to say that he would not recommend I write a book unless I felt like I had something very important that I wanted "out there."

Recently some planets aligned, and I found my "out there" calling—a book on parenting. Maybe I'll write about marriage or relational growth one day, but for now, if I have the chance to put my ideas out into the universe, my first longing would be to speak into the lives of our little people, the most vulnerable of us all.

Way back in 1979 I had discovered psychology, and at the same time I began to more deeply reach for and understand my relationship with God. My professional goal was to become the best clinical psychologist I could be—but I wanted to learn how to do that within the context of my faith. For the last thirty years that is what I have done. I have worked to help people, spiritual or not, with depression, anxiety, OCD, porn addiction, marriage problems, etc.—and, of course, problems with their children.

This book will mirror that same kind of open door policy. This is a book for parents—every faith, creed, and color. My own spiritual heart will necessarily be a part of our discussions, because that is who I am. But whether you have a faith life or not, we can all learn together about loving kids well—my goal today is simply for you to have a richer more life-giving family. And I also know about thirty years of stuff as a parent and as a shrink regarding how to do that.

By the way, if you *are* interested in how God can speak into families, and if you want that for your kids, then we're gonna turn that stuff up to '11'! After all, he's got like seven billion bad kids. I think he gets it.

Regarding this book, one of the reasons that I delayed in writing was that for years, I found that I was constantly changing and learning from my clients or my audiences. Just when I thought I had a good model for marriage, parenting, or spirituality, someone would ask a question and turn my whole thinking upside down—in a good way. This book is a snapshot of where my heart and my mind are now. Hopefully within a couple years I will cringe at some of the things I have said, because I hope to be continuing to learn.

The content of this book is also the fruit of my own parenting, years of being a therapist to both adults and children, and experiences I've had while doing conferences. As you read, you'll also encounter countless randomly gathered ideas and categories, turns of phrases, and quotes from innumerable sources—movies, speakers, book authors, comedians. I've forgotten where I've gotten many of these ideas—they just live in the gumbo of my brain. So, though I will try to footnote and acknowledge their sources, I fear I will consistently fail. But, dear reader, know that I am the recipient of many gifts from many people, and I hope to pass them on to you. And to those of you who have given me categories, perspectives, theories, quotes, and even personal healing, I hope to acknowledge you, but if I somehow misstep, at least know that I thank you deeply. JLC

Table of Contents

Parenting is tough.

— Kate Middleton

Introduction

We're all in this together

A couple of parents approached me during the break at one of my conferences. "We had to tell you this," they chattered. "As we were leaving the house, our teenage daughter walked through the kitchen and said, 'Oh my gosh. Like, where are you guys going?' 'To a parenting conference,' we replied. She looked at us with that classic teenage look of disgust and said, 'Good!'"

I love parents. I don't care where I'm speaking around the country—over and over again, CEOs, school teachers, mothers who daylight as corporate attorneys, artists, pastors, and cardiologists, all come up to me. They've taken a Friday night and a Saturday morning out of their lives to learn about their kids. They stand in line or raise their hands with eager eyes, hoping maybe I can bring some clarity to a problem that they have with their children. (And if the Duchess of Cambridge would like any help, I'll do my best to work her toward the front of the line.)

It's hard being a parent

If you think about this parenting task, it's actually kind of weird. In our culture, you can get training on just about any subject in the world. Click on YouTube and you can learn how to change the washer in your faucet. You can go to weekend seminars on how to better use Keynote—but we receive no real formal training in this incredibly important task of raising little humans. *Parents feel uninformed.*

Most parents just parent on the fly. We don't think about what we're doing or have any real sense of being strategic. We just go with our gut. Maybe we parent the way we were parented—or the opposite! Maybe we parent out of our *emotions*, "Oh my gosh, I can't stand to see her struggle! Let's swoop in and rescue her!"

Regardless, I see parents just frantically reacting to the situations their kids create! And most parents *know* that they are this lost! We feel impossibly outgunned by this incessant, challenging, fluid, high-stakes tennis game of parenting. *Parents feel ill-equipped.*

Furthermore, most parents feel like they are constantly "returning serve" in this tennis game. We live responding or reacting to what this child might throw at us next. I encountered some parents recently whose three-year-old had just decided he no longer liked eating! What's up with that? I read the other day about a couple of siblings. The little sister ran to her mom, tattling, "BJ is stealing my air!" The mother went back to find out what the hullabaloo was about, and she found BJ grabbing fists of air and screaming, "Mine! Mine!" I was told about another little girl who started crying because her "drink was too wet."

This is the kind of stuff we are dealing with!

Parents tell me, "We can't ask our boys to do anything without them turning it into a competition." "Veronica, the teenager, stopped acknowledging us months ago, and now just disappears into her room." "My four-year-old has a limp-legged meltdown every time he doesn't get his way. What do we do, Doc?" I had a parent tell me just today, "I love my kids, but I get overwhelmed with the millions of decisions that parenting requires. It's just constant! And they are making up new problems faster than I can figure out the solutions to the old ones!" (Personally, I was always an expert on the developmental stage my kids just *completed!*) *Parents feel overwhelmed!*

Lastly, parents feel *guilty and afraid.* Today's parents often feel like they need to parent *perfectly.* We need to be at every ball game. We need to make sure our kids get in the right school with the right friends (beginning with pre-school). And, oh yeah, we need to protect our kids from all harm and make sure they feel loved every day while we're at it!

So let's take a look at this situation so far, shall we?

We parents aren't free. We live feeling ill-equipped, overwhelmed, full of questions, guilty and afraid! For real? That's a walkin' talkin' reason to rehabilitate if you ask me! Our culture has turned being a parent into something that can feel burdensome. It's no longer just a "family of four" living life together; it's a pressure-packed performance that you have to do perfectly or else! Yuck! Somebody ought to write a book and throw these poor guys a bone!

You're in luck. This is not just a book about parenting. This is a book for you, the parents. Let's take care of you for a change.

Let's get free

In order to "set parents free," I want to give you two simple things. I want to tell you how to best care for your kids, and then I want to teach you how to handle it when you become "screwball parent of the year" and mess it all up. These will be our building blocks for parenting freedom.

The first thing that parents need in order to feel free and to enjoy raising their kids is to know that their children are *getting what they need to thrive*. Otherwise we're going to worry about them, right? And that's not freedom! So I want this book to help teach you what your kids need in order to grow up whole and happy—how you can give good things to their lives and hearts. I want you to finish this book feeling more competent, heads-up, and aware about how to care for your kids. The freedom to enjoy being a parent partially comes from knowing what you're doing.

Now if you are like me, we can't stop there. If all we did in this book was talk about what your kids need to grow up happy, healthy, and groovy, you still aren't free. You just have a new set of rules to follow—a new standard to live up to!

So, secondly, we are also going to have to talk about how to handle it when you *screw it all up. Fall on your face. Fail.*

Because you will. And I don't want that to be something that frightens you.

In other words, I want to teach you how to give to your kids, and then teach you how to handle it when you goof it up. In fact, I want to talk about how we can handle our mistakes in such a way that not only will keep our screwups from damaging our kids, but might also actually *help them out!* Regular ole humans actually make pretty good parents—once we get set free.

So let's look at how to give our kids what they need, and, then how to handle it when we drop the ball!

How do we give to our kids?

If you think about it, kids come to the table without much to offer. I mean, when they are first delivered as infants, they don't bring much to the party. There's basically just something going in, or coming out of, one end of them or the other— all the time. And somewhere between then and college commencement, they (hopefully) have learned enough about love, wisdom, relationships (and how to clean their room) that they can function in the world.

So what happened? No magic voodoo. Someone just *parented* them.

When I was a graduate student, I worked for a while in the L.A. school system. One afternoon, I witnessed two boys fighting on the playground. In the midst of the fray, a little girl ran up to me, desperate—"Quick, Dr. Cox! Use your psychology on them!" I wasn't sure whether to assume the "palm-out Iron Man pose" or not. As much as you probably deserve to be a superhero, there's no psychological superpower when it comes to dealing with kids. They just need teaching, loving, guidance, and support. They need us to teach them the heart and the skills to do life. Napoleon Dynamite understood this. "Hey Pedro, you've got skills!"

So freedom step one is, I want to teach you how to give to your kids. I want you to know what they need, and what they don't need, so you can relax. Freedom comes when we have the confidence to know that we are doing our job and that our kids' hearts are getting filled up.

I'm going to guide you through how to give to your kids by asking *seven questions* that parents often ask me. These questions will serve as the chapters on our journey.

Chapter 1   Am I screwing up my kids?
Chapter 2   How do I help my kids know that they are loved?
Chapter 3   How do I get my kids to do what I say?

Now, at this point our kids are going to respond with an issue of their own! Since they've all seen Harry Potter, and since their question fits somewhere between chapters 3 and chapter 4 we're gonna call it –
Chapter 3 ¾.

Chapter 3 ¾ But what if I don't want to do what you say?

So we're going to respond to their question too! That's only fair, right? Then we parents get to keep asking questions.

Chapter 4   How do I help my kids learn to be strong?
Chapter 5   How do I help my kids deal with pain in life?
Chapter 6   How do I teach good values to my kids?
Chapter 7   How do I teach my kids about God?

I believe these seven questions (plus one objection from our snarky kids) capture the ingredients that kids need for life—what kids need in order to develop the emotional/spiritual/functional "software package" that will set them up to be rocket-hot and ready to go for life in the world! (And also, to keep bath time from becoming another dumpster fire.)

Also, you will find that different kids will need emphasis in different areas of growth. So, we are going to also use these categories and questions as a guide to help you spot your children's "blindspots." You probably have one child who came out of the womb always oriented toward love and nurture—"Cuddly Carla." However, those same kids often struggle with the difficulties of life—bullies, disappointments and conflict. She might need more help later from the "building strength" chapter. On the other hand, your next child is little Napoleon, wanting to rule your home like the Ottoman Empire. His blindspot is submission and obedience, so you'd better study up on that chapter! Different kids will need different emphases. Our chapters and categories will help you sort that out and better "make the call" on those parenting conundrums.

So, we are going to start freeing you by giving you clear, strong, and hopefully fun, answers to the questions regarding what your kids need. I want you feeling confident.

Sometimes, however, you will miss by a mile.

What do we do when we screw up?

I imagine that you want to be an amazing parent. Well, every party needs a pooper, that's why you invited me. *You Won't Be!*

That's right, you heard it here, folks. You're going to be as bad of a parent as I was. So, our second way to set you free has got to be about having room to fail—an alternative to the "what if I mess them up?" anxiety that makes us all crazy.

Here's our new hope. *What if we don't need to be amazing?*

What if our kids don't need "perfect" parents? What if all they really need is for us to be regular ole people just like them? What if all this pressure we put on ourselves to be "practically perfect in every way" is actually counterproductive? I mean, usually when humans are under a ton of pressure, they perform *worse*, right?

"But, how can we be free to fail our kids?" you exclaim. "How dare we not be amazing parents? Don't our kids deserve better than that? Doesn't letting go of the pressure mean I'm settling for being a slacker parent?" (No—but you get points for dramatic presentation.)

To be honest with you, I don't think that I was that great of a parent. And I think my children would agree. Like many of you, I looked inside and saw what an empty tank I often had. I wondered how was I supposed to teach good things to my kids when I barely possessed those things myself? Our kids turned out to be pretty cool people (which was one of our goals). They all have jobs and none of them live at home! (Each of which, I think, qualifies me to write a parenting book!) But Norma and I were not perfect parents. I'm thinking that you guys reading this book probably feel the same way. Let's start a club. *The Screwed-Up Parents Club!* And the first rule of The Screwed-Up Parents Club is that we *have* to talk about The Screwed-Up Parents Club!

Let's ask the question this way: What if you being *you* is enough?

What if parents having the freedom to just be humans with their kids—working together to help everyone grow—is what our kids really need in the first place? What if they don't need "perfect parenting" out of a "perfect parenting" manual? What if they just need *you*? What if being a goofball parent is okay? In fact, what if having imperfect parents is actually *better* for our kids? I believe it is. And we are going to talk about how.

This is not a manual

So we are going to talk about how to richly give to our kids, and then we are going to talk about how to handle it when we fail. If you think about it, that's the way God talks to us. In his word, he talks to us about the ways that lead to life, and then he tells us where to run when we mess it all up. We're just going to apply the same principle to our parenting.

This book is not going to be just a "how-to" manual on parenting. What I really want to do is to help create a "heart" for your family—a vibe for making your family a haven for loving, broken, growing people to be together, to learn together. I want to help set you free.

If this is a "manual," it's a manual for how to be *you*, as a parent. I don't want to just give you parenting advice. I want to help make parenting something that is fun and natural for you—something that reflects the heart of God, as well as your heart and your child's. I want you to feel free in your parenting. So, walk with me. Learn alongside of me. Parent along side of me. Fail along side of me. And let's talk about how to create something great with our kids!

Anything worth doing is worth doing poorly.

— **Phil Sutherland Ph.D**

Chapter One

Am I screwing up my kids?

Parents need a break

The other day I googled the term "child friendly." I got almost two *billion* hits. Then I googled "parent friendly"—I found a measly half million. Need I say more? Our contemporary culture is tough on parents. It is distressing to me the amount of pressure that is put on parents—and how much pressure they put on themselves. So, before we get started helping our kids, let's have a little "Mommy and Daddy time." I want to take care of you guys first. Besides, "in the event of rapid cabin depressurization, parents traveling with small children, please place the oxygen mask on yourself first before assisting your child and other passengers." Let's get you an oxygen mask and help you get free.

The first step in getting free is knowing that *it is safe to fail.*

My oldest daughter, Callie, is a therapist in Nashville. One weekend I was doing a parenting conference in North Carolina. The same weekend Callie was speaking to a group of mothers of teenagers. After the weekend, I called her and said, "Well, my conference went well. How did your conference go?"

She replied exasperated, "Oh my gosh! Parents are *so* anxious! They are afraid all the time that they're going to do something wrong and screw up their kids!" Then she added, "At one point, one mother's anxious question just pushed me over the edge, and I said to them all, 'Look! My dad is currently being paid "too much money" to speak on parenting in North Carolina! He is and always has been considered a "parenting expert." And I know that he and my mom both tried to parent us with all their hearts and souls. And get this—I *still* needed therapy! Okay? So let it go!'"

The ladies of course got the "joke" and laughed! Which reminds me of one mom who told me, "Yeah, I think we're just gonna give up trying to parent well and instead start a trust fund for our kids to go to therapy one day!" Another told me that she had taken up pottery. That way, when living with her kids sent her to the mental institution, she would already have her craft!

This is where most parents exist! We live in an age of what I call "Psychological Legalism." Since our culture has lost a lot of its moral foundation, the new morality is psychological—emotional. Think about it. The biggest taboo in our culture is doing anything to hurt anyone's feelings or being "insensitive." And if you commit such a crime, you are pilloried in the public square! It's the new puritanism.

In the parenting realm, this means that today's parents live terrified of screwing up our kids. We're afraid for our children to suffer any pain, fearing that pain will harm them in some way. We're afraid of parenting poorly and our children turning out to be dysfunctional, codependent, or insecure. Then that child is going to resent us for their horrible childhood and probably write a tell-all book, unveiling all of their family trauma—which will later become a Lifetime Movie called something like *Family of Fear!,* starring Lindsay Wagner as YOU!

Parents need to be set free.

This reminds me of the mother who told me that she had walked into her living room one evening and caught her two-year-old urinating on her new rug. (He had escaped from bath-time preparations and apparently needed a pit stop.) Seeing him, she screamed so loudly that it scared him. He ran to the bathroom crying—and then proceeded to sit in the bath, inconsolable, wailing "I tee-teed! I tee-teed!" lamenting his possibly unforgivable sin. Her question to me? "Have I screwed him up for life? Is he going to have some kind of weird 'urinary neurosis' one day?"

See what I mean? Too much pressure!

We parents can even put more pressure on *each other!* You know those "know it all" parents—the ones who are always announcing their expertise in a superior tone? "Oh, you think it's hard with just one—just wait 'til that second one comes along." Or, "Enjoy these years now, it only gets harder!" Then there are the "Mommy Shamers" on Facebook—"You shouldn't have your child in a car seat like that yet—he's too small!"

Something in these people needs to take all of their anxiety and spray it on us like that bug man who squirts insecticide along your baseboards. What is up with these people? Parents need more freedom and comfort, not more high stakes fear—especially from one another.

Personally, I never really liked going to parenting conferences or reading parenting books. The reason was because I always came away from them with the same sort of feeling I had after visiting my financial advisor. He would say things like, "No problem. All you guys gotta do is start putting aside another two- or three-thousand dollars a month, and you'll be fine!" Thanks a lot, pal!

In other words, I left feeling more overwhelmed, not helped! I didn't feel set free; I felt avalanched with more demands.

So, point number one as we kick this parenting book into gear—*I do not want you coming away from this book feeling more burdened!* ("Awesome! He gave us seven bullet points on how we are screwing up our kids! Thanks a lot, Doc!") Even though I'll be giving you a lot of pointers about how to love your kids well, this *is not* a book about how to parent *better!* This is a book to help you create something wonderful with your kids. And if you are anything like me, that's gonna have to take into account the fact that we are all knuckle-headed, screwed-up, fallen parents! If the solution to having great kids is that we have to be perfect, then adios muchachos! Nobody is going to have a happy day.

So, what's the alternative?

Relationship not rules

Here's the secret: Good parenting is not a task, a performance that you execute better or worse. Good parenting is a *relationship*! (Albeit a relationship with people who take your money, and throw up on you, and tell you you are unfair all the time, but a relationship nonetheless.)

Now, think about it, what do we do in relationships when we screw up? What do we do with a good friend? What do we do in our marriages when we hurt our spouse? How do we manage our blunders in relationships?

We swing back in! We repair it! We talk to the person about our mistakes and we heal it. We restore!

Let's just do the same thing with our kids!

What does this sound like?

For an example, let's look at the life of a somewhat incompetent parent—me. One of the places that Norma and I both struggled with parenting was in the realm of getting our children to stay in their rooms and sleep. (Notice there is no section in this book about helping your children "stay in their rooms and sleep.")

Anyway, one night the kids seemed committed to another glass of water/gotta go to the bathroom/I'm afraid I won't be able to go to sleep. Pick a card, any card. I finally just lost it and shouted at them, "I am so sick of this! It's 10 p.m. and this place feels like a girls' dorm! Get back in your rooms, and I don't want to hear another word out of any of you!"

Now, I haven't mentioned this yet, but we had three girls.

And I don't want to go too fast for you, but if you yell at three little girls at 10 p.m., the result is lots and lots of tears! Pretty soon, the sleepless household was now a house of mourning—a tearful, screaming, sleepless household. Good job, Dr. Cox!

Norma looked at me with those "wife eyes." You know the ones I mean. Those eyes your wife gives you when she is wanting to communicate, "Well, that helped a whole lot, Dimwit!"

Immediately realizing that I had lost control and made a bad night even worse, I gathered the kids to me and said, "I'm sorry girls. That was really not okay. We really need you guys to go to sleep, but there's no excuse for me to yell at you."

I just repaired. That's all I'm talking about.

And this isn't just about your mistakes. It can also be about your limitations. A friend of mine had all good intentions of attending his son's last baseball game. However, work and reality overruled, and he never made it to the ball fields. By the time he got home, his son seemed mopey and sad. His wife said, "Honey, he was so disappointed that you didn't make his game."

Now, if you're like me, it's so tempting at this point to make excuses or be defensive. "Come on! I'm doing my best to support this family!" Or lots of us try to make it all better—"I promise to take you to get ice cream." This dad just *owned* it. He sat down next to his son and said, "Hey buddy, I really understand that it felt terrible that I missed your game. You want to talk about it?"

So here's our starting point. It's okay for you to let your kids down. Just repair it! Let's relax and be *people* here!

Basic parenting principle: *A good parent learns to become comfortable with their own limitations, and helps their child learn to become comfortable with the parent's limitations as well.*

Not only does this make room for you to not have to be perfect, it also teaches your children about real life relationships. Just think how ill-equipped for life your kids would be if you were always perfect! When our kids see us manage our own failure with poise and kindness, it teaches them *experientially* what grace looks like—grace that says our love for each other trumps the ways in which we fail. Our children need that freedom, and for goodness sake, we parents do too. So as we let our children down and repair it, we are teaching them how to be broken, fallen people in relationship with others, and even with God.

It also creates funny, delightful encounters. One mother told me that she had been having an especially difficult day. She had made that deadly mistake of flipping through family photographs and having the terrible realization (you know the one) where you see how much weight you gained. (I remember thinking once, "Who's that fat guy in the picture?")

Anyway, this mother (who this morning had suddenly developed a very negative "body image") was now in a bad mood. Things soon went awry with her four-year-old daughter, and the mom snapped, responding harshly and unkindly to her child. Remembering this principle of repairing, she quickly swung back in and told her little girl, "Honey, I'm so sorry. I was really unkind to you. Mommy doesn't mean to be mean this morning. To be honest, I just looked at a picture of me, and I feel fat—and I think I took my bad mood out on you." Her empathetic, forgiving four-year-old looked up at her and replied, "That's okay mommy. It's all right if you're fat."

One day I was in the car alone with the girls. By this time, they were probably ten, seven, and four. I had botched something regarding parenting, and we were discussing it as I drove. I acknowledged that I had not handled a certain situation very well, but then I foolishly continued. I added, "Yeah, ya gotta kinda work with me here. This is the first time that I've ever been a dad, and I'm sort of learning as I go."

Callie, the oldest, piped up from the back and said, "Well, is there like a book you can read?"

The second oldest joined in and added, "Yeah ... or maybe like a class you can take or something?"

I dared not broach the subject that parents actually take classes from *me* on parenting well. Why make a ridiculous situation even more ridiculous?

So here's our bottom line. Loving our kids is really no different from loving anyone else. When we screw up in our relationships, we swing back in and repair it. And that's what we can do in our parenting as well.

This is how God relates to us. God tells us about the most life-giving ways to live—how we "ought to" act. But if he left it at that, then "which of us could stand?" We all mess it up all the time! The only way a relationship with God works (and he figured this out) is if there is some way for our fallenness and brokenness to lead us back into a forgiving relationship with him. *In other words, his grace and patience with our screw-ups is the basis for our relationship with him, not our perfection.* And he invites us to live out the same principle with one another. And of course, with our children!

Humble parents

So why do you not need to be afraid that you are a bad parent? Why can we really be free? I'll tell you why. And I want you to get your grandmother to needlepoint this and hang it on the wall over your cupboard. It's one of the Secrets of the Solar System when it comes to parenting, and it is this: *The only thing better than a **perfect** parent is a **humble** parent.* A parent who can see their mistakes and learn. A parent who can swing back in with their kids and ask forgiveness.

This is what it means to get free—and to set your kids free. Your kids know that they are not perfect, and probably suspect that you aren't either. Let's just own it and be fallen, imperfect people together.

I used to say to my kids, "The only difference between you and me is that I was born twenty-something years before you (so I know some stuff you don't know)—and that God has put me in authority over you (which is just a job description, saying basically that you need to do the stuff I say). But other than that, I'm a knucklehead like you. I make mistakes like you. I have gifts like you. And I am learning just like you."

Get it? Parenting is a relationship, not a performance.

Good Enough

The fun thing is that the research bears this principle out. D.W. Winnicott was a pediatrician and a psychoanalyst in the early-to-mid 20th century. Aside from writing brilliantly on child development and psychotherapy, he spent an enormous amount of time with parents. He noted how parents parented, and then followed up on the outcome—noticing how those kids turned out. Years later, when he checked in on the kids who had had technically "perfect" parents, he found out that, frankly, they were a little weird. I mean, what do you think someone who had had "perfect" parents would be like? They weren't very well-adjusted to the real world.

Then Winnicott went back and looked at the kids who had turned out to be the most functional adults—the kids who grew up to be adults who loved well, worked well, and managed life in a kind and powerful way. Then he looked back at what kind of parents they had had. His findings?

These parents were *unremarkable!*

They loved their kids, but they screwed up sometimes. They were attentive and involved, but sometimes they really dropped the ball. But they had a *relationship* with their kids—a bunch of "pretty good" people living together in a family. And he called them—*"Good Enough"* parents!

I read this years ago and felt enormous relief! "You mean I'm not permanently scarring my kids when I lose it?"

Not if I go back and repair.

We don't have to live as perfect, doting, attentive, never-failing parents. We just need to be "good enough."

But there's more! Good enough parenting is great news for parents who fear failing their kids, but Winnicott did not come up with the good enough notion just because he wanted to make parents feel better about themselves (I mean, he was British! Hello!) He supported good enough parenting because it was the best thing for *the child!*

It works like this. For most kids, having "perfect love" and constant availability from their parents was fine and all. But Winnicott observed how there was something about the *dance* of a parent actually messing up, and then swinging back in and repairing it with their child, that was like a magic ingredient that made love more solid for kids. Those kids became stronger, more trusting, and felt more loved. Children actually need the periodic failure and repair of parents in order to learn the truth about love—that it is strong enough to endure our screw-ups and failures, and that even when we let one another down, love remains. Good enough parenting is actually what is best for your child!

Living with your kids as a "good enough parent" is great news for us pressured parents, and it's the best thing for the child!

It's freedom for us, and it's the best thing for them!

"It's a floor cleaner and a dessert topping!"

I want to free you from the prison of believing that your kids need you to be a wonderful parent. What they need is for you to be a *person* with them. They know that they aren't perfect—how lonely for them if their parents were! I want to free you to be good enough. I want your life as a parent to stop feeling scary.

You're probably doing this already

One nice thing about writing a parenting book is that I know that I'm preaching to the choir. By definition, if you guys care enough about your kids to pick up a book and try to learn, I'm assuming that you are "good enough." You care about how you treat your kids. You are curious to learn more. You are engaged with their lives. And you often fail.

I know you want to always be a strong, wise parent. I know you don't want to get frustrated while helping your kids with their homework. You don't ever want them to see you blow up in anger. I know that you don't want to feel too exhausted to give to your kids when you get home from work. And if you are like me, you also don't want to get sick of hearing their long imaginary stories ("... then the princess got lost, but then the magic pony found her, and then they all rode back—all the way to the castle ... and then ...").

But all of these things will happen. You will let them down. You will not love perfectly. Sometimes, you will even hurt them.

If you are looking for a magic parenting book that will teach you how to parent perfectly, guaranteeing your kids turn out to be Rhodes Scholars, go ahead put this book down. Give me "one star" on the Amazon review. For that matter get off of Amazon altogether, because I don't believe that any book can make you into a perfect parent who raises perfect kids. Your kids will be as incomplete and broken as you or I. Instead I want to teach you be a group of people who are strugglers together. A family where everyone is fallen but loved—messed up, but belonging to one another.

The good news is that you will be strong and wise, *sometimes.* Instead of getting frustrated, you'll be loving, *sometimes.* Maybe sometimes you'll actually enjoy playing with ponies. You will be good enough. And when we love our children "good enough"—and when we repair when we don't—it's like we are building a "water filtration system" in our kids that can sift out our failures and be nourished by the pure water that remains. As a result, they feel loved *and* their hearts grow stronger.

Screwed up families

So, are you screwing up your kids? Well, if you're like me, you probably are! But instead of trying to fix that and make everybody perfect, I recommend that you just be screwed up *with* them! A group of fallen people who live together in grace, learning to make room for one another's failures. That is a family filled with love. *That is a family that is not screwed up.*

I was watching my son-in-law, Steele, deal with my grandson recently on a family trip to the beach. He was trying to get twenty-month-old Whit to wear his beach hat. As they sat in the sand, Steele would put the hat on Whit's head. Whit would (naturally) rip it off. Steele would then put it back on his head. Whit would rip it off. (You get the drift?) Ultimately, I saw Steele swallow his frustration, look up at me, and sort of shrug. He was failing, but apparently he was letting that be okay. Welcome to parenting. Ultimately, I joined them on the sand and we got the hat on—sort of. It was good enough.

Basically, having kids is like living in a frat house: Nobody sleeps much, everything is broken, and there's a lot of throwing up. So, we have to just do what we can. And what we "can do" is what our kids really need.

I'm tired of parents being afraid. I don't want you wondering if everything you are doing as a parent is wrong. I don't want you bullied by the "latest research." I want to help set you free to love, give, and parent your kids out of your heart.

Do not think we are leaving this topic here. We are going to weave this theme throughout everything we are going to talk about in this book. We are going to do two things together to set you free. I want to tell you all I can about how to love your kids well, how to set limits on them, how to teach them about pain and strength, and much more. And then we are going to swing back to this chapter over and over again, remembering the grace to fail and be human parents. Remember—the only thing better than a perfect parent is a humble parent! You're going to get sick of hearing me say that. But, then again, maybe not.

This is home and home is not something you remember, it is something you see every day and every moment.

— **Rick Bragg**

Chapter Two

How do I help my kids know that they are loved?

In the upcoming two chapters, we'll dive into our next two questions, which are, **How do we help our kids know they are loved**, and, **How do we get them to do what we say?** These questions really touch on the two most basic elements of parenting. We are at ground zero here.

I call these two ingredients—*Love* and *Limits*.[1]

There's a sense in which we could say that all of our parenting choices boil down to playing ball between these two "end-zones." We need to *love* our kids enough for them to get a wonderful grounding that they matter and are cherished. But we also need to set enough *limits* on them so that our houses aren't being run by little terrorists with bazookas.

These are constant themes for God as well. He calls them things like Grace and Truth, or Peace and Righteousness. He says things like, "I am the Lord your God who led you out of the land of Egypt, out of the house of bondage." (What a loving guy!) But then, in the very next line, he says, "Thou shalt have no other gods before me!" Boom—Limits! He relates with both love and limits as he cares for his people. As we go along, you'll see that your parenting needs to balance them both as well.

Now, as a pair of parents, you probably will find that between the two of you, you will tend to err on one side or the other. One of you probably tends to be more "lovey." The other tends to be more about limits and discipline. In fact, I often tell parents that if we could put you both into one of those transporter thingies like on *Star Trek*, beam you off somewhere, and then bring you back as one person, you would be one perfect parent! Those of us without "Scotty," on the other hand, tend to err to one extreme or the other. Personally, I tended to be Capt. Von Trapp blowing his whistle and making the kids walk in line, while Norma was busy singing with them in the bed and making clothes out of the drapes!

So love and limits. They are such the brick and mortar for parenting that we are going to devote an entire chapter to each. In our next chapter we are going to look at how to set powerful limits on the little outlaws who may have taken over your home. But first, let's talk about love.

The greatest of these

How do we help our kids know that they are loved? I mean, getting your kids to obey is cool and everything, but I believe that in the relational and spiritual world, authority is never an end in itself. Authority always functions as a handmaiden to something else—a tool to create something else. And I believe that that "something else" is loving, abiding relationship. We're going to talk in Chapter Three about how to keep your kids from running your home like their own personal Al Qaeda. But we're gonna do that, not just to create wisdom and peace in our family; we're also going to do that in order to create the safety and context for abiding, loving relationship—the epicenter of our hearts.

Now, this doesn't mean that we have come to the touchy-feely, group hug portion of our program. The kind of love we're going to teach is not *schmoopie schmoopie*, Mr. McFeely, "make them feel good all the time," kind of stuff. Sometimes parents can get a little squirrelly when I start talking about the relational side of parenting; the whole world of engaging how your kids feel; embracing who they are. They're all good with the "keep 'em in line" discipline part, but then we start talking about teaching your kids that they matter, and those parents say, "Uh-oh, he's going soft on us! He's turning into one of those West Coast hot-tub types! Save it for the chapter on moon juice and mindfulness, Doc!"

No! What we are teaching here is not psychobabble. It is about asking what it looks like to give our kids a core sense of belonging and safety—a background of being seen and connected and wanted in their hearts. We are going to be building the grounding that makes adults feel whole and loved in their lives—that "battery pack" that becomes my fuel source so that I don't always need other people to approve of me. The opposite of insecure. In other words, we are going to be building the grounding that makes adults feel whole and loved in their lives. So suit up and let's ride!

Core questions

Here's a way I like to think about it: Kids live their lives asking what I call *Core Questions* of their parents and their inner circle; questions about their world and their hearts.

Implicitly or explicitly, kids are asking questions with their eyes, ears, and experiences about who they are, how life works, and how relationships function. Questions like "Do you want *me*? ("You know, 'real me'! Not just 'good boy' me.") "Does what I *feel* matter?" "Do you care when I'm hurting?" "How big a deal is it for me to screw up? Can you give me a vibe for that?"

Get it? Core Questions.

Inside their hearts, kids are constantly asking these core questions.

Now, fortunately and unfortunately, they are getting answers to these questions all the time in the relationships they have with us! (No pressure or anything, right?) So, as we're talking about loving and relating to our kids, this is not about having a little Kumbaya time. Instead, I want us to unpack how we can best be giving good answers to these "Core Love Questions." How do we core communicate to a child that you matter, we want you, it is good that you are here? Once they get that, (and are shown with good limits that they aren't Kanye West), they will be unstoppable adults. So we're not just rolling chicken bones here. This is powerful heart juju.

Now, I will go ahead and tell you that this doesn't mean

that they aren't going to blow us off sometimes when we try to lovingly connect with them. I remember one of our kids won a goldfish at the state fair when she was about five-years-old. She named the fish Goldie. One day, I walked into the bathroom where Goldie lived and found him floating belly up in his little bowl, bobbing above a seafloor of blue rocks. Being a wise and insightful therapist, I thought to myself, "Oh my gosh! This is my daughter's first brush with death. This is an important opportunity. I need to tread carefully here. I need to walk with her through this meaningful and possibly traumatic time."

I walked to her room where she was busy coloring, the only sound, the soft scribble, scribble of a red crayon rubbed down to a nub. I softly knocked on the door and said, "Callie—baby. We need to talk, honey. It's about Goldie. Darling—Goldie is dead." She briefly looked over her shoulder at me and stopped coloring. She said, "Okay. Well, why don't you just flush him down the toilet or something?"

Wow, good thing she had such a sensitive, wise, nurturing father, eh?

Also, even if we try to be loving, kids are notorious for distorting things. I've always liked to cook. For some reason, I was walking through the house one day carrying one of my chef knives—a big ten-incher! Suddenly I rounded the corner and there was our middle child, Katherine (about age four at the time), standing there in her little footie pajamas looking up at me, towering over her with a knife in my hand.

Her response—"Daddy? Are you going to *cut us?*"

I mean, what am I supposed to say to that? "Come on honey, I'm trying to put those days behind me!"

I can just hear her telling her therapist one day, "Growing up in our home was terrifying! My evil dad used to chase us though the house with a butcher knife!"

So, regardless of what we do here, your teenage boy is probably not going to plop down in the kitchen with you and say, "Gee Mom, let's just sit and share." Nevertheless, our kids need us to engage them and connect with them.

Let's look at two ways we can teach our kids about love.

We're going to *tell them*. And we're going to *show them*.

Teaching our kids that they are loved
Tell them

Showing love to our kids is going to be our most important and powerful tool for teaching heart love, and it's where we're going to spend most of our time, but let's get real—you need to *tell* your kids that you love them. It's not rocket surgery!

I want your kids to have memories of you taking their face in your hands and looking them in the eye. I want them to remember you picking them up and brushing their hair out of their face, and saying things like, "Do you know that you make your dad really, really happy?"; "I smile when I think of you"; "I like the way you play"; "I love your songs"; "You don't know this, but we look at you when you're asleep"; "We love you!"

I was talking to a dad a few years ago who worked out a little game with his school-age kids. They would tap one another three times, signifying the three words in "I love you." *Tap*

Tap Tap! It was their little secret sign, communicating love wherever they went. Even with teenagers, as they ignore us on their way up to their room, they still need us to say, "Hey buddy, I love ya big!"

We're about to get all developmental and psychological, but I don't want you to miss this basic way to teach love. I have so many adult clients who tell me that their family was one in which no one ever said, "I love you"—out loud—with words. Words of love were not spoken. Remember those core questions? Kids are asking all the time at some level, "Do you love me?" We need to verbally answer—"*Yes*"! Don't miss that.

Show them

Telling our kids that we love them is super important. But, to coin a phrase, we gotta make our "walk match our talk." Unfortunately, the most powerful place that kids learn about love (and most things) is from how they are *treated*! I tell parents all the time that there is a vast difference between *loving* someone and *doing love* to them—*showing love.*

I've always loved plants. But there was a long season of my life in which I had no idea how to care for them well—how to "love" them well. I would buy a lovely plant and joyfully bring it back to my office. Weeks later it was dead. So, I would go back and buy another plant. I imagined the plants at the nursery seeing me coming back, as I selected another one of their buddies, and thinking, "Dead man walking!" I loved plants, but I didn't know *how* to love them!

We all love our kids. But if you really want to teach them how loved they are, let's learn to *do* love to them; *show* love to them. In other words, let's ask ourselves what kinds of interactions make love *feel* powerful to them? How do we show love to them in their language? Kids have a love language too, and teaching our kids about love involves understanding how they hear and experience love, and speaking that language back to them.

So, how do we *show* love?

Not like this

A lot of folks in our culture equate loving their kids with "coddling" them. In other words, if you make sure your child is never unhappy, then they will feel loved. This is where we make sure to attend every ball game or music recital. (Wouldn't want them to feel like they aren't a priority, would we?) We make sure every kid gets a trophy and each child gets the same number of toys for Christmas, etc.

Now, boys and girls, this does not create a feeling of being loved. This creates a sense of *entitlement*, which actually *prevents* children from feeling loved. In other words, when I live in the "I deserve, I deserve, I deserve," mentality of self-centered entitlement, then when love *does* come along, I don't feel the warmth and undeserved joy of it. I just feel like, "Well, it's about time!" Coddling has been uber-popular in the last two generations of parenting. Beginning with mine! I mean, my generation raised the millennials! (You're welcome.)

Other parents can confuse loving their kids with adoration and praise. Here, "loving" kids means, "I'm so proud of you!";

"Look at you, you're *amazing!*"; "You ride your bike like an Olympian!"; "You're a special snowflake!"

Remember the old joke where the parents are all watching the high-school marching band from the bleachers. Suddenly one boy marches the opposite direction of the rest of the band. His mother pokes her friend and says, "Look! Everyone's out of step but my Johnny!"

Parents can get obsessed with adoring their kids. Years ago I did a conference at a school. After speaking, I stood for a moment and watched the carpool line. One mother, driving a big Suburban, had a license plate that read JIM'S MOM. I found myself wondering what it would be like to be Jim and have a mother whose identity was that wrapped up in him.

"Who are you ma'am?"

"I'm Jim's mom." (And, apparently, that's all.)

Frankly, it made me feel the most sorry for JIM'S WIFE one day.

Another reason to be careful about praise is that once you begin relating on the basis of *praising* a child as "*good,*" you open the door for their ears to begin listening for *judgment* that is "*bad.*" In other words, praise sounds sweet, but it lives in the universe of judgment—and that is a two-edged sword. If I can be praised for my goodness, I can also be judged for my badness. I see adult clients all the time who had parents whose "love language" was "I'm so proud of you." So, they learned to relate to their parents, not out of love, but out of performance. And they learned to fear shame as much as they danced for praise. Love just says, "I want *you*—good or bad"; or "I bet that felt so good to *you* to score that touchdown! You've worked so hard to be able to play that well!" When we talk like this, we are connecting to the *child*, not their successes or failures.

Mattering

So, if we avoid coddling and praise, where do we land? What does *showing* love sound like? Teaching grounding love to kids isn't long division; it involves simply this: Living in such a way that says to our kids, "What's important to you, what's hurting for you, what it feels like to be you, *matters* to me. I think about it. I talk to you about it. I don't discount it. I try it on."

Whether we are talking about your children, your marriage, or your best friend, one of the most powerful ways we show love is by treating people like they *matter*. In this sense, loving your kids is really not that different from loving anyone else. We try on what it's like to be them. We treat them like a person—just like us. We love our neighbor as ourselves. We let them matter.

I mean, think about it—what would it be like to be one of your kids? Psychologist Bruce Narramore has a great analogy for what it's like to be a kid. He says something like this: Imagine living in a house in which everybody is two to three times taller than you. In other words, imagine living with two *eighteen-foot giants*! They pick out your clothes and then dress you in them. One of them cooks your food, and the other one makes you eat it!

What would it be like to live in "giant land?" Let's try that on. What would it be like to be our kids?

Callie was diagnosed with Type 1 Diabetes at age thirteen. The crisis that resulted in her diagnosis was an almost fatal health emergency that put us in the ER in the middle of the night. A couple of days later as things were more stabilized, I went to retrieve her younger siblings from the grandparents. On the way home, five-year-old Bonney asked, "Is Callie going to die?" Tenderly I reassured her, "No! No!, Baby! She's not going to die! No way!" "Well, then why do they call it *die-abeties?*" she replied. My heart collapsed hearing her little child mind, struggling with such a terrifying thing. What is it like to be them? Let's try that on.

One of our sayings in our home with our children was, "*You matter more than what you are like.*" (The whole truth was that we sort of had *two messages.* You're completely loved around here, unconditionally, *regardless* of your choices. However, how much you actually *enjoy* your lifestyle around here is completely contingent on your choices. But that's another chapter.)

But our bottom line message was, "You matter more than what you are like." Our point to them was that your knuckle-headed choices or your bad behavior will not change how much you matter to our hearts. You matter! How you feel matters. (It might not change our choices, but we care.) What you need, what you love, the things that are important, meaningful and scary to you—matter to us.

Different ages—different love languages

So, what does teaching real love look like? How do we *do*

"mattering" to our kids? Let's get specific. I'm going to gloss over the obvious relationship builders, like "spending time with your kids"—board games and Boy Scouts kind of stuff. You can get that anywhere. I want to go a little deeper and ask, *How do we relationally/emotionally live out the "Actions of Love" to our kids.* True love always has hands and feet, and since kids are concrete thinkers, what we *do* is far more important than what we *say.*

So, what does it look like to *do* love for our kids? It's different at different ages—Infant, Toddler, School-Age, and Teen. Let's look at them.

Infants

How do we teach love to a squally baby?

Actually, this is one of the most important ages developmentally for learning about core love and mattering because the questions here are so basic and preverbal. So tune in!

We are going to teach an infant about love by giving them two things:

Nurture and Trust

And *Bonding and Connection*

Nurture and Trust

Think about it—what's it like to be an infant?

Number one, they need lots of stuff. Babies have lots of problems. They're always hungry, sleepy, gassy, or poopy. (Norma and I used to hear noises from "down below" and muse, "Is it solid, liquid, or gas?")

And, little bitties have all sorts of feelings! They feel loneliness and fear and anger and joy. Babies feel a lot. And they don't even understand all that's going on, much less can they do anything about. So, they're unhappy a lot. (And then they're *happy*, and then they're *unhappy*, and then they are *happy* again ...)

But herein lies one of the beginning points of teaching a baby about love. They have all these problems—*but!*—there's this nice lady and her big friend, and they keep coming around and somehow making it better! They change his diaper and feed him and hold him and make everything okay.

I remember each of my kids as a baby. They would be desperate for their bottle, and as you prepared it and began to hold them, moving the bottle toward their mouth, their eyes and hands would get this desperate look like, "It's not going to happen! It's not going to happen! It's not going to happen! *Aaaaaah*, it happened!" And over and over again for baby, it *happens*! And the nice lady and her big friend give him these loving things. And pretty soon, baby starts to learn the first part of the infant love language: that his *needs are attended to*. That there is *nurture*. "Maybe I will be *okay*. Maybe I'm all *safe and sound*."

I've encountered parenting theories over the years that miss this. I've heard some people tell parents to push their infant too quickly to live on the parents' schedule, rather than learning to develop an ebb and flow with their child's needs. Some far-out notions even claim that the baby's schedule should be brought under parental rule, lest the baby usurp the authority of the home. Come on, people! A baby's only two question are, "Am I going to be okay?" and "Am going to be alone?" The correct answers are "Yes!" and "No!" respectively.

So, the first thing any baby learns about love is that *the bad* can become *good again*. That being needy isn't wrong or dangerous. That people are there. If I'm needy and vulnerable, it's safe and okay.

And as this nurture and mattering goes on over time, baby starts to get that comfort and safety tattooed on his heart—on the inside! He learns another wonderful part of love—*trust*—that love isn't going away. In other words, baby is tuning into the fact that it's not just okay now; it can be okay in the future. How many of us adults live with that inside of our hearts? These are the protons and electrons of love.

But that's not all.

Bonding and Connection

During this season even more "love stuff" happens for baby. Sometimes even when everything is okay, the nice lady and her big friend just *hold* him. They sort of gaze into his eyes and goo-goo him and hold him close and play with him. His eyes meet theirs and their eyes speak back how much they delight in him. The room is quiet and soft, and he begins to feel this nice weird wonderful feeling that I'm special and dear to them. I am "*with*!" I am *one* with someone.

This is what the textbooks call "mother-child reverie" or "bonding." Baby learns that it's not just food that feels good—

people feel good, too. And this becomes the foundation for love and intimacy for the rest of your child's life—that feeling of just being with, of being held.

It is core hardwired in babies (and adults!) to need this kind of connection. When our first child, Callie, was in utero, we didn't know her gender, so in order to talk to her, I nicknamed her Peewee. I would tap on Norma's tummy and say, "Hello Peewee, we love you already! Grow and grow, and come out and be with us!"

Months later, when she was born in Los Angeles (Our OB drove a red Porsche with a license plate that read, STORK1), they brought her out, covered in goo, screaming and red. They weighed her and tended to her, and all of that time she continued screaming. Then they wrapped her in blankets and handed her to me, still red-faced and yelling. I looked at her and said, "Hello, Peewee. Welcome to life!" And as she heard my voice, the one she had been hearing for nine months, she immediately stopped crying and looked into my eyes.

Quiet. Safe. Loved.

We humans are hardwired for connection—and especially for our children, emotional connection speaks the deepest kind of love.

On the other hand, I was holding a little baby boy a few years back. His eyes were locked on mine, as I swayed and cooed with him. I was delighting in the oneness and connection with this little fellow. And then, suddenly, his eyes rolled back in his head, and he fell asleep. I exclaimed (half in jest), "Wait! What just happened? I thought we were having a moment here, and he just rolled back and went to sleep!" From across the room his mother replied, "Welcome to what it's like to be in a relationship with a man!"

So, the first way in which we *do* love with our children involves steady care and attending, coupled with sweet bonding with our babies. And here's what I want you to get. When you do this stuff, you're not just "tending to the baby." You are literally *teaching love.* You're building layers of core connection. You're writing "motherboard software" for mattering. Congratulations.

Someone once said that from zero to eighteen months we are basically teaching our children that the world revolves around them. And then we're gonna spend the next eighteen years un-teaching that. And that is good. For them and for us!

Good enough

I'm sure you remember how constant and exhausting having an infant is. I remember pacing back and forth with one of ours in the middle of the night and wondering, "If I just put her outside in the flower bed for just a little while and got a little sleep, would that really damage anything?" It's demanding, but this season of nurture and bonding is critical.

On the other hand, don't let all this "wonderful attending" stuff spook you. I hear a lot of anxious parents who say, "Oh my gosh, if we let him cry a bit, it will mess up his 'core bonding!'" Good parents find that ebb and flow with their child. "Good enough" remember? I want you to be loving *and* free!

Another extreme I see is parents who *only* think about

bonding as they live their lives with their children—for the rest of childhood. Their kids sleep in their bed, and they never push them to develop any of their own coping skills. As we will see later, bonding is important, but so is building autonomy and strength. Good parents find a balance there. There is a time to grow up.

Toddlers

Infancy passes more quickly than we expect. Soon they are up and about. So, how do we show love to a toddler? Well, you can start by not locking them in their room and drinking Chardonnay out of a sippy cup at 10 a.m.—that would be a good start. But in the plus column, how do we show "mattering" during the one-to-four years season?

Well, let's put it this way. What can a toddler do that an infant can't do? Almost everything, right?

Around one year of age, all of that oneness and bonding starts to get a little boring, and all of a sudden Little Kahuna starts seeing cool stuff to do! There's a whole cabinet full of colorful cleaning products. There's nothing like a toddler and a Tupperware drawer. And what are their favorite words? No. Me. Mine. (All very charming.)

So suddenly they start entering this world of having a *me* and developing mastery. They start walking around—vertically! (I mean, how exciting would it be to stand up after being on your *back* your whole life. "There's a world *behind* me too?") They start saying words and playing with toys, throwing tantrums, and basically making your life more difficult. Suddenly they've developed a *will!* They start having some power.

Now, this a pain in some ways, but try it on! Remember, "mattering" is about trying on what it's like to be our child. I remember watching my fourteen-month-old grandson sitting on the floor of the kitchen, digging plastic silverware out of a little box. He would pull out a handful of forks, spoons, and knives, hold them over his head, and then cast them all upon the floor. They would jangle and dance and spread out, scattering on the hardwood. I remember the look of amazement in his eyes and his little sounds of delight as he reached in for another handful, pulled them out, lifted them over his head, and scattered them again across the floor. It was like he'd suddenly become Harry Potter, full of magical powers! This boy who had basically spent his entire life so far lying in a crib and having other people do things to him was suddenly making the world happen before his very eyes!

So how do we show love to a toddler? Well, the toddler is still going to need that comfort and nurture that we began to show in infancy. They still thrive on that cuddle time in your lap. They love their little routines such as listening to you read that favorite book or watching videos (often of themselves). This shows love to them just like it did when they were a tiny one.

Also, you'll often see them do what developmental psychologists call "rapprochement." One minute, they will be deeply serious with their "baby work" across the room, concentrating studiously on putting things in containers and then dumping them back out again. And then, suddenly, they will run back to your lap and pat your legs or reach up for you to hold them. "Even though I'm big and strong, I need a mommy to check in with." The good toddler parent welcomes this ambivalence.

But since a toddler is ready to move beyond just nurture and cuddles, we're going to add a couple of new pieces to our love story. The most exciting thing in their world is all their new little abilities, so a powerful way to teach love to a toddler is to meet them there. So, we are going to do two things again. At the same time. Kind of like patting your head and rubbing your stomach.

We're going to:

Celebrate and embrace these new little abilities, and *set limits* on these new abilities.

Let's look at both of these.

We celebrate their abilities.

Since the most exciting thing about being a toddler is this magical newfound ability to make life happen, one of the ways that we show love to them is by looking for opportunities to affirm them there. Look for times where it is fun and safe for them to assert themselves and be big! In other words, we say the *opposite* of the *Runaway Bunny*: "If you run away from me, I will jump up and down and clap and throw a party and say, 'You go girlfriend!'"

Callie separated early and enjoyed her newfound autonomy even while still crawling. One afternoon we went on a picnic at Echo Park in downtown Los Angeles. You've seen it in movies—the L.A. skyline, palm trees, and a big lake with a fountain in the middle. Anyway, as we spread a blanket on the grass and got out the cold fried chicken, we turned around, and Callie was gone! We looked up, and she had crawled almost thirty feet away. She then rolled around and sat facing us, her shoulders shaking, and her head thrown back in laughter. We waved and cheered! "Hope you make it in Hollywood!" Of course, we retrieved her, but there was that intoxicating moment in which we all celebrated her independence. When we join with a toddler in that celebration, we are speaking love to them in their language.

I remember Katherine (second child) loved playing with the TV remote. She'd pick it up in the middle of a show and push the buttons, changing the channels. Her eyes would go wide with amazement and power, as if she had just reengaged the hyper-drive of the *Millennium Falcon*! We would say, "Wow! Look at you! You are Thundar the Powerful! Sheena, Warrior Princess!" (Though we often missed the best part of the TV show!)

So, we speak strong love in a toddler's love language as we look for chances to say, "We are proud of you"; "You are cool"; "You're learning amazing things!" And when they mess up, they will look to us to see what happens. This is another opportunity to show love.

A friend of mine has a four-year-old little boy who dropped her phone and broke the screen. He realized what had happened and looked up at her with frightened eyes. Lovingly, she swallowed her frustration and anger, looked into his eyes, and told him, "It's okay, man! We make mistakes. We can fix this. This is *easy!"* He melted into her arms. Our message is also that "your power isn't going to *ruin* everything either!"

A parent's delight in this busy stage called "practicing" is a huge way toddlers hear love. We celebrate with them in this most important thing in their life. This is mattering! (And, by the way, they need this mirroring and celebrating now, so they don't spend the rest of their lives looking for it—"Everybody look at me, look at me, with my Porsche and my hair implants.")

We limit their abilities.

As you can imagine, not all of a toddlers antics can be responded to with such enthusiasm. "Oh wow, look at you drinking water out of the toilet again! It's organic—like composting!" Or, "You hit your baby brother so well! He'll be out for hours!"

That kind of thinking won't help anyone with their personal growth. This is why we are going to show love by *limiting* their independence and power, too. In other words, "We love you enough to not let you hurt yourself or us." So, when they suddenly run out in the street, we grab them and strongly tell them "No!" We let them have a few moments in the playpen if they hit their sister! We don't give in or get angry when they fall to pieces on the grocery store floor. We set limits on their power.

Once when Callie was a toddler, I realized that things had been quiet for a while —too quiet. Those of you with toddlers know what that means—somewhere in the house, DEF CON conditions exist. Indeed, I discovered her playing mailman in the "mail slot" of the VCR. (Remember, I was a parent in the nineties.) If you think about it, the opening for a videocassette player looks just like the mail slot in your front door. She had stuffed all of our mail up inside of the machine. Cute? Yes. But not a good "love language" for VCRs! We've got to limit that kind of stuff.

When I was a kid, I painstakingly drew an art project for my social studies class. Foolishly, I left it lying on the table. When I returned, my baby sister had "finished" my drawing for me with a crayon, scribbling the whole thing into oblivion. (I should have saved it. She is now a professional artist!) But the point is, turn your back on toddler and your house will look like one of those films the highway patrol shows you during Drivers Ed. Disaster time.

Toddlers need us to lovingly limit them. This is loving too.

Pulling your hair out

As you know, the toddler/preschool years are one of the most challenging stages of parenting, simply because they're so constant. I think researchers should refer to it as the "one-armed paper hanger" stage. During this chaotic season, we parents can feel like the fish in the *Cat in the Hat*. The moment you turn your back, Smallfry is pulling the Ming vase off the shelf. As one of my friends says, "You fear for their lives every second."

Unfortunately, the psychologist genie has no magic cure for that. Parents of toddlers are always telling me that they are completely exhausted after a day of chasing their little one around. Of course you are. Hang in there. It doesn't mean you're doing anything wrong. Soon these little guys will develop more self-control. I promise. We are going to talk more about how to help toddlers develop that in the next chapter. In the meantime, keep hangin' paper—good enough—and don't let the incessant chaos discourage you!

So, again, we *show* love to toddlers by doing two things. We *celebrate* their abilities, and we *limit* their strength. We make room for them to *say* no, and we teach them to *hear* no. Both.

Each one of the "Cox kids" went through a peculiar phase when they were toddlers. Perhaps this will sound familiar. The family would be riding in the car, listening to some kid music on a kid's CD (You know the one—that CD your kids insist upon listening to every time in the car, until you're so sick of the songs you want to scream.) Anyway, each of our kids went through a phase in which they wanted to be the *only one* who got to sing. I remember countless times in which they might be singing along to a song, and I would merrily join in.

"*Noooooooooo!*" they would protest, hands flailing. "Don't Sing! Only me!"

Well, we wanted to *delight* in their independence but also to *limit* their independence, right? So we would say, "We understand you want to be the only one to sing, but sometimes other people get to sing too. So, you can sing this verse but the rest of us will get to join in later."

We're teaching love here, but we're also teaching that other people matter. A big way we learn about love is by learning how to love others as well.

School-age

What does *doing* love look like for the five to twelve year old? Well, we will still *bond and nurture*. A mom was talking to me the other day about putting her eight-year-old to bed one night. He's typically busy with baseball, *Star Wars*, and playing the Wii (and maybe some homework). But on this particular night, as he was going to sleep, she told me how her rambunctious son just settled and drew close to her. "He just let me rub his back, and we just were so quiet and still together." Kids never stop needing that kind of closeness.

Besides continuing to nurture them, we will also still *celebrate* their new abilities. ("Look Ma, no hands!") We'll also still set *limits* on their choices (for the rest of childhood). And we still *tell* them we love them, of course.

But remember, teaching our kids about love is not just about sweetie sweetness. It is also about meeting them at their heart's need; touching what it's like to be them; trying on what is most important in their lives. So, what is most important in a school-ager's life? How do we speak love in their language?

Two things again.

Number one, school-age is the first time that kids start making sense of *life outside of the family*. They begin having their first forays interacting with other kids, teachers, and coaches. And they're going to need help with that.

Secondly, school-age kids start to really tune into how *unideal* things are in life. Think about it—what does your school-age kid complain about? "There are thingies in my soup." "We have too much homework." "That's not fair." "I hate our minivan." "Her piece is bigger."

You've heard this kind of stuff, right?

School-age children are beginning to develop a greater awareness of how the world is not the way they want it (and *they themselves* aren't either!)—and they're going to need help with all that loss and disappointment.

So, to teach a school-ager about love, we are going to meet them in these two places. We're going to call them:

- *Empowerment* to deal with life's challenges, and
- *Empathy* for how difficult life can be.

(And I realize that "Empowerment and Empathy" sound like the title of next week's episode of *Dr. Phil*, but indulge me.)

Empowerment

Entering the world on your own for the first time is a scary proposition. For the school-ager, life suddenly gets dramatic—there are homework, strikeouts, bullies, and spend-the-night parties. Suddenly your child is having to learn to navigate such challenges apart from you. During this season, lots of kids can get scared, and they need to know that we've got their back.

One of the most powerful ways we can teach a school-age kid about love is to come alongside of them as they are making sense of life's challenges—helping them learn that they are strong; helping them learn mastery and confidence in their abilities, and helping them see that they are not alone. I like to call this *empowerment*.

Learning to deal with real life and to feel powerful in it is something that is "caught like a cold" from the people we love.

All of us need loving, strong parents who walk alongside of us and help us learn that we can do it and learn to do it well. This is a huge way that we parents get to show love to our school-age kids. The way we respond to our children and our children's challenges can actually build in them a sense of love and power to do real life. And we get to do this!

Here's one of the Secrets of the Universe that we will discuss more in Chapter Four. It's key for teaching love and strength to our kids. The secret is this: There's a real sense in which *kids get their view of themselves and of the world from the eyes of their parents, mentors, and inner circle.* In other words, as kids encounter the challenges and difficulties of life, they need to be able to look into our eyes and see those eyes looking back at them with confidence and strength in their abilities. This kind of empowerment pours love into their hearts.

For example, half of the time when children struggle with school anxiety, I can trace it back to anxiety in the parents. Once I worked with a parent who reported that she had been talking with the school counselor about whether to hold her child back a grade. She said, "I told that counselor that I just wanted to make sure that my daughter did not struggle in *any* way!" Now, what are those mother's eyes saying to her child about her ability to handle life? An overprotective parent's eyes are implying to her child, "You're tiny and fragile, and you need your mommy to make sure you never struggle." Is that the message we want to communicate? Is that loving?

I want my eyes to say, "I've got news for you, Cowboy. You are loved, and you are strong! You can do this. And I will help you. We can do this together!" That's what it sounds like to join a kid in their challenging world.

And when they succeed, I want to talk to them about *them*! Instead of "I'm proud of you!", I want to say, "Wow! That must've felt really *amazing* to hit that home run!" "I bet it feels really good *to you* to have worked so hard and made that good grade."

What a gift of love for our children to be able to look into our eyes and see their *own strength* reflected back—not just our pride.

So, a huge way that we can show practical love to our school-age kids is by engaging this new challenging life with them! We engage their homework with them, throw the baseball with them, and teach them that they are strong. Trust me, you're already doing this stuff! I just want you to understand how powerful it is. This is strong Love Kung Fu!

I've always been terrible at math. I was terrible at math as a kid, and I'm still terrible at math. I remember struggling with my multiplication tables as a school-ager. One night my dad was calling out the tables to me. I was doing okay, but every time I got stuck on eight times seven. I could *not* remember what eight times seven equaled. So Dad started marching around the room, his arms moving up and down as if he were beating a giant drum. He began to chant: "Eight times seven is fifty-six! Eight times seven is fifty-six! Eight times seven is fifty-six!" Soon I joined him, and we marched through the house, "Eight times seven is fifty-six!" I aced the math test the next day. And I still chant "eight times seven is fifty-six" when

I do multiplication.

Years back, I spent a season teaching laypeople how to lead small groups at a church in Atlanta. One week we talked about how our own eyes and hearts can be like healing "mirrors" to help those who are hurting. As we "see" the hurting hearts of other people with grace and truth in our eyes, and as we speak love back to them, we help free them from their pain. (*Everyone* gets their view of themselves from the eyes of the people who love them.)

One guy in the group came back the next week talking about how that image of a mirror had deeply impacted him, and he told us a story. His school-age daughter had a mild facial deformity and lived haunted with shame about it. Borrowing our image of a mirror, he decided to speak to her. He invited her to join him in front of a real mirror, and to look at herself, and to see him seeing her. As they stood together, their images reflected in the glass, he told us what he said to her. He said, "I want you to know what *I* see when I look at you—Me, your father. I see a beautiful young lady whose face lights up when she sees me. I see a girl who reflects God's image in radiant beauty, and a young lady who makes my heart happy every day." Her eyes filled with tears seeing herself in the "mirror" of her father's eyes. And so did his. (And so did *ours*, hearing the story.)

But there's more to this tale. I was talking with one of the members of that leadership training group just this week. It's been more than ten years since. She told me she had been to a church retreat recently and had encountered a confident young woman there, whom she described as having "an unusual but stunning" appearance. My friend asked who that lovely young woman was. The answer—it was the child in the mirror, who had apparently grown up to reflect her father's view of her.

What I want you to understand here is that when you do things like speaking healing words to your children or helping them with homework, you are not just calling out spelling words or pitching baseball. You are being "boots on the ground" for *showing* heart level love to your child, by meeting them at the point of their most felt need. Just like nurturing an infant, you are writing those lines of software that speak love. I can still feel my dad's love now as I write about those stupid multiplication tables a half century later. And apparently the "mirror girl" still feels her father's love as well. Love for our children happens in these day to day places.

Empathy

Now, all this real-life stuff is hard! Let's talk about how we can love our kids by walking through that hard stuff with them. Let's talk about how *loving* it can feel when someone "Gets it"—when someone shows *empathy*.

When I do marriage conferences and talk about conflict, one of the things that we discuss is the fact that most humans do not know how to heal hurt. Once we hurt someone, we often don't know what needs to happen in order to make that hurt feel better. That's why your wife is still bringing up stuff from like, ten years ago. "This is like that time on our honeymoon!" The reason she's doing that is because the hurt she feels has not been healed.

In the conferences, I always ask the crowd, "I want you guys to tell *me* what you need in order to make your hurt feel better?" Invariably the answers land on themes like "... that someone understands"; "... that they care"; "... that they 'get it.'"

These folks are right! Good shootin' guys!

Secret of the Galaxy: The Three H's! *Hearing Heals Hurt!*

For some reason that I don't understand (and I should understand it because it's my job), pain in our hearts gets better if someone understands it.

It's called "empathy."

Empathy means I try on what it feels like to be *you* and talk to you about it. "That hurt you!" "It felt like I was attacking you." "When I said that, it must have felt to you like I didn't care." ("Sympathy," by the way, is where I talk to you about how your pain feels to be *me*. "*I'm* so sad you are hurting." Both are good. At least you're not still fighting!)

So, how does this relate to our kids?

Well, in the midst of all the challenges of young childhood, our kids end up facing a lot of yuck. And as we'll discuss in Chapter Five, there is plenty we can do to help them there. But this is a chapter on love. For now, our question is simply, how can the difficulties our kids face give us an opportunity to infuse their hearts with love?

The answer lies in understanding the world of *feelings and empathy*.

I know—you were wondering when the shrink was going to get around to talking about feelings. Well, here's your big moment. Feelings are actually quite an interesting phenomenon. When it comes to discerning facts about reality—"Is that truck going to hit me?" or, "Do you really love me?"—feelings are pretty unreliable. God loves me regardless of how I feel about that fact on any particular day.

But regarding the *heart*, regarding *relationships*, feelings touch the center of our souls. If you and I had a discussion about something practical and pointless, like how often you should change the oil in your car, you'd probably forget about that conversation by next week. But if I hurt your *feelings*, you would remember that indefinitely. And I might come do a conference for your group years later, and you would say to someone, "You won't believe what that guy said to me like five years ago!"

Why?

Because I had hurt your *feelings!*

There is a direct link between how much I *get and understand* what you feel, and how *loving* my heart feels toward you. *To the degree that I don't care about what you feel, it's gonna feel to you like I don't care about you.* (Again, cross-reference your marriage here.)

So how does this relate to our children? Well, you don't have to hang out with a kid very long to discover that they are very emotionally driven. I mean, how logically does your nine-year-old act when he strikes out at baseball? He doesn't say, "You know, Father, there are many things we wish for in life that we cannot have. Success at baseball is just one of them." No, he feels like a total loser, and after the game he runs to his room and cries! So, a huge way we teach love to our kids is by "getting it" and caring when our child is hurting. God made us in such a way that when our pain encounters love, understanding, and empathy, it metabolizes—it gets better. (It's one of the reasons therapy works.)

I hated junior high. I felt afraid and out of my element. One day some ongoing tension I had with one guy blossomed into a fight. We both ended up in the principal's office. (I'd call the fight a draw.) But I remember crying about my life at school that night at home. I was sitting on the bed in my room, and my mother came in and sat next to me, her hand rubbing my back. My father stood close by, and they were just quiet and loving and *with* me. They listened to my hurt and kindly comforted me. (I also remember overhearing my mother whispering to my dad, "I wish I could just turn that little brat across my knee!" Mom's are the bomb!) Life was hard in that season, but I was so comforted knowing that they "got it" and cared. *Hearing Heals Hurt!*

Real love and empathy say to that kid who didn't make the team, "Oh my gosh, dude! Come here buddy! Nothing hurts worse than that. I know that you wanted that so badly. That's right man, it's okay to cry about it. We're going to figure it out together."

Real love and empathy say to that child who is angry about being grounded, "Yeah, man. I get it. I know you are mad. I hear ya. You're still grounded, but I care that it hurts so bad."

One of the most powerful ways that we *teach* love to school-age kids (and everyone else for that matter) is by making room for them to *feel*, even as we stand our ground with firm limits. We don't try to make them feel better. We don't try to fix it. We don't blow it off and tell them to think about the "starving kids in Africa." Instead, we try it on. We let it matter. And when we do that, we are letting our *child* matter—we're teaching love!

The added bonus of empathy

By the way, engaging kids at a feeling level is not just a "love" thing. Empathy and emotional connection also help kids learn to *manage their emotional world*—to be able to have feelings and not let them run their lives.

Here's how that works.

Little kids are concrete. Firstly, they are concrete *thinkers*. (That's why *Sesame Street* doesn't talk about the lofty concept of "Threeness." It talks about three *cookies!*)

Secondly, kids are concrete *feelers*. They *do* what they *feel!* If you don't get your four-year-old that Bubblicious at the checkout counter, they don't say, "Gee, Mom. I am really sad and disappointed. I was really looking forward to that big gooey bubble gum!" No, they throw themselves on the floor and scream like you are dragging them to the orphanage! They *do* their feelings!

This can be a lot of the reason for crazy misbehavior in kids. Sometimes, acting like a spoiled brat is not about "disobedience." It's about a child having so many feelings that the emotion just bubbles out of them and turns into violent or impulsive behavior. (It's also one of the causes of ADHD.)

Anyway, somewhere between the Bubblicious stage and adulthood, we develop an ability that allows someone to cut us off on the freeway, and we may say, "What an idiot! I'd love to run into the back of that guy and teach him a lesson." *But we don't!* (hopefully).

So what happened in the years between Bubblicious and road rage? Emotional maturity happened! *Emotional maturity* involves developing the ability to *have* a feeling and not necessarily *act* on it. Talking to our kids about their feelings helps them develop this ability! I call it helping kids learn to "mentalize" their feelings. Make them mental, not physical.

You know that stereotypical psychologist phrase, "It seems like you are feeling very angry." Well, we're not just doing psychobabble when we say this. We're actually naming a feeling. It's taxonomy. A ton of people literally do not know that what is happening inside of them is that they are being driven by a feeling. And naming a feeling begins to give us power over the feelings that control us.

When we talk to our kids about their feelings, we are engaging them with love, but we are also teaching them to manage their emotions. We are essentially saying, "That feeling that just washed over you—the one that made you hit your brother—that's called 'anger.' And that's okay, but I can't let you hit your brother."

We used to say to our kids all the time, "You can be angry, but you can't hit your sister!" God says, "Be angry but sin not." Same thing.

After many conversations about angry feelings, Katherine

(then about age five) walked into our room one evening looking very serious. She had her fists clenched and her face set. She looked at us and said very seriously, "I'm feeling really angry at Callie, but I'm trying real hard not to hit her!" Now, she wasn't just giving a shout out to Jules Winnfield, who is "trying real hard to be the shepherd!" She was making sense of having a feeling, but not *acting* on it. It was all we could do not to laugh at her stone-faced commitment, but she was getting it!

Feelings happen inside, and as we grow, we learn to not let them control our lives. Empathy and understanding not only feel loving, they give us power.

So, feel free to go grab your school-age kids right now and *tell* them that you love them! But every time you tie on those soccer cleats, or coach a child on how to deal with a bully, or talk to them about their hearts when they are sad, know that you are folding love into their hearts, *doing* love at the deepest most wonderful level.

Teenagers

How do we show love to a teen? Well, we're still going to *tell* them we love them, even though they will probably groan and walk out of the room. (Though it's always moving to me when I see teens in therapy, observing how even when they "cannot stand" their parents, their hearts still seem to crave their parent's love—and they hurt so much when their parents are unkind.)

We will still *attend and nurture* sometimes (usually on their terms). Our teens wouldn't speak to us for three days and then suddenly would appear in our room—inevitably during the best part of a movie—and collapse sobbing on the bed, needing nurture and comfort. (I'm thinking, "I thought you hated our guts!")

There will also be limit setting, empowerment, and empathy. But let's be honest, showing love to teenagers is complicated. Do you remember the old analogy that warned us that little kids are like dogs, but teenagers are like cats. You come home from work and your little kid "dog" jumps up and down and runs to your arms! They can't wait to play and tussle and tell you about their day. But one day, one fateful day, your wonderful little puppy dog turns into a big surly teenage *cat*. Now you walk into the room, and they sort of turn up their nose at you and walk away as if to say, "Who died and made you emperor?" You present them with dinner, and they groan, roll their eyes, and disappear upstairs. Thirty minutes later, the Dominoes guy is knocking at your door.

So why can teenagers be such annoying little snits? Well, if a toddler is working to develop power and separation from *mommy*, a teenager is working to develop power and separation from *family*. That's why.

The teenage years are a transition time from childhood to adulthood. Teens are not just children anymore, but they're not quite adults. And the teenage years are like a flight simulator to help kids begin practicing to function independently in the world.

We'll talk more about this in Chapter Four, but this is why

you see them wanting to be different from you, disagreeing with everything you say, and generally being annoying. This is why they disappear into their room, off the grid like Jason Bourne. This is why they are humiliated if they're seen in public with you and why they say things like, "Oh my gosh! You guys are so dumb!" All of this behavior is charming, of course, but what they're trying to do is find out who they are apart from you.

So welcome to today's brainteaser: How do you connect with and show love to a child whose *job* is to get away from you?

Here's the secret: *Loving a teenager is not necessarily about being close!* So for us parents, the rules have to change. Suddenly, we are not just parenting, we're *de-parenting*—where your goal (and theirs) is to work yourself out of a job. (I mean, who's going to nag them in college?)

In our culture, many parents have lost the perspective that parenting has two goals, not just one. Sure, we "parent" them to the point that they feel loved and safe, but also we need to begin (earlier than you might think) "de-parenting" them toward strength and separateness. De-parenting is about letting them go. De-parenting is about pushing them to be strong. And with most teens, de-parenting is about permitting them some of the separateness they are begging for.

One of the most powerful ways that we show love to a teenager is through de-parenting. In other words, *fostering a child's independence is as important a gift to our kids as nurturing them.* Good parenting jujitsu does both!

Let's look at two practical ways you can love your teen by de-parenting:

- Learn what it means to *talk with them,* and
- Work to *embrace their attempts at separation.* (as many as we can, at least)

Talk with them

If you really want to show love to your teen, learn what it means to talk *with* them.

One of my teenage clients actually taught me this. He said, "I like talking to you, man. You don't just talk *to* me, you talk *with* me." (I thought to myself, "I'm so stealing that!")

As we said earlier, showing love to our kids is really not that different from showing love to anyone else. How do we love other people? We treat them like they matter. They are people just like us.

Since your child was born, you've had the *role* in their life of being their parents. But as they get older, and especially during the teenage years, true love looks for opportunities to relate to them not just from the *parent role,* but also as *fellow people.* Despite the way their room looks, they are people too!

Simply being an authority in the lives of our kids is pretty staightforward. We are the parents; they are the children. "You can't have any dessert before supper." "You can't put the cat in the bathtub." Not a lot of ambiguity there. But a major love language for teenagers involves their longing to be heard and treated like *people* whose opinions matter—whose feelings matter.

A very powerful way we do this is to *talk with*.

We do this all the time in real life. Right now, you are reading my book. And I am speaking as an authority. But if we met one day at a conference, say, in the parking lot of the conference center, it would be bizarre if I continued to relate to you as the *authority*. "I noticed the way you parked your car," I would say. "I have three points on that. You may take notes if you wish."

No! That would be weird!

Instead, I would step out of my role as authority and relate to you as a *person!* I would talk *with* you. "What's a good pizza joint nearby?" I might ask.

That's "talking *with*."

To show love to teenagers, we do the same thing. We sometimes need to step out of our role as authority and talk *with* them. One of the biggest mistakes I see parents of adolescents making is still trying to parent their teen from that "authority parent" role only. "This is what we say and that's final!" If you do that, your teenager will rebel, shut down, or become your compliant little automaton (which doesn't work very well long-term). So yes, as we will discuss in the next chapter, we need to set limits on teens. But to love them well we also need to look for opportunities to add the "human to human" element—to talk with.

What does Talk With sound like?

Let's put some legs on this. How do we "talk with"? Your teen says something like, "I hate school!" The dimwitted authoritarian parent responds by saying, "Well then, I hope you like being a garbage man one day, because that's what you gonna be if you don't buckle down!"

The "talk with" parent says, "Oh my gosh! I hated school sometimes too! I remember I thought I was going to flunk chemistry in eleventh grade, and going to that class felt like going to prison. What do you hate the most? Is there anything you like?"

Hear it? I'm saying to my child that I love them enough to step out of my own parental anxiety (hello!) and let them matter—to hear *their heart*.

That is teenage love!

Now, don't panic. We are just *adding* the "talk with" part. We're not turning your family into a groovy encounter group with no discipline. So, we're also going to say, "... and, by the way, if you flunk that test tomorrow, you're grounded this weekend like we talked about."

We do both—like walking and chewing bubble gum at the same time!

Let's do another example. They say, "I've gotten into rap music." The anxious controlling parent says, "Oh my gosh, with all those filthy lyrics! I want to wash that 'Lil Wayne's mouth out with soap!"

Now, to the degree that you talk that way, gangsta boy is going to come home tomorrow wearing gold chains and a flat bill.

The "talk with" parent says, "Really? What you like about rap? Who's the best rapper? Can you make your whole car shake and vibrate at the stoplight? ... *and* by the way, if you get into stuff that's too nasty, we might have to set some limits there—maybe you could get into Lecrea—but I'm glad to know what you're into. Make me a CD."

You talk like that, and your kid's going to be borrowing your Chris Stapleton soon.

People often ask me, "Why is my teenager not talking to me?" A lot of times it's simply because they are trying to forge some healthy independence. But sometimes it's because you're wanting to talk *to* them, not talk *with* them.

A mother raised her hand in a group once and asked me, "Why won't my son talk to me?" (Like I knew him or something.)

Smelling a rat, I asked her, "Well, what would you like to talk to him about?"

She said, "I want to know what he's doing, so I can make sure he's not acting up."

Wow! I can't imagine why he didn't want to talk to her!

I often have parents bring their teen to my office and say, "She won't open up to us, Doc."

I usually say something like, "Well, let's ask her something, and see what happens!"

"So, Cher, how did you feel about coming to the shrink's office today?"

And she'll say, "Oh, my *Gaaaaah*—I didn't want to. They just told me I was coming, like, an hour ago. Oh, my *Gaaaaah!*" Suddenly the parents leap up, bellowing, "We did not! We told you two nights ago, and you just weren't listening. You never listen. See—this is our problem!"

And I'm thinking, "*Hmmm.* I wonder why she won't open up to you."

Another Secret of the Universe—*Your teenager will listen to you (in obedience) approximately to the same degree that you listen to them (regarding their hearts).* This is love for a teen. It speaks the same thing to them that rocking a baby speaks to an infant.

Embrace their separation

Another way that we de-parent and teach love to a teen is by having a category for *loving and embracing* as much of their separation as we can. (And yes, I said "loving.")

Remember, teens are all about separating, having their own space, and being different from you. It's their job. They are trying to become adults here. Go girl!

That's why it feels like the worst thing in the world to them when you make them come downstairs and play monopoly with you and their eight-year-old sister! Why don't you be merciful and just give them molten lava to drink? They are practicing to be adults and asking who they are apart from you. All of our anxiety and panic that they are "not wanting to spend time with the family" feels like a suffocating octopus to them. Which tends to make most of them pull away even more. (Cue the dance of the clingy parents and the "pull-away" child.)

So one of the most powerful ways that we can teach love to our teenagers is to embrace as much of their separateness as we can. Kind of like we did with toddlers, remember? Don't tell your teen I said this, but a teenager is just a big toddler with a nose piercing. Their developmental tasks are the same—learning to be separate and independent.

So a huge way we show love to a teen is to look for their attempts at separation that we can accept—and *accept* them!

Now, there are three big fat reasons I'm telling you this.

First reason: Because it feels profoundly loving to them. To their ears, it's like you are welcoming them to adulthood. You're not just treating them like they are a kid. You know how, at family gatherings, there will come a year in which the teenager slides over to the grown-up's table after dinner? Moving toward adulthood is a big deal to them.

Second Reason: Consider the alternative—your thirty-eight-year-old son, still lying on the couch in the bonus room saying, "Hey Mom, do we have any more Hot Pockets?" Let's help them leave while there is still time!

Third Reason: They can make this *harder* if they need to. In other words, we can do this the easy way, or we can do this the hard way.

Let me explain.

There's a sense in which having a separating teenager is like being carjacked. You're sitting in your car in a parking lot, and some guy taps on your window with a gun. Now, this guy could take your wallet. He could take your car. He could kill you and take your car and your wallet! But if all he wants is your *wallet*—give it to him! You are the luckiest person in town! The people who get killed are the ones who fight the carjacker and try to not give *anything*.

Your teen will separate (hopefully). How *bad* that experience will be has a lot to do with how much you work with them. Mine used to like to call me "John" sometimes—or "Papa Shrink." I'm like, "DEAL! If that's all you need to be separate and sassy, then where do I sign? How do I lock in at that rate?" It's the parents who bow up and say, "No, that's disrespectful! You will call me 'Father'!" Those are the ones who have the kids who shave their heads. They can take this as far as you want! Their tactics are downright Archimedean! Look for the independence you can accept, and accept it—this is a carjacking remember? No way around it.

So they say, "I want to paint my room." Or, "I want to get a stud in my ear." Or, "I want to go to the football game with my friends." Try to stretch. Look for separateness you can embrace and embrace it! This is a major love language for teens!

This is hard

By the way, why do we resist this separation/independence thing in our teens? Usually it's for two reasons. Because we're *anxious* and because we are *sad*. Let's touch on these briefly.

Hear me on this. Fear and anxiety are your enemies as the parent of a teen. Anxiety creates a situation in which your teen makes stupid choices (which they *will* do)—so the anxious parent tries to control them more. Which, A) doesn't work, and, B) the teens who are the most controlled tend to be the ones who make the most and the stupidest choices! So beware your fear! As Yoda said, "Fear leads to anger, anger leads to hatred, and hatred leads to suffering."

Secondly, separation may mean we have to do some

grieving—the sad part. We don't want to let our babies go!

Our oldest, Callie, went to TCU. I'll never forget dropping her off and driving back from Texas. I think I cried all the way to Shreveport. One night during the first semester of her freshman year, Norma and I were literally sitting watching baby videos of her and crying. Suddenly the phone rang, and it was Callie! Frantically, we turned off the TV, straightened up, and wiped our tears away.

Upon answering, she asked, "Hey, what are you guys doing?"

"Nothing!" We replied. "We're doing absolutely *nothing*."

Our relationship with our children is the only relationship God created which was designed to move toward lesser and lesser intimacy—and that goes against our grain. But sadness and grief are our last great gifts to our children. When our kids see that we are strong enough to let them go, it speaks deep mattering to them. And we can be comforted by the fact that there will be an ebb and flow. To the degree that we welcome their separation, they will swing back and share their hearts. It also lays the groundwork for good adult relationships with them—I'm living that now.

I wish I could do this

Loving our children is not just about touchy-feely, "Who loves you baby?" It's about living in such a way that says, "Who you *are* matters more than what you are *like*." Let's look at a master at work. The best way to learn to cook is to watch Thomas Keller, so let's peek in on someone who *loves* like a gourmet chef.

One of my mentors told me about a day in which he had come home from work and found his wife and teenage daughter talking in the kitchen. His daughter often borrowed and wore his T-shirts. He felt like it was a sweet gesture and enjoyed it. On this afternoon, however, he noticed that she was wearing his *favorite* T-shirt! He had worn it during one of the greatest adventures of his life and kept it folded away, separate from the others. Walking through the kitchen, he said with a smile, "I see you have graduated up to wearing my *favorite* T-shirt!" He then went back to change clothes.

When he returned, there was a tangible, sober atmosphere in the room. Sensing this, he asked "What's going on, guys?" His daughter stood up and turned around. The T-shirt was covered with pink paint. She had worn it while painting a piece of furniture and ruined it. My mentor told me that he felt rage and loss flood over him. He wanted to let her have it! Both barrels!

So he did what we will discuss in the next chapter: He took a *timeout!* He knew that anything he said in that moment would be something he would later regret.

He walked in the next room and collapsed on the bed, flooded with anger. But then, as he lay there, something happened in his heart—something warm—like what happened in the Grinch. He got up and walked back in the room and looked at his daughter. He said to her, "You know, dear one, saying 'I love you' is *cheap.* It's just these words that we throw around like they really mean something. But it is a very rare gift to be given the opportunity to give love that *costs something.* That was my favorite T-shirt. I loved it. But the loss of that in no way compares to how much I love you. Today I get to love you with some *cost.* That is a rare gift. Let's get some turpentine and see if we can at least turn hot pink into soft pink—together."

Get to know love, kid.

Getting free

If you are anything like me, you don't love *anybody* as well as my mentor did his daughter. Let's talk about a couple ways the rest of us screw this love thing up! Let's talk briefly about what I call the "*Love Un-doers.*" And then let's get free.

We've been talking a lot about putting love in our kids' plus column, let's talk some about the ways in which we can detract from love in the negative column. The Hall of Famers here being *anger* and *shame.*

I had a kid once in my practice whose father screamed at him and called him a stupid idiot if he lost a ball game. And the kid said it didn't bother him because he deserved to be yelled that for how he played. But he was super insecure, and he struggled with friends. Fun for the whole family, right? We'll talk more about anger in the chapter on discipline, but regarding love, to the degree our children feel our frustration, anger, and exasperation boil over on them, they will feel love sucked out of the room.

We parents are just humans. We have our own junk, injuries, and longings—things that often go unfulfilled and unresolved. Our hearts can hurt. And then we have kids! And as we do life with our kids, it is so easy for that garbage we are carrying to emerge in frustration and fear, and come pouring out of us as anger. So our kids don't do what we want, and we say things like "I'm surprised at you!"; "I'm so sick of this house being such a wreck!"; and "This is why we don't get you nice things!"

Maybe you had a hard day at work, and you turn around and catch your four-year-old walking away from the refrigerator with a whole gallon of milk—which they then proceed to drop. You scream at them. Or those two boys are fighting *again,* and you pop your cork! Please tell me you do this kind of stuff too!

So what do we do when we act like a total whacko? Just decide to go act better? Make a New Year's resolution? Good luck with that!

Certainly, do some of your own growth work. We'll talk more about that later. But more importantly, remember—this is not just another "go be a better parent" book! We need to remember good enough—Quick! The only thing better than a perfect parent is a humble parent, remember? So what do we do when we blow it?

We swing back in! We repair it!

We say, "Man, I totally screwed up and was so harsh. Obviously, I need to do some growing there. Will you forgive me? I treated you like you didn't matter at all." (You're still going to time out), but that's no excuse for my being a jerk.

Now, parent, look at what you've created!

You've just turned a total screwup into a moment of deep, precious intimacy and humility with your child, which *is* the love and mattering we are talking about giving them!

Mischief managed!

God's strength made perfect in weakness!

You win either way, and so does your child—all because you *were* a screw-up!

This is the gospel at home, boys and girls. This is good enough parenting.

Sometimes (on a good day) we can show our kids love though our wisdom and compassion. And when we mess up, we can still show them love through our humility.

Because of our safety and forgiveness in Christ, we all get to live now in what I call the "Grace Effect." The Grace Effect is the wonderful backwards way in which, in the context of grace and love, our screwedupness makes us *closer* to one another, not *further apart.* We all think that if you really knew me, you would think I'm horrible and run off screaming. But the truest truth is that if I am really humble and honest about my mistakes, and if our home is filled with such grace and safety that you can be humble too, then we get to be screwed up *together.*

"You too? I thought I was the only one!"

The result is a deeper richer love than "perfect people" will ever experience. Try it sometime. God made this paradoxical miracle possible—and living it out teaches Jedi-level love to our kids.

So study your kids' love languages. Learn about nurturing and bonding and empowerment and empathy. But also learn to fail well. And bring that to your kids.

I want to free you, remember? Love is not about doing nice things to each other. Real loving intimacy is about people being close and honest and real. I'm a person, you're a person. Let's be close and broken and fallen together. This is how I want you to love your kids.

Q&A time

Many people say that one of their favorite parts of a conference is the question and answer time. One of my friends calls it "Stump the Chump." And since there are a thousand complications and permutations to the principles in this book, let's have a little Q&A time at the end of our chapters, and talk about the kind of stuff I'm often asked.

> **Hey Doc—you talk about how hearing our children's feelings feels loving to them. But we have a child who emotes about *everything*. Constantly. Where do you draw the line between loving their heart and being driven crazy by their constant *emotions*?**

Great question! Emotions are certainly the language of our hearts, and it feels loving to us when those emotions are cared about and heard. But every now and then, you run across a child who doesn't *feel* their emotions—they are *run* by them. Your question is insightful because that child *does* need something besides just empathy.

As we said, children came out of the womb with very different personality styles. Some are born feisty and independent. With them, we might need to lean harder into the chapter on teaching about love and connection. On the other hand, that next child is sweet, cuddly, and loves being touchy-feely and relational. Oftentimes, that's the same child who is getting picked on by their peers. With them, we will need to lean harder into the building strength department. Different kids, different blindspots

So what do you do with that histrionic, emotional child? That "Desdemona" whose blindspot is that she's always emoting all over the place? You could do *empathy and love* with her until the cows come home, and it will get you nowhere. She's got the "lovey/touchy-feely" thing down! *Her blindspot is not being strong.*

I remember one of mine was acting pitiful and treaded upon after being given a consequence for her misbehavior. She spotted one of my handkerchiefs nearby. Picking it up, she looked up at me with pitiful eyes and asked in a quivering, manipulative voice, "Daddy, do you mind if I use this to dry my tears?" I'm like, "Knock yourself out, Slick. Whatever floats your boat." More empathy won't help her here. She needs a "buck up" moment—learning to be strong and to contain her emotion.

Emotions need the love and understanding of intimacy, but when emotions begin to run a child's life, we need to swing in and help create limits for that child in their emotional chaos. They are not able to say "no" to their flood of feelings yet, so we need to do that for them. Just like we tell a child that they can "be angry, but they can't hit their brother," we tell an overly emotional child, "We love you and your feelings, but we cannot let them run your life or our family."

After you have given that child some moments to express

their strong feelings and you've engaged them with a caring heart, swing in and say something like, "Hey buddy, I understand that you are so sad that the party got rained out. And we care about that. However, I also want you to reach inside and tell those emotions they don't get to ruin your day. If you need, we might let you do a little timeout until you can get a handle on that tantrum. We want to help you not let them take over. You are loved and you are strong. And we're going to help you learn to be stronger than all these feelings."

When we say this kind of thing, we are supporting and strengthening the child in their war against the power of their feelings. They have us on their team, and they are not just loved, they are strong.

> **My husband is not a very "relational" person. He admits that he doesn't do intimacy and closeness very well with the kids or in our marriage. This whole chapter is on how to love our kids well. What if he doesn't know how to do that?**

As we unpack all the things that our kids need throughout this book, you will certainly find at least one area in which you have your own blindspots. (The advanced students will find about *seven* areas in which they have blindspots.) But you said one thing about your husband that is the linchpin for dealing with any blindspot, be it relational or even spiritual. You said, "He *admits* it!" In other words, he is what God calls "repentant," and God can do amazing things with repentant people.

I'll tell you what I did with my blindspots. Number one, I let them be a very talked-about part of my marriage and my parenting. I tried to talk to my kids about the things I could not do well. Fortunately for me, "The only thing better than a perfect parent is a humble parent!" Good enough freedom means that I am relating to my children in the areas where I am strong, *and* in the areas where I am weak. Remember, grace sets us free to bring our mistakes and failures to the relationship. That's the best kind of love there is.

Secondly, get in your own growth process. Find a therapist or a pastor or a growth group and began asking them to give to your heart and hold you accountable regarding your struggles. The good news is that our growth and development does not stop in childhood. God made us to where we can continue to become more and more like him if we receive the ingredients for healing.

(Check out the Q&A Bonus Round appendix for more thrilling Q&A action!)

---

[1]*While these two categories are quite common now in the vernacular of parenting, I learned them originally from Bruce Narramore.*

You can get a lot with kindness. You can get more with kindness and a gun.

— Al Capone

Chapter Three

How do I get my kids to do what I say?

The goal

Be honest. If you're like most parents, you read this book's contents page and just skipped straight to this chapter, right? So welcome to, "How to get your kids to do what you say 101," otherwise known as, "How to get Godzilla out of Tokyo!" Your child's corresponding question, by the way is, "Why can't I just do anything I want?" (And we are going to have to give them a good answer.)

As we said in the last chapter, there's a sense in which we can boil the whole parenting universe down into two elements: Love and Limits. Personally, I think it would be great if we could just *love* our kids. Being the discipline warden was never my favorite role. However, we all know that kids would take advantage of a home that was just "Pleasure Island." They are red-blooded American gangsters.

One Saturday, I took our kids out for the day. I told Norma

to take the day off, and I was going to be "Disneyland Dad." We rode go-carts and played video games and had pizza and went to the mall! One of the things they loved to do at the mall was to sample the perfumes at the department stores. With three girls, that meant the car smelled like a seraglio on the way home, but they loved it!

All was going well that day—"well," that is, until *I* needed something. On our way home, after hours of joy, I pulled into the parking lot of my cleaners. I needed to pick up my shirts. The girls gasped.

"Where are we going? What are you doing?"

"Oh," I replied, "I just need to run in and pick up my cleaning ... be back in a scooch!"

Suddenly they erupted into wails of protest!

"*Nooooo*, Daddy! We don't *waaaaant* to stop at the cleaners! This isn't a fair! We want to go *hooooome!*"

To be honest, I wasn't quite sure how to respond to this performance. I parked right in front, got out of their blast radius, and ran in the cleaners. As I was walking back to the car, I could see them still screaming and crying. The windows were rolled up, so I couldn't hear them, but what I saw was like a silent film of the condemned souls in the lower levels of Dante's *Inferno*—silent screams displayed behind the glass.

This is who we're dealing with here. I mean, everything with your kids will go along just fine as long as you do their bidding. But then you do something stupid—such as take them to the grocery store! (Ha! You fools!) You know how at the grocery store every little cherub turns into an international terrorist. Carlos the jackal. Isis operative. And the child's basic message is, "You will buy me this Zagnut or I will scream so loud that everyone in the store will hear the cries of my people!" Or with teens, you ask them to do their chores, and they're on the phone to the Department of Human Services, reporting you for abuse. "Yeah, they're doing that 'chores' thing again. Can this go on their record?"

As we'll discuss later on, there are actually two reasons that we discipline children. One is to help craft them into people who can make wise choices and function well in the world (and do what we say). But the second reason is simply to make them people we can stand being around! I mean, there's no commandment against singing *Naa Naa Naa, Naa Naa Naa* for three hours in the car. But if you don't hit the kill switch on that stuff soon, you're going to want to sell them to the next caravan.

So, all that love stuff in last chapter was great, but as our friend Al Capone said, "You can get more with a gun." So we also need to *Bring Da Noise!* Besides, I don't think you're going to enjoy parenting (much less feel free) until you feel strong and competent engaging in powerful discipline with your kids.

If the way you are currently trying to discipline your kids makes you act like a maniac, take comfort. I actually came up with the model of discipline I'm about to teach you in order to deal with my own anger issues. I was feeling powerless trying to get my kids to do what I wanted (feeling powerless is usually what triggers our anger). I would say, "Do this," and they'd refuse. So I would get louder, and they would pitch a fit. And we did that every night. "Happy, Happy, Joy, Joy!"

At some point I thought, "There's got to be a better way! Use your magic powers, Mr. Psychologist!" So I did. And I came up with this model. And I'm gonna teach you what it is.

Here's what we're going to do in this chapter.

First, we're going to look at how we often try to solve these problems, usually ineffectively, using two inadequate measures I call "Coddling" and "Control." Then we're going to look at a more powerful way of engaging our kids—an approach I call "Teaching Discipline." Initially, I'm going to give you some examples and stories to help you get the vibe of Teaching Discipline, then we're going to go step-by-step and look at the process. Lastly, we will look at more examples, and finally some question-and-answer time.

The ways we usually discipline
Coddling

Our first "bad idea" approach to discipline I call Coddling. Coddling is basically Good Cop/Good Cop. The parents aren't the authorities here, we're all just friends!

With coddling, our kids might be throwing plates at the neighbor's house ("Mind you don't cut yourself, Mordecai!")—and we're saying stuff like, "Hey, amigo, didn't we talk about this?" Or at home we say, "Hey, buddy, let's pick up your toys, okay?" Like we're making sure we're getting their permission—don't want to step on any toes here. (In our culture, *parents* are the ones who are "seen and not heard!")

Here's another one I love: Since coddling parents often feel like they can't just *tell* their kids what to do, they feel that they have to sort of *pitch it,* sell them on it. One technique that amuses me I call the "Good Cop/Better Cop Team Parent Approach." It goes something like this: One parent poses a proposition to child, and then the other parent jumps in excitedly to encourage it—hoping the child will bite.

Here's what it sounds like.

Parent One: "Hey guys, we're going to do bath soon, okay?"

Parent Two: (Gasp!) "A *baaaaaath!*"

We're not going to spend any more time on the coddling thing because it barely counts as a persuasive technique. You've already abdicated your authority here. So let's move on to option number two and spend a bit of time on it because it's our default mode when we are frustrated.

Welcome to Control.

Control

Let me introduce you to Control, one of the most popular approaches to "discipline."(Though, as you will soon see, this approach needs no introduction. I think you already know it well.)

Control usually begins by our issuing a *command.* We tell the kids to clean their room. And what are they going to do?

Well, I'll tell ya—they're going to *refuse!*

But not just refuse. (They have more finesse than that.) They are going to refuse by using one or more of the following sophisticated techniques:

- They will do nothing—staring like there's a gas leak in the room.
- They will put away two things, and then stand in the middle of the squalor and say, "I cleaned it."
- They will demand to know "Why?" Like, "Unless you have a cogent, persuasive reason, the deal's off."
- They will say, "I don't want to." (One of my friends responds to her kids by saying "That's okay, you don't have to *want* to.")

One of our daughters would play the pitiful card. "I just feel too sick. I can't even sit up. And I feel really bad about it, because I know I *should* clean my room. I mean, I want to. But I just feel too bad!"

In other words—using a variety of creative methods, they r*efuse*!

Now, at this point, what does Control do? What is our part in this waltz?

Kiddo *refuses*, so basically—we e*scalate*!

And we are going to escalate using one or more of the following sophisticated techniques:

- We say it louder and meaner.
- We threaten really *big* things. "I'm going to rent your room out to someone who appreciates it!"

- We try to g*ive* them that "reason" they demanded.
- We use their whole name. (Just in case they thought we were talking about some *other* "Callie Cox.")
- We count. (Remember Tina Fey and Steve Carell in the movie *Date Night* as they try to deal with their daughter? Tina's character says something like, "I can't get her to do anything." Steve Carell: "Well, did you "one-two-three" her? Tina Fey: "Yeah! I "one-two-three-ed" her. ... it *still* didn't work!")
- We say, "I'm not going to tell you again!" One time my mother used this line on me, and I responded by saying, "Good! Things are looking up!" (Little safety tip. Don't ever say that!)

Anyway, these are the tools of the trade with Control: *Refusal* and *Escalation.* They are the coin of the realm. And don't look now, but the room still isn't clean.

In other words, *Control doesn't work.* After all, can you really control anybody? I mean, how do you "make" your child clean their room? Take a nap? Be polite at grandma's? As they say in *Cool Hand Luke,* "What we got here is a failure to communicate." And it's called a p*ower struggle*—a battle of your will against theirs.

The power struggle
A power struggle is officially defined as: *When your child*

challenges your authority, and you attempt to prove it, (thereby tacitly "agreeing" that your authority is in question).

So, there are two parts to a powerful struggle:

1) The child challenges—"Not gonna do it!"
2) And you say—"Oh yeah? Then I'll show you who's boss!"

And if you play the power struggle game, I promise, it will be "hasta lasagna don't get any on ya!" You will lose! They are better at being immature than you are! You will lose in one of two ways:

1) You will lose by *their* winning and never cleaning the room; and now you have an honest-to-goodness south-of-the-border coup d'état on your hands—and you're living with the Kardashians.
2) Or, you will lose by actually "winning," but you've won by becoming bigger and louder and "threateningier" and meaner and naggier and shamier. And you have forced them. And you've "proven your authority"—you think.

So ultimately, the room may get clean, but everyone is exhausted and angry and resentful. And their takeaway is, "I swear I'm going to win next time," or, "I'm so mad at Dad," or, "Okay, I will just submit and live in a one down position my whole life."

The bottom line is that you lose. And so do your kids.

In fact, what I've seen when Control is used with kids—when that power struggle style is enforced—is that we get one of only three kinds of kids as a result. When Control is the norm in your world, it produces either a *compliant child*, a *rebel*, or a *sneak*. Let's consider each of these.

Compliance

Firstly, we can produce a kid who is *Compliant*. In other words, if you are "successful" at making your child do what you want, perhaps they'll never disobey you—*or anyone else in their life!* Not to go too fast for ya, but if you force compliance, it often "forces compliance"—and then it's real easy for that kid to develop compliance as a life strategy. And that's lots of fun when you're proud of your little soldier at grandma's house. But let me ask you, how are the "compliant adults" doing in life? I see these kids in therapy when they are about twenty-two, and they can't say "no" to anyone. They live sort of paralyzed of upsetting the parent figures in their world—at work, with friends, with their spouse, or with that guy in the back seat of his Camaro. In other words, they're compliant. Not the best life strategy for adults.

Rebellion

Secondly, Control can create a *Rebel*. With a rebel, you draw a line in the sand, you start a war—and he is *glad* to finish it! A rebel says, "In your face! You want a piece of me? White meat or dark meat?" And in the rebel's home, we can often see an escalating war zone take place, especially with a teen.

You ground him, so he sneaks out. So you nail the windows shut, so he builds a meth lab in the basement. And you'll be thinking, "Boy, that escalated quickly."

A lot of times when parents say, "Nothing we are doing is 'working,'" it's because what they are doing is taking place within the culture of a power struggle—and nothing "works" there.

Sneaks

Thirdly, Control can create a *Sneak*. A sneak makes you think you are winning and that "your little angel" is complying—but just wait. You've told them they can't eat in their room, and they've sweetly said, "Yes ma'am." But later you find like two-hundred Twinkie wrappers hidden in their sock drawer.

I have a friend who grew up in a strict Baptist home where her parents only allowed her to listen to Christian music. Problem was that she loved AC/DC, Prince, and Bon Jovi. Her solution? She hid her naughty rock 'n roll cassette tapes inside of Christian cassette cases. So, if you looked inside the case of Amy Grant's *My Father's Eyes* you would find Bon Jovi's classic album, *Slippery When Wet!*

Anger and control

Another problem with power struggles and control is that *anger* is usually a major player. Let's talk briefly about anger and discipline.

Secret of the Galaxy: Anger is what humans feel when they *don't* feel powerful. Anger is essentially a defense, a way to *not feel* vulnerable. For most people, anger is the *second* thing they feel, not the first. In other words, instead of feeling helplessness, shame or fear, we get angry, the gift that keeps on giving.

Think about it—you're in a hurry for a job interview, and you miss every red light along the way. You top the next hill, and the light turns red right in front of you. If you're like me, you curse and bang the steering wheel. You get angry. But that was the *second* thing you felt. The first thing you felt was *helplessness* or *fear* that you'd be late. Tell me I'm wrong!

Here's another one. Your wife tells an embarrassing story about you at a party. You get in the car and the first thing you say is, "Oh my gosh! What were you thinking telling that story!" You're angry, right? But the first thing you were feeling was *embarrassment* and *shame*. Anger is a defense against more vulnerable feelings.

So, how does this apply to parenting? Well, think about it, your kids are out of control. Bedtime starts to feel like a border war. You feel *helpless, powerless,* and *overwhelmed*. But that's not where you *stay*! Quickly those vulnerable feelings morph into anger (the second thing you feel), and you start screaming and yelling at those rotten kids. Anger is a way to not have to face our helpless and powerless feelings. And if we aren't careful, it will corrupt our discipline.

How does anger undermine our discipline?

Number one, it makes discipline *personal*. Bruce Narramore talks about how angry consequences put a child in the position of getting "punished" because we are mad, not "disciplined" because of their choices. Notice, I never use the word "punishment" anywhere in this book. Punishment is a *retaliation* for a crime, usually done in anger. Discipline is *education* for the future—an opportunity to teach. Discipline is a non-angry consequence. Punishment is angry payback. And, with punishment the child's takeaway is, "Man, I won't ever make Dad mad again!" or, "Now I'm mad at Dad!" or, "I'm gonna learn to never get caught." As opposed to the "wisdom" we are shooting for—"Wow, that choice cost me a lot. I think I'd better *learn!*" Which, as we will see, is the goal of discipline.

Secondly, anger lessens our power. Here's yet another Secret of the Cosmos: *There is an inverse relationship between how angry we are and the effectiveness of our discipline.* The angrier we act, the less powerful our discipline.

If we act like a total gizmo—screaming and yelling at our kids—their takeaway is going to be *"Gaaaagh,* she's going off again! How 'bout a little more positivity, Mom?"

If instead, if you calmly take away your child's Xbox, the arrival of the consequence isn't going to get lost in your hissy fit. There's no angry mom to point at—just a lonely empty dust spot where the Xbox once stood. Power quotient maximized!

I sometimes struggled with my anger as a parent. Maybe the girls were acting like hooligans, but I would often snap and be unkind. I worked on it in my own therapy, but also, I invited my kids to hold me accountable for my anger. I told them, "If you guys act up and need discipline then that's one thing. But if I'm a jerk, you get to call me out. My anger is my immaturity and my responsibility, so I want to give you a stun gun to help me with it." It wasn't too long after that that I railed on them again. Callie, about eight-years-old at that point, entered our room in tears saying, "I know we did bad, Daddy, but now you're just being mean." Ouch! Instant anger management therapy!

So anger is what we do when we don't feel powerful. Let's get powerful!

The new goal: Teaching Discipline
Obedience needs to be taught

So how do we get our kids to do what we say? Well, we can't coddle them into obeying. And we can't control them into doing what we say. So what are we going to do? Well, I'll tell ya! We are going to teach them to obey. That's right. They don't know how, so we are going to teach them! In fact, we are going to call this approach "Teaching Discipline."

Here's the secret. Kids aren't born with the ability to submit to authority. They aren't born with the inclination to obey—any more than they are born with the ability to manage pain or to trust love. We have to teach our kids the software they need to do life.

The "do it because I said so" authoritarian types act like submission and obedience are abilities that we can just require and expect out of children. As if here is this five-year-old walking around with this incredibly sophisticated internal capacity to humble themselves and obey—and the problem is, by golly they just *aren't* willing to do it! And those guys say things like, "Well, when I was a child, all my parents had to say was 'boo!' and I jumped." (Which is why we are all in therapy.)

I disagree with the "do it because I said so" guys, not because I don't wish for that kind of simple parenting. I disagree with them because I don't believe that *submission* is included in our kids' factory specs. A child having the *ability* to obey is the end result of some real learning and maturity, not a baseline to begin with. So instead of requiring them to obey, which leads to power struggles and all the problems therein, we're going to *teach* our children to obey!

Teaching Discipline flyover

How do we teach discipline and submission? How do we get our kids to do what we say? I'll give you the fifty-dollar fancy answer, and then I'll explain it:

Instead of controlling our kids, Teaching Discipline is going to help them develop the ability to wisely control *themselves*—by *experiencing* which choices lead to good things and which choices lead to bad things. In doing so, a child *learns* to choose wisely.

So, first we are going to get ourselves out of the "make-them-obey-us power struggle." We are not going to "make" anybody do anything anymore.

Secondly, we are going to let them *choose*—even if it means that they disobey! (This isn't about control anymore, remember?) Given the freedom to choose, they will probably thumb their nose at us, or continue hitting the heirloom furniture with the plastic golf club, or mosey in late for curfew, again.

At which point, thirdly, we're going to be smokin' sure they experience *consequences* (good or bad) for their choices.

The result?

If we get our anger and control out of the way, and we let them experience the costs of their choices—our kids will begin learning to choose well and obey. IT CAN LEARN!

Kids are pretty clueless at first

If you think about it, the only reason that adults make wise choices in our lives is because we have *learned* what choices lead to what consequences. "Choosing this will help me get a promotion at work." "Saying what I really *want* to say would hurt my wife." "Eating that cake will make my pants not fit." Well, read the news! Children don't yet understand the relationship between what they are choosing and what it will cost them. They arrive on Earth pretty clueless.

Five-year-old Callie and I were killing time once while Mom shopped. In the courtyard of the shopping center there was a big fountain full of pennies.

"Can I make a wish, Daddy?" she asked.

"Sure, babe," I replied, fishing a penny out of my pocket.

She took it, squinted her eyes in concentration as she selected her wish, and threw the penny in the fountain.

I asked her, "What did you wish for?"

She looked up at me and said, "I wished that I had a penny."

(I'm still scratching my head about that one.) Kids don't live making choices based on consequences. They live reacting impulsively. So we have to *teach them* about choosing and obedience.

The new goal of discipline

Now, as you have perhaps already deduced, the goal of Teaching Discipline is not necessarily immediate obedience on *this* occasion. That bugs some people; but remember, immediate obedience *can't* be the goal at first! That's called Control! The goal is for them to choose what they choose, and learn from the consequences if they disobey.

In other words, here's today's Zen/Grasshopper moment: the only way kids learn to obey is by *disobeying* and reaping *experiential consequences* for those choices. (Not our yelling and controlling.)

Stated another way, the goal of Teaching Discipline isn't obedience right now. The goal is obedience *tomorrow,* and the day after that, and the day after that, because your child has *learned* to choose well. That's what healthy adults do, and after a little schooling it will get them in the bath without all of the hullabaloo. I promise.

So good news for you: Your child's disobedience is not a failure in your discipline—it is *"school"* (as long as it costs them with an event.) So, we aren't going to demand obedience, we're going to *teach* it. Let's start explaining how this works. Let's put some faces on this theory.

Let's learn from Buck

I knew a kid once who was always getting in trouble. His name was Buck. Of course it was. Let's look at how Teaching Discipline works by having dinner with our old friend, Buck.

Think about what usually happens. You tell Buck to stop doing something. "Hey Buck, stop bugging your brother at the dinner table." In other words, we usually begin by giving a *command*. And that's cool, but let's go ahead and say what's going to happen next, because we all know, right? #Notfirstrodeo

Basically, Buck's going to wait One Mississippi, Two Mississippi, and then what? He's gonna bug his brother again! I mean, who wouldn't?

Now part of that is because Buck's a little renegade. But part of that is because all we've done so far is issue him a *command*. And commands aren't powerful. They are just words.

If you want real power here—if you want to begin *teaching* obedience—then the next thing to do is not just to intensify your command. "Buck, I TOLD you to quit bugging your brother! And that's final!"

If we want to teach Buck to obey us, he will need an *event*, not just words.

Teaching Discipline Secret of the Universe: *The most powerful way a child learns to make better choices is by experiencing an event based on their choices.* In other words, kids only learn to obey with events, not words. They are concrete thinkers, remember? A bunch of conceptual words, be they nagging, arguing, threatening, or begging, just sound to a kid like Charlie Brown's teacher *"Waa wah, waa waa wah."* (Maybe you've noticed this.) In fact, a lot of disobedience in kids is due to the fact that all they are encountering is a bunch of *words* back and forth, and never an *event/experience* based on their choices. So, to teach kids to do what we say, we don't *demand* obedience, we *teach* it—with an *event!*

So now, when you feel push back from Buck, instead of more words, we are going to give him a *choice*—predict an *event*. "Buck, *if* you touch your brother again, *then* you're going to timeout." Or "I'm taking your plate until the rest of us have finished eating." We are not trying to stop the brother-poking at this point; we are just setting the stage for the bright and shiny teaching moment that is about to round the corner, because we know that good ole Buck is already raring back to poke his brother again.

The stage is set. The players are ready. The audience is hushed.

Now, when Buck strikes, we **under-react!** "Oh, dude! Sad call there! Lemme get that plate out of your way." In other words, we *follow through* with what we promised (otherwise we'd be teaching him that we are just full of hot air!). And you can say all of this *nicely*. In fact, it's better if you're nice.

Now, at this point, Buck will probably protest and cause a scene (and we'll talk about how to handle that). But ultimately what will happen is that Buck will begin *learning* that this isn't about Me vs. Dad anymore. Dad's not mad. Dad doesn't have a dog in this fight. This is Buck's choice! This is about whether Buck's hiney wants to end up in timeout; or whether he loses his dinner while the rest of the family dines. An event! An experience! It's the only place that irresponsible people (of any age) learn to submit to authority.

We are *teaching* discipline here!

Now, I'm gonna introduce you to Teaching Discipline by giving you some more examples. But here's the strategy: When you encounter that "In your face," that "No"— when they "Throw down"—what we're going to do is work to change the conflict from *You vs Your* child to *Them vs What they reap in their reality*. The moment we realize they are not going to do what we ask, we're going to back up and give them a *choice*—"If you do A, then B is going to happen." And if we can get our anger and control issues out of the picture and let their choices cost them, then suddenly school will be in session! It's learning time.

Examples
"OMG!"

When our older two children went to college, our youngest daughter, Bonney, about sixteen at the time, lived a few years alone with just us. She claims they were the Golden Years. The way it should've been all along!

One night the three of us were having dinner. As we finished, Norma and I began cleaning up the kitchen. As we worked, Bonney pranced through the kitchen, heading upstairs to her room. I looked up at her and said, "Hey Bonn, will you come help us do the dishes?" She paused on the stairs, looked at me through the railing (with a horrified adolescent look of astonishment on her face), and said, "Are you on pills?" and proceeded up to her room.

Now, before we proceed any further, notice that feeling that you are having right now. It's very similar to the one you have when your toddler looks at you and throws food on the floor again, or that pre-teen refuses to get ready for school, again. We're going to have to address that feeling in a big way. It's one of the biggest threats to Teaching Discipline. That urgency, that anger, that disbelief that a child could possibly talk to her parents that way—and that we *need to stop them!* If you conquer that feeling, you will have conquered discipline.

Back to our story. Norma and I looked at each other, mouths agape. How dare she? How could we let our daughter be so disrespectful? What were we supposed to do? I played through the scenario of storming upstairs, bursting through her door, and saying, "You will come back down here this minute, young lady, and help us do the dishes." I've ridden that merry-go-round before. No thanks.

To be honest, I was pretty stumped. (Which, as we will see, is okay. Often you will be stumped in the moment. That's why we aren't going to *act* in the moment.) I decided to breathe. Wait. Take my time. (Unfortunately, she's not going anywhere.)

I began wondering how I could I keep this *event* from becoming a *power struggle*. How could I make it an experience that could cost *her*, not a conflict between the two of us? How could I use this to *teach?*

Suddenly it hit me. I got her car keys off the rack and put them in my pocket. Norma and I then settled in our room and began watching a TV show. About thirty minutes later, we heard Bonney coming down the stairs in her clacky Barbie high heel shoes. (You could actually smell her before you saw her, lathered up in perfume.) I heard her looking for her keys, jangling through other keys hanging on the rack.

"Oh my gosh, y'all!" she demanded. "Where are my keys?"

"Oh, I've got them!" I replied. She appeared in our room, hands on her hips.

"Well, I need to go to Kris's!"

My reply? ... *"Are you on pills?"*

Checkmate!

I continued. "I left you a few dishes in the kitchen. Once you wash them you can have your keys back."

The moment you feel that power struggle—and you will *feel* it, like a disturbance in the force—slow down, take your time (most of the time there really is no rush) and look for the cost. Kids only learn from an event.

Let's do another one.

The mysterious case of the pigsty room

Let's go back to that messy room we mentioned earlier. You walk back in the room and see that it is still not clean. Let's employ some Teaching Discipline!

One option is to say to them, "Wow! You guys really are committed to not cleaning up your rooms, eh? That's impressive. Come to think of it, you actually *don't* have to clean up your rooms. Electronics aren't coming on in the house until you clean your rooms, but that's up to you. I don't have a monkey in this circus. You can do whatever you want—without electronics! You can read the classics!—in your filthy rooms!"

At this point, our kids would inevitably exclaim, "Oh my gosh, *Full House* comes on in ten minutes!" (nineties parenting, remember?), and they would start scrambling to clean up. The *event* gets to be the bad guy, not you.

Another option with the filthy room: "Hey guys, it's not a problem if you don't want to clean your rooms. And if you don't clean them, I'll be *glad* to! I mean, *somebody* needs to clean your rooms right? But here's the catch—if I clean your room, anything I pick up goes in the "Sunday Box" until Sunday. (We actually used the trunk of my car.)

At first, they're usually fine with that plan, lying on their bed playing a video game as you clean. ("Excuse me, Housekeeping, you missed a spot.")

But then tomorrow's soccer game arrives and their soccer cleats are in the Sunday Box. (Oh no! I'm so sorry dude!) An *event*!

I was talking to the parents of a slovenly teenager recently. They aptly call him Pigpen after the iconic Charlie Brown character. Our intervention? If he doesn't clean, his mom will. But she charges five dollars a day for her services—to be deducted out of his allowance. You choose, Pigpen!

Are you getting it? They challenge our authority, but we

don't attempt to prove it like a power struggle would. We let them choose anything they want. We don't "make" them do anything. We back off, let them reap the consequence, and learn through experience!

Basic principle of discipline: *You can have anything you want in life, you just have to pay for it.* And if we can get the power struggle (who's going to win?) out of the way, then our kids can choose anything they want. They just experience the consequences for it. This is the only way anyone *learns* to make wise choices or obey. This is Teaching Discipline.

Whine connoisseurs

You can start primitive versions of this as early as eighteen months. Ours would become quickly discontent and began whining for juice or more snack or to be picked up. Don't say, "Stop whining!" Instead say, "We're not going to help you if you're going to whine and cry. Can you say, 'Juice ... please?'" (A simple form of event.) Invariably, they would begin pointing and asking in their little baby talk for what they wanted. With little ones it's important then to immediately swoop in and quickly respond. "Oh wow! I love how you are asking! Thank you! Here is your juice!" We are *teaching* obedience and self-management.

Dressed for success

That seven-year-old won't get dressed? Don't fuss and fume. Put them and their clothes in timeout. They can *all* come out when they are all together. And, *your child* gets to pick how long that takes! They can take two minutes or thirty minutes. We don't have a taco on this enchilada plate, remember? The event does the talking, not a nagging, frustrated parent!

Grounding for grades

Older kids who refuse to study need an event too. Let's not leave them out! That wouldn't be right! That wouldn't be fair! What I often do in my practice is to get the parents to retrieve teacher grade reports on Thursdays. If their student has more than one or two C's, (whatever standard you choose), then lazy Mr. Peabody is grounded for the weekend. And, you know what? Mr. Peabody doesn't even *have to study* over that weekend. He can do anything he wants. We don't have a pony in this horse race. So, Mr. Peabody is free to not study—but there's always next weekend to consider. His choice—not our fight. Suddenly I find sullen resistant teens asking their parents to please call out their Spanish words.

The legend of the Slo Mo Kid

Your child dillydallies and procrastinates, always making everyone late for school. If you're like a normal parent, you rant and rave, and soon you'll all get free crazy bread.

This child needs an event. "We're not going to fight you anymore about getting ready for school on time. If you're late, that's cool. It's up to you. Your father's going to go ahead and take your brother to school, and I'm just going to wait until you are ready. However, you can deal with the school's detention policy, and I'm also going to *time* you. I'm going to clock how late you ultimately are. Then when you walk in the door from school, you are going to give me three times that amount of time in timeout. (Twenty minutes late to school is an hour in timeout! Ouch!) So take your time. I don't have a Ferris wheel in this carnival.

And, yes, this will cost you as much as it costs them, but that's what good parenting does (remember labor?). But this cost will pay off. I guarantee!

And by the way, remember that to the degree that you can address all of these scenarios without anger, you will have more and more teaching power. (Though at the same time, to the degree that you begin learning that you have this *power*, you will find yourself being *less angry*.)

Midnight Madness

I remember pacing around in my bathrobe one night at about eleven-forty-five, angry at my teenager for not coming in on her curfew. I mean, I was fuming! I wanted to ground her until her first child was born. So I asked myself, "Dude, what do you need to stop being this angry?" My answer: For her to suffer at least as many consequences for this as I was.

Since she had missed curfew before, we had told her that being late would cost her the use of the car for a week. As she walked in, we didn't rant and rave and act like dingbats. We simply said to her, "I'm glad you're home safe. Remember, since you're so late, you'll be needing to make other plans about driving next week."

And when you enforce these kinds of consequences, your

kids will probably rage and argue and protest, and we'll talk later about how to handle that. For now, just get the principle. We don't respond with anger and control; we respond with an event. That's true "powah!"

Preschool purgatory

Now, you parents of children ages one to four, you're rolling your eyes right about now. You're saying, "Yeah, like that's going to work for my four-year-old! I spend my life chasing him across the Walmart parking lot!" One mother told me she looked up and saw her three-year-old headed toward the electrical outlet with a pair of tweezers in his hands. Where do they come up with this stuff?

Admittedly, we will need to modify our plan a bit for Littles. To teach them, we'll have to be more hands-on.

Children don't even understand cause and effect until about eighteen months of age, but then there is a gradual increase in their ability to understand basic forms of discipline. In the meantime, we have other little teaching tools at our disposal.

With toddlers we begin with *restraint*, not discipline. We grab little Electrical Boy, take the tweezers, and say, "No! No!" We may even pop the hand of a repeat offender. We run and grab him before he heads out the back door toward the pool. We say clearly, "No pool!" If he hits us, we grab his hand and say, "No hit!" Again, maybe a little bit of playpen time for the chronic hitter. Some of the earliest discipline involves teaching a child self-restraint by lovingly restraining them *ourselves*—they will then begin taking that ability inside as they get older.

With Littles, we also *redirect.* "You can't play in the garbage can. Come play with your toys instead." Just attempting to stop a negative behavior can leave them a little lost at this age. It helps when we can introduce them to a positive behavior instead.

We also *praise* them when they give us their listening ears. We say, "You are doing so good obeying me!" By the time they are in the late threes and fours however, we ought to be able to lean in with more events and choices. We can start to say (and they will understand), "Come on now and let me put your pajamas on you … or there's not going to be a treat."

Strangely, some of the most incorrigible children I hear about in my practice and travels are four-year-olds who are literally *running* their families. With four-year-olds, I am very comfortable putting them in timeout. And that may mean more than *four minutes* if they aren't getting the message. I don't know who it was who came up with the rule that says, "We should only put children in timeout for the same number of minutes as their age." I wish I could say *anything* in the universe that had that much far-reaching impact. It's not true. I've seen countless four-year-olds who needed much longer in timeout after terrorizing their family. It's not like they don't have object permanence, i.e. feel abandoned in the universe if left alone. The wild ones sometimes need a serious consequence. Over and over I've seen that once their parents stayed strong and consistent, the four-year-old was blessedly dethroned—to the betterment of all concerned.

So, parents of Littles, expect this season of frustration. Don't let it get you down. One mother told me that it helped her to wake up and tell herself, "I just know that there are going to be lots of interventions and tantrums today. And that's my norm for this season. It will get better. Relax."

She's right. I promise it gets better.

I was talking to the mother of a three-year-old a while back and asked her, "What is it you need to hear most from a parenting conference?"

She replied "Hope! Hope that it will not always be this way. Hope that the rest of my life won't consist of having my child melt down every time we leave the toy section at Target!"

It's normal for you to feel frazzled, like you've been on "24/7 baby patrol." But that doesn't mean you're parenting incorrectly or that your child is a budding terrorist; it's just *that* constant during these years. Don't let that discourage you.

I mentioned earlier that Callie, my oldest, is now a therapist. I was talking to her about Littles one day, and she said, "A preschooler can accomplish more in the two minutes that you turn your back than most adults can accomplish in a day!" But they will grow up. And they will learn.

Remember that you're not Batman
Speaking of incorrigible children, don't forget that this model is powerful, but it's not *all*-powerful. No approach to discipline is guaranteed to make your children obey. You can't control anybody remember? But control's not our job. Teaching is.

One of our girls went through a season as a teen in which she seemed immune to discipline. Regardless of what consequences befell her, she continued to rebel. Now that she is an adult, we are still hearing stories (confessions?) of things she did that we didn't even know about. This was, of course, a painful season, but don't let such times discourage you from disciplining with this clear method and goal.

Your job is not necessarily to change your child. Your job is—regardless of their response—to demonstrate to them that there is a *cause/effect* nature to the universe. To teach that, whenever you do A, then B will happen. Your job is to teach that principle, not to "change" your child. Our child ultimately turned around; I think she's the most responsible of our brood now. And in the vast majority of situations, if you can manage your fear that "we're losing her," yours will too.

Teaching Discipline: Step by step

Now that you know what Teaching Discipline sounds like, let's break it down into some steps. Let's slow it down like the fights in *The Matrix* and look at what we're doing.

Step one: Check the emotional rush

Remember that feeling? The "Are you on pills?" feeling we talked about earlier? If you're anything like me, when they blow you off, or sass you, or refuse a request, or throw a tantrum at bath time—again!—you will feel that "feeling." That "helpless, angry, how dare you, I cannot believe this kid" feeling.

Well, step one is to resist those feelings of anger, and helplessness that are flooding you and *think!* Those feelings will make you do stupid things, and they will give away your power. To teach these little stinkers, we need to *think.* And this may mean stepping away for a bit as I mentioned. Put *yourself* in timeout if necessary. The emergency exits are clearly marked.

Let me tell you why this is so vital. When we're really challenged in our parenting (or in any conflictual relationship), what happens is that we get triggered back in our midbrain, our hypothalamus, our amygdala—what I call our "Caveman Brain." And our only options there are fight or flight (or control or coddle), and those are emotional reactions, people, not strategic thinking. Living out of that reactive anger and frustration throws us back into that power struggle. We will yell and scream, and it's *Goodnight, Vienna!* We are being as immature as they are!

We need to *think,* not *emote!*

Remember when Obi Wan says to Luke, "Luke, trust your feelings"? Well, Master Kenobi needs to read my book. He's wrong! Obi Wan is wrong! You can't trust your feelings here! They will lead you to the Dark Side! (That's why Obi Wan had to give away Baby Luke and Leia to Uncle Owen, Aunt Beru and Bail Organa to raise! Nobody can be a good parent thinking like that!. Get real!)

So, leave the messy room and step away. Let them tantrum. Sit on all those feelings that are making you want to act like a kook. Maybe take some time to settle down. I want you to think. In the vast majority of situations, there really is no rush.

I often tell parents that conflicts with our children should be "golf, not tennis." Often in our interactions with our children, they "serve" some problem at us and we feel like we have to swing right back, immediately—Topspin forehand, back at cha! No. This conflict with your child is a game of golf. Take your time. See how the green breaks. Talk to your caddy. Plan your shot.

They say, "But I don't want to take a bath." Take your time. Walk in the next room. Think about what would be a good "or else" to present to them? How 'bout, "That's cool, I'm not going to fight you. You can go to bed dirty. But if you don't take a bath, there won't be any bedtime story tonight. You get to decide, Chief." And let them choose!

Now, if you're like me, in order to think this clearly, you will have to wait. Take a timeout yourself. Check your emotional rush. Put the pin back in the grenade That's the only way we can get to the place where we can *choose* how to handle a situation rather than just reacting to it.

We can get creative. We can be strategic. We're smart too—*if* we stop being emotionally reactive. In some ways this is the hardest step of all, so take notes.

Step Two: Give them a choice

Remember that one of our Secrets of the Universe was, "The only way that children learn is by experiencing an event." So, what event awaits them? As we said earlier, one reason that kids will often not do what we command is because all we've done so far is issue a *command*. And it would be great if kids just did what we said because we said so—by command. But they're not gonna do that! Face it!

Actually, if you think about it, many of us adults wouldn't make some of the choices we make unless we knew the cost, right? I mean, if they came on the TV and said, "The state troopers are all on strike, but don't y'all speed between here and Las Vegas." What would you do? Are you kidding me?

How 'bout the IRS? "There's no real penalty if you don't pay your taxes, but boy, are we going to be mad!"

"Ha! Sorry, Uncle Sam. Hope that works out for ya!"

I need a choice, not just a command. That's how adult life works, and that's where we're taking them.

So the next thing to do if your kids resist you is not to just intensify your command. The next step in Teaching Discipline will be for us to get *you* out of this conflict and give them a *choice*, a *consequence*—that *event* we've been talking about.

Not, "I *said* get off the computer!" (More intense commands.)

Instead, I want you to sound more like this. "*Hmmm,* interesting, I told you to get off the computer, and you're not. Fascinating choice. So, you're just going to refuse? Well, I'm not going to fight you, but if I come back in a few minutes and you're still on the computer, I'm going to ground you from all electronics for a couple of days. So you choose."

As we said, when you respond this way, they will ignore you, or go ballistic, or have a tantrum—all of which we will talk about. But the point here is, when you feel that refusal, don't fight. Don't try to *make* them. Put on your gypsy scarves and pull out your crystal ball, and do a little fortune telling. "I see a cold dark timeout in your future. I sense loneliness, regret, a sore bottom. I see you going to the library to use their computer—a beige 486 with Windows 95 on it!"

Tell them their choices! These are not "threats." These are "promises."

Positive Rewards

And this can be positive rewards too. We've been talking a lot about negative consequences because we've been trying to eliminate the power struggle (it's the only way). But once you are no longer in the wrestling ring, it's great to engage our kids with some real positivity when they are making good choices. We can say to that school-ager who's being responsible. "Look at you, Amigo! Doing those chores! The 'Chore-meister!' You da man! Thank you for how much you work to pull your load around here—feels really good."

Look for chances to catch those little ones in the moments where they are being good. They are playing "spaceship" in a cardboard box while you are cooking (Do kids have imaginations anymore?). While they are being good aliens, say to them, "Hey, guys—sending a high-five your way! Y'all have been playing so well and letting me cook. I smell treats in your futures!"

Once you conquer the power struggle, positive rewards are great—as long as they don't become *bribery*. The difference between a reward and bribery hinges on whether you have a dog in the fight. A reward says, "Hey pal, if you make all A's, we'll give you a reward! Good luck to ya." A bribe says, "Come on baby... Go study... Please? If you do, we will pay you!" (Hear your agenda there? They still own you.)

But with positive or negative consequences—Teaching Discipline gives them a choice.

Littles

Now, remember, you parents of little ones. They are going to be slower to get this, but I want you to go ahead and start understanding the model and teaching these principles. That four-year-old is screaming because you won't give her any more Laffy Taffy. She needs containment and choices. Lean down and tell her you understand that she is so upset, and that she may tantrum for a while if she wishes. However, if she continues, she will complete her tantrum in timeout. If necessary, carry her there like a sack of potatoes. She needs a choice. (And we'll talk later about what to do when she tries to come out!)

Littles require more "hands-on" engagement, but they will start to get it. A mother I was working with the other day has a three-year-old who was refusing to do what she said. She kept her cool and casually said, "Well, then I guess you don't want to play with the Wii anymore tonight, huh?" And he backed down. They have more self-control than you might think—if you stand your ground. And they do get older and easier. (Well, maybe not easier.)

Teenagers

As always, teenagers raise the stakes, so they need clear choices and events more than ever. Don't tell that teenager, "You'd better not drink at that party!" Instead, I want to say, "We've talked together about our policy on drinking. If you drink at that party tonight, we are bound to find out. And it will mean that you lose your phone for a week. You make the call!" (Like Monday night football—"*You* Make the Call!")

By the way, parents of teenagers often live with a ton of anxiety about their kids making stupid choices about things like drinking, smoking, texting, etc. Consequently, they tend to get very controlling. Attention: Anxiety and control totally contaminate this discipline/learning process. Your agenda gets shoehorned back in. The dog gets back in the fight. And you're off to the power struggle races again.

As we said, fear is your enemy as a parent! Besides, I would rather them go ahead and make their stupid choices *now* and reap some consequences for them, than to make them later in college. The consequences just get bigger. Let's go ahead and train the lad.

Step Three: Let them choose

Let them Choose! Don't warn. Don't say, "I mean it!" Don't count.

Let. Them. Choose!

Walk away if necessary—just walk away!

Why is this so important? Well, with our "if/then promise" of a consequence, we've changed the conflict from Them vs

You (who wins?) to Them vs their *Choices*, remember? We've finally got them where we want them—in teaching mode! Don't get back in the power struggle! We just got you out. They're not at war with you anymore. They're in school!

Basic principle: *Our kids will never learn about the fruits of their choices if they are constantly being nagged, reminded, and demanded to choose our way.* Remember, the only way kids learn to obey is by having the freedom to choose unwisely and by reaping consequences for that.

And hopefully they will suffer some.

Sometimes I call discipline "Safe Suffering." In other words, with Teaching Discipline, kids get a chance to learn about the way the world works. Only first time through, with nice, safe, loving parents—and nonlethal consequences! How great is that!

So, why do we take all electronics from that teenager we catch texting inappropriate things? Because we are saying, "This little trip back to the Stone Age reflects in a safe way what would happen if you didn't learn." Safe Suffering!

This is why the Bible says that the man who spares the rod *hates* his child.[1] ("Rod" being an ancient Hebrew symbol of authority, not a literal *stick* of course—but you'd be surprised at how many people need to hear that.)

This opportunity to experience safe suffering is a gift, because the consequences only get bigger. Psychologist Tom Elkin said this Secret of Life: *A small amount of known pain in the present is infinitely preferable to an unknown amount of pain in the future.* Let them choose and suffer now. There are few gifts more loving.

Step Four: Follow through

The final step in Teaching Discipline is to follow through. In other words, make sure your kids experience what you said they would experience. Otherwise, you're a *liar*!

We were visiting friends a while back and the mom and her little boy were fussing. She finally said, "Okay, that's it! You are in timeout!"

But then they *kept interacting*!

"But I don't want to go to timeout!" the boy replied.

"Well, then stop making so much racket while we talk," Mom responded.

I wanted to say, "Wait—I thought you just made a *promise* to your son. You *are* in timeout. Where you lying to him? Bluffing? Posturing?"

This is where a lot of parents drop the ball. The child acts bad, we are desperate to control, so we threaten all sorts of stuff. Then we regret it, feel guilty, feel like it's too much hassle—so nothing ever happens. And we wonder why our kids are out of control. I had a teenager tell me a while back, "Yeah, they threaten a lot of stuff, but they never really do it. It's actually kinda confusing."

Kids are riverboat gamblers with their hat pulled down low over their eyes and a cheap cheroot between their teeth. They are betting that the tenth time, you'll finally give in. And those one-armed bandit odds are enough to keep them at the gambling table far into the night. We must be consistent.

Furthermore, if we don't follow through, then we are depriving them of tasting that bad fruit that is the *only thing* that teaches them. Kids only learn through experience, remember? So they have to actually *have* that event to experience Teaching Discipline!

In fact, the least effective tool in your tool box for getting through to your children (or any impulsive acting-out person for that matter) is your *words*. You can tell, coax, beg, reason, cajole, explain—and what is your kid going to say? "Wow, Mom! That's a great point! I've never seen it that way! I'm glad you explained it to me. I think I'll go be kinder to my sister."

Right!

Kids only learn through an event.

Don't make promises you can't keep

Now, since kids only learn through an experience, and we have to *follow through* with an event in order to give them that experience, it's therefore pretty stinkin' important that we be careful to only pick consequences that we are really willing to follow through with! Right?

I see parents threaten these giant things: "If you don't stop screaming, there's no summer camp!" or, "If you're late for curfew, I'm going to *sell* that car!" And everyone involved knows that you're not going to follow through with all that baloney, so let's get real!

Besides, consequences don't have to be really bad in order to teach. The pattern for Teaching Discipline is—short, sweet, to the point, painful, *certain*—followed by, "Here, try again!" It's education, remember? Nothing personal. Nothing ultimate. That's the point! It's not punishment, it's discipline.

Besides, scary, angry consequences just scare. They don't teach. The stakes are too high, and your child is mad at you. And those long-term consequences, like summer camp or being grounded for six weeks are so far in the future that our kids don't get that educational experience *today*. To teach well, don't take away summer camp in July. Take away their dessert right now.

And you can do this nicely! As Patrick Swayze said in the classic art film, *Roadhouse,* "Be nice ... Until it's time to not be nice."

You don't have to say, "That does it! I told you! Now you're going to *suffaaaah!*" You can be nice. "Oh, Dude, remember I told you that if you left your bike out in the rain I was gonna hang it up in the garage? Well, I found it out the rain again. I'm so sorry, man."

I call this being "Lovingly Ruthless." No need for violence or anger—we let the consequences do the talking. And you can be the nice guy—"Gee, I hate that for you!" We don't have a toy in that Happy Meal, remember?

Now, frankly, just between you and me, most parents cannot stand being this lovingly ruthless, which is why we have a child-centered culture.

Stay free

So those are our steps. Everyone wants four simple steps to

everything. Your wish is granted. (Long live Jambi!) These are the four simple steps to powerful Teaching Discipline— four steps to "get your kids to do what you say."

However, as you'd probably tell me right now, *simple* does not mean *easy*. That is true. What I've seen for thirty-something years is that, at first, parenting this way is like learning to write with your non-dominant hand. It takes a little getting used to. And I have parents moan and say, "There's no way I could learn to do this." However, after spending some time in my dojo, and after a bit of practice at being creative, most parents get it.

A couple of parents who had asked me questions about their incorrigible little girl at a conference, grabbed me a couple of days later. "We have used your stuff with our daughter over the last day or so. After a few good consequences instead of all the talking and fussing, she has really changed—already! At one point she looked up at us and said, "Is this what you learned from that parenting conference?" Boom goes the dynamite.

Okay, that's our model. And if you're feeling like it's too late; like you've screwed up discipline too much, then let's go back to our soft landing spot—Good Enough! This is not a book to tell you that you should be a better parent, remember? I want you to enjoy parenting, not feel overwhelmed by it!

I didn't figure this model out until my children were well past preschool. And, as I told you, I was an angry jerk sometimes. So don't use this chapter as a lens to look at your failure. Somewhere, you learned Control or Coddling. You can learn Teaching Discipline just the same! And when you do, it's going to be double rainbows all the way. Trust me. You can do this! At least you can do it good enough.

The return of the examples

So those are the steps and the goals of Teaching Discipline. But I find that the place that parents really learn to discipline like this is through examples. So let's look at some more. Of course, my examples won't cover all of your contingencies, but use them to get the principles and then get creative. Then you can freestyle the model on your own to fit your particular circumstances.

Timeout

When Bonney was about four-years-old, she had a cold, and her mother called her to come take her medicine. It was a bottle of that sticky, sweet, red medicine that you put in a big dropper and try to get your kid to swallow. Bonney hated it, and immediately upon hearing her mother's call, scampered upstairs and disappeared. Norma looked at me and asked me to do something that was essentially impossible. "Go *make* her come back and take her medicine."

Really? How do you make anyone do anything? Even a child!

Besides, what happens when you try to force a four-year-old to take their red syrupy cough medicine? What are you supposed to do, hold them down and pour it down their throats? They cough and spray it all over your clothes! It's like waterboarding!

Again, I was stumped. (And at first you will often be stumped, too.)

I thought for a moment and then said to the silent upstairs (Bonney was under a bed somewhere), "Bonney, you need to come take your medicine. If you don't, I'm going to put you in timeout, and you can come out whenever you want; whenever you are ready to take your medicine, that is. And that can be three minutes or three hours. That's up to you."

She soon grimly slumped down the stairs.

You've probably noticed that I like timeout, though it's by no means the only consequence I employ. I like timeout because it is nonintrusive. Remember, our goal is to shift discipline from a conflict between you and your child to a conflict between them and their choices. So I like timeout because I believe a nice stint in the "cooler" is a good consequence your child can experience *apart from you*. Teaching Discipline is between them and their consequences—in this case, the consequence is isolation.

I believe that the timeout experience should take place in a room, not in a corner or a chair. Preferably a room that is very uninteresting, i.e. not *their* room. I like a half-bath or a utility room or a walk-in closet. Something boring. An egg timer is helpful when they are small because Littles don't understand what "time" is. "You get five minutes in timeout" is meaningless to them. However, "When the little pointer goes to 'zero' and it dings"—that's more their lingo.

We used the half-bath downstairs so much that one day we were leaving on a vacation. The car was packed, and we were ready to go.

Norma looked at Katherine and said, "We're leaving soon, Kat. Go to the bathroom!"

Katherine looked at her and said, "Why? I didn't do nothing!"

Spanking

Another discipline example: When Katherine was about three, we were on our way to church. She was buckled in her car seat in the van, and about halfway through our journey she unbuckled herself from her seat, dismounted, and started walking around the car, strolling up and down the van's center aisle as if she were in an airliner.

Nothing we said changed her agenda of strolling the van while in flight. (Do you feel the helplessness? How do you "make" her get back in her car seat?) We had to find an event! Being on the road, my options were limited. So I had to draw from one of my least-favorite means of discipline. I told her, "Katherine, this is dangerous. You need to get back in your car seat or I am going to pull the van over and pop your leg and *put* you back in your car seat."

She ignored me, of course.

I literally pulled the van off to a side road, got out, put her in her car seat, buckled her in, and popped her leg with a firm (yet not injurious) smack. She started wailing and crying of course. The goal was not obedience on this occasion. It was to help her learn that there was a consequence for (in this case) dangerous behavior.

By the way, her big sister in the way-back seat of the van, sat observing all of this. She just shook her head and said, "She chose unwisely!"

Let's talk about spanking for a moment. People tend to go to extremes on this issue. Some people, fearing abuse and having read *some* of the research, claim that all spanking is bad. Other more authoritarian types maintain that it is the *only* appropriate discipline. I disagree with both parties. I dislike spanking, but not because it's bad or harmful. (Any form of discipline can be that.) I dislike spanking because I dislike *inefficient discipline.* It is very, very difficult to communicate, "This is not a conflict between you and me, but a learning experience," while you are literally striking your child.

However, I have used spanking at times—like I sometimes use a Coleman camping stove. A camping stove is not my go-to if I'm going to cook, but if I am out in the wild, and have no other options, it can be useful. Quick little "pops" can begin by age eighteen months if little Hondo is into repetitive, dangerous behaviors (though try distraction, praise, and strong commands first). Rarely spank after age six (they are smart enough by then to respond to more sophisticated discipline, and hopefully so are you). Never spank after age ten. To the degree that you are angry, never spank—at any age. For that matter, to the degree that you are angry, never do *any* discipline.

In general, I would advise you to use spanking as a last resort. Spanking gets its bad reputation because of angry, authoritarian parents who discipline reactively (and are too lazy to be strategic and smart). We can be more savvy, creative, and controlled than that, for crying out loud.

Natural consequences

Timeout is a favorite go-to for me, but the best disciplines "fit the crime." This form of discipline is often called *Natural Consequences*. If you don't share a toy, it gets taken away. If you make a mess, you clean it up. If you don't feed the dog, we'll keep your dinner warm while you do. Once you take your time and practice a little, you can come up with some effective, cunning natural consequences for your little cherubs.

When Callie was in the full-blown throes of adolescence, her father greeted her one morning with a cheery smile. (And I use the word "morning" loosely.) Her response was a sullen grunt as she shuffled back to her room with an Eggo waffle and a cup of coffee.

I'm thinking, "Wow, that nasty response takes practice. She must have sisters."

Later that morning she came down, heading out the door. Her sweet father asked, "Where are you headed, darling?"

She looked at me, rolled her eyes, groaned, and replied, "I'm going to Elizabeth's, okay?"

Later that afternoon as she returned, I asked, "How is Elizabeth?"

"Oh my gosh! She's *fine!*" she retorted as she stormed back up to her room.

Now, if you think I wanted to jerk a knot in her at this point, then by golly, you'd be right! But I was trying to avoid the head-to-head conflict, knowing that waiting always pays off. It did.

About four o'clock that afternoon, as I was minding my own business, Callie pranced down the stairs with a cute look on her face. "Um, Daddy! Would you fix my broken necklace?" she chirped.

I replied, "I would be glad to fix your necklace, darling—if you could answer me one question first. Why might I *want* to fix your necklace, given how you've talked to me all day? (*"Quid pro quo,* Clarisse!")

She backed off and replied, "I guess I *have* been kind of a jerk all day."

I replied, "Yep!"

Events don't have to be in the form of "discipline." Sometimes they can just be the natural consequences of your child being a sap. I'm amazed at the number of parents who complain that their children are disobedient and disrespectful, but who continue to serve them dutifully, driving them to events and baking cookies—all for the kid who's just berated them all morning.

I fixed the necklace much later that night.

Reality

This "consequences" thing is not limited to misbehavior, by

the way. This isn't punishment, remember? It's education.

One day, one of the girls insisted upon playing 'tennis backboard' against the garage door. I'd told her not to, but the moment I turned my back, she was back at it again. Only a few strokes later, she planted a tennis ball right in the middle of one of the windows, shattering it. I felt the anger rise in me. I had *told* her to not do this! Now I was going to have to change all of my plans today. I was going to have to go to Lowe's and by a sheet of plate glass. I was going to have to sweep up all of the broken glass and replace the pane! Day ruined!

Again, I asked myself what I needed in order to not be an angry jerk. The answer was for her to experience as much painful cost for this event as I was going to experience. I knew then that what I needed was a *special assistant!*

I went to her and said, "I'm not angry at you (anymore), but this is going to cost you the same thing that it's going to cost me today. I'm going to have to change my plans and fix this broken window—and guess who is going to be my 'favorite deputy.' You!"

She responded desperately, reminding me of a birthday party she had that day, as well as a softball game. "I am so deeply sorry, sweetheart. This isn't even a punishment; this is just repairing the damage you created. I'm sorry it's going to cost us both so much."

Discipline is to teach out kids about reality, not to punish.

Tantrums

What about tantrums—a popular go-to for children of all ages?

First, let's remember that tantrums can have different meanings. Sometimes a *toddler tantrum* is just a boil-over from a child's inability to manage intense emotion. Remember how we talked about how Littles *do* their feelings? The ability to manage emotion is a very sophisticated, cognitive process that most of us don't complete until adulthood (mid-fifties in some cases). So sometimes, a tantrum in a toddler is just the result of a child being flooded with anger or disappointment, literally not knowing how to contain it—so it just erupts into a hissy fit. They need us to keep our cool, not scold them, and help them settle down—and, if necessary, carry them away from the crime scene.

This can also include helping "mentalize" their feelings (remember?). As we put words on their emotional world, they get a better handle on it—"I know you are so mad that I won't give you more juice, but (throw in some distraction) let's come over here and look at this book together." You are doing what we shrinks call "containing" their emotion, and your poise will help build in them the ability to contain it themselves, later.

Preschoolers can tantrum out of childish protest. We told one of ours that when she learned to use the potty, we would take her to Toys "R" Us to get her own special little-girl potty! After several weeks of back-and-forth (potty training is not an event, it is a slow patient, teaching process), she finally became victorious.

We all piled in the car and headed to Toys "R" Us to retrieve her prize. I pulled a box off the shelf containing the little potty and put it on the floor for her to inspect. Something distracted me, and when I looked back, Katherine had her pants down to her knees and was pulling the potty out of the box. Apparently, she wanted to take it for a test drive right there in the store. I gasped and dove to the floor, trying to pull her pants back on her. She arched backwards screaming in a tantrum, clamoring for the potty seat as I pulled it away from her, both of us tangling on the floor. She raged and squealed that she was not getting her way. (At that moment, I had this image of looking up from the floor and seeing all of my clients standing in a circle around us, observing this scene.) Sometimes a tantrum is an emotional protest.

Here's how I respond to a preschooler tantrum (after you get their pants back on them). I just *squat*. Like a baseball catcher. I don't say much, except maybe, "Yeah, I know it's hard, man." Don't try to get them to stop their tantrum. Just squat. To the degree that you try to *stop* a tantrum, you have tipped your hand that this is unpleasant to you—and then they know they have you. Their strategy is to make you miserable, helpless, and humiliated so that you give them what they want. They are Machiavellian, remember?

If you can deal with the "shame voice" in your head telling you, "All the other parents in the store are wondering why you are torturing your child over on aisle eight," you've won half the battle. Just squat. I might continue calmly, "Yeah, I know you really wanted that so badly. And I know it feels terrible to not get it. I care." (I'm being kind here, but I'm also making it clear that I'm not budging. I'm also mentalizing their feelings.)

Typically, after a few minutes of screaming, my kids would look up at me and ask, "What are we doing, Daddy?" I would reply, "Well, you needed to throw a fit, so I thought I would just wait until you were done. Are you done yet? Cool, let's finish shopping." Many parents will claim at this point, "Well mine would just lay there and tantrum until closing time!" Maybe at first. Usually in these situations, however, you guys have just played out this power struggle for so long that it will indeed take a while for your little terrorist to realize that the rules have changed. Don't discount the power of this intervention just because it may take him a season to learn.

With *older kids*, tantrums can be *weapons*. Remember Carlos the Jackal back at the beginning of this chapter? Sometimes children tantrum in order to "punish" us for not getting what they want. I was talking to a mom recently whose child rages and screams at them if he doesn't get what he wants. So how shall we engage our friend, Carlos, and the "Terrorist Tantrum"?

First, remember that you *cannot stop him*. In fact, don't even try. Nothing you do right now will get him to change his behavior *today*. So let's shoot for changing it *tomorrow*! (Teaching discipline, remember?)

So, point one—do not engage him. Keep your cool. Under-react.

Secondly, let's do some teaching. Say quietly (*don't* try to make sure he hears you—sometimes I even whisper), "If you can't stop yelling at us, I'm going to call your coach and tell him you won't be pitching at the game tomorrow, so you can choose, buddy"—and then disengage as much as possible. Leave the room if necessary. He, of course, won't hear your discipline because he is still busy having a tantrum.

The chickens will come home to roost however, tomorrow after school when he says he's ready to go to the game. "Oh! That's right, you probably couldn't hear us last night because you were raging at us, but we told you if you continued to tantrum you weren't going to be playing ball today. I'm so sorry, buddy."

This kind of non-angry *cost* will be what teaches him, not a big loud power struggle trying to *make* him not tantrum.

By the way, if he *rages* at his consequence for *raging*—that's cool, we can do this consequences thing all week. He can miss every game if necessary. However, I find many parents are often fearful about putting the hammer down on Carlos —fearing his retaliation. One mom consented to my counsel regarding setting limits on her little terrorist, but added, "Okay, but it's going to be an ordeal!" Another told me that taking a ballgame away from her raging child "felt like too much." This kind of thinking is why Carlos is currently still El Presidente'.

Home field advantage
Ever notice how when you are at the store, grandma's house,

church, school, a parking lot—or on the phone, kids get especially out of control? They know your power over them is limited in these places, so they turn up the shenanigans. I call these places your child's "home field advantage." They *own* you there! It's like playing LSU in Tiger Stadium—on Halloween night!

Here's the ultimate secret to the home field advantage debacle: The best place to address the field advantage showdown is at your *home*, where *you* have the home field advantage. If a child has learned that their choices will certainly lead to consequences at home, then it will be easier to maintain our authority out in the wild. Apply consistent Teaching Discipline at home and you will be building the software in your child to obey you at the grocery.

Also, you can *predict* their behavior. You're on your way to Aunt Sally's. (And you *know* that they always act up at Aunt Sally's. You've done this before, right?) So with school-age kids and older, you can go ahead and *predict* that. "Hey Bud, you know how you always act like a goon at Aunt Sally's, and we always end up fussing and causing a scene? Well, we're not going to do that this time. In fact, we are not going to correct your behavior at all. I'm just going to be taking notes regarding the number of times you act up. Then, when we get home, you're going to give me twenty minutes in timeout for each infraction." Again, "You make the call." No. Dog. No. Fight. Etc.

Learning to predict and plan ahead for discipline is super helpful. You know that they always give you fits when you call and tell them it's time to come home from the neighbor's house. You *know* that right? You live here. This is Earth, remember? So go ahead and predict it.

"Can I go to Billy's?"

"Sure, kiddo. But if you give me any hassle when I call you to come home (like you did last time/every time), go ahead and know there won't be any TV tonight."

Now you're ahead of the game.

Parents always ask me, "What do you do when they throw a fit in a restaurant?" Well, given that that is a "home field advantage location," your power is indeed more limited. I see many parents use shame to try to control their kids in restaurants. "This is why we don't take you to nice places!" "Look at that little boy over there. *He's* not misbehaving!"

That kind of talk isn't discipline, gang; that is your own public embarrassment dumped on your kids. Let's shape up. Shame is a love un-doer, remember? And like anger, it will undermine your discipline (not to mention your child's heart).

Instead, let's engage some Teaching Discipline mojo. I would silently take my screamers outside of the restaurant and just sit on the front steps. Again, not saying a word. Inevitably they would ask me what we were doing. "Well, you needed to pitch a fit (which you can't do in the restaurant), so I thought I would bring you out here where you can scream all you want. You done yet? No hurry."

They would say, "Yeah, I'm done."

You get a cold meal, but you also get a child who's learning to control their own behavior. Good trade.

Teaching after the fact

So much of the Teaching Discipline model we've been talking about has been about some *future event:* if you do X then Y will happen. Or about a power struggle where your child is warned about the consequences of their future choices. Well, you can't anticipate everything, right? So what if they pull some stunt that you never saw coming? How do we use Teaching Discipline then?

When Katherine was about five, she and one of her little friends found their way down to my workshop. By the time we had discovered them, they had gotten a can of orange spray paint and painted each other orange from head to toe—like Oompa Loompas. You guessed it; I never saw that coming. I never thought to say, "Oh, and if you paint yourselves orange, you're going to timeout." There's no way to give an if/then for everything.

In these surprise attacks, just catch your breath (take that timeout yourself, if necessary) and just give them a *non-angry consequence* for their knuckle-headed choices. The goal is simply to *learn*, remember—and they can learn after the fact! "Wow, since you decided to cut your little sister's hair, I think that you are going to lose all electronics for a week." The power of the Teaching Discipline will still be there. (Of course, Katherine and Grace's stunt came with built-in consequences—a scrub-down with mineral spirits after their trip to Loompaland!)

Don't forget Love and Limits

While you are mastering all of these rockin' discipline skills, don't forget that we're still engaging with both love *and* limits.

I mentioned psychologist Tom Elkin earlier. He used to refer to love and limits, calling them "Bologna Sandwich Discipline." A bologna sandwich is two slices of bread with a greasy slice of meat in the middle. Bologna sandwich *discipline* is two slices of love with the "meat" of limits in between.

Like this. "I know you don't want to do your homework, kiddo. I get it." (Love.) But if you don't, there's not gonna be any TV tonight. (Limits.) But I totally understand and care." (Love again.)

Get it? Discipline is limits surrounded on both sides by understanding.

So as you practice Teaching Discipline to help your kids learn to choose well, don't forget to reach back and fold in the love piece as well. In Psalm 85, the Bible speaks of how in God's salvation, "Lovingkindness and truth have met each other. Righteousness and peace have kissed."[2] God balances love and limits perfectly. We will just do it good enough, but let's give it a shot anyway.

Conclusion

Ok, let's wrap this up. The original question was, "How do I get my kids to do what I say?" The answer? There's a sense in which you can't. Ultimately, we can't control anyone. Instead, like the little bald-headed kid in *The Matrix* says, "Do not try and bend the spoon, that's impossible. Instead, only try to realize the truth ... There is no spoon."

In other words, every parent's go-to when they encounter a disobedient child is to try to "Bend the Spoon." To "make" their child obey. This will create a power struggle, and you will lose.

Instead, what I've invited you to do is *teach* your child to obey, rather than to *require* it. Teaching Discipline! And, Secret of the Galaxy: The most powerful way that we teach children is through an *event*. So when we encounter that pushback, we back up, give a choice and predict an event.

Then we let the child *choose*. We don't warn them or scold them. They are free to choose anything they want (we don't have a Peep in that Easter basket). Then, as we *follow through*, we're teaching them that their real choices have real consequences. This is not about their war with us anymore.

Not only will this teach them to make wise choices now, it will also start teaching them and preparing them for life as an adult.

One last story before we move on to the next chapter. One afternoon I was left alone in the house with one of my children. As her mother left with the other two, her final words to Katherine were, "Before I get home, I want you to clean up the playroom."

Later on, I found seven-year-old Katherine still watching TV and lying on the couch. "Just curious," I said. "Do you have any plans to clean up the playroom like your mother said?"

Her response, "I don't want to. I'm tired."

I was in a playful mood, so I responded to her saying, "I tell you what, you need to clean up the playroom, but you can pick *any way in the world* that you would like that to happen."

She replied, "Okay, I want you to wrap me up in a blanket and hold me like a little baby while *you* clean up playroom." (I kid you not.)

But like I said, I was in a playful mood. So without cracking a smile, I walked over to the couch, wrapped her in a blanket, and, cuddling her like an infant, began to pick up toys and put them away. Suddenly, we both dissolved into gales of laughter, and I threw her back on the couch like she was a bag of sand. "TV is going off until you clean the room, smarty-pants. 'Kirk Out'!"

Play with this model. Help each other with this model. Let this model set you free from the back-and-forth, power-struggle nonsense. Learning Teaching Discipline requires the same thing as getting to Carnegie Hall: Practice. Take your time. Screw it up. Be good enough. You can do this.

Q&A Time
Hey Doc—What if we're giving our kids consequences and limits, but it's not working?

Well, there could be several things going on here. One of them could be that you, the parents, aren't both on board. Oftentimes when I see a child having too much power in the home, one parent is *enabling* the disobedience. Maybe they're playing the softie, being sympathetic, letting the child off the hook, or maybe they're just absent. Two good parents who are unilateral in their discipline are hard for any child to defeat. Ask yourself—"Are we on the same page?" "Are we backing up each other's discipline?" "Is one of us a silent partner?" "Is one of us undermining the other's intervention?" If you're not on the same team, then go upstairs and fight it out until you can come down arm in arm, parenting as One. If you can't accomplish that, then that's a marriage issue, not a parenting problem.

Here's another possibility with the repeat offender: Sometimes you will find a child who just thumbs their nose at your consequences. You spank them and they say, "That didn't hurt." Or you put them in timeout and they respond, "Great, I *like* timeout!" So what are you supposed to do then? Put them in timeout and cut the *heater* on to teach 'em a lesson?

No, when a child acts like this, they are not really immune to your discipline. They are just living out of the *power struggle*. They just want to be sure you know that you aren't "winning." Somehow, your discipline has stopped being about choices and consequences, and you've started sending out a vibe that "we're going to be the *winners* here, and you are not." At this point a compliant child will just roll over (which is a problem too). But a more adversarial child would rather die of starvation in timeout than let you think you have won. They don't care about consequences at this point. They just care about you *not winning!*

The way out of this is to quit playing. When mine pulled

this stunt, I used to say, "That's cool! Then we have a win-win. My job is to discipline you as best I can, and you don't mind timeout, so we're both good, right? High Five!" In other words, I'm not trying to win here. You can choose anything you want, you just have to pay for it. Once your child starts to pick up on the atmosphere that you are no longer trying to "win," the chemistry of your interaction will change.

Here's another dynamic that might be happening when discipline doesn't "work": Sometimes children can be so filled with emotion—sadness, anger, fear—that you could send them to San Quentin, and they still wouldn't obey. My rule of thumb here is that before that child will bend the knee, they need to be "heard." In other words, there is so much going on for them emotionally that they don't have the bandwidth to learn from the consequences. In that situation it's probably good for you to get with a therapist of some sort and try to understand what's going on emotionally for this child. Only then will they be able to have ears to hear the teaching of discipline.

> **We have two boys constantly in competition and fighting. They have gotten the "adversarial sibling" thing down to a science. And whenever we try to hold one accountable, he just blames his brother. What do we do?**

Sibling dynamics are fascinating. There's a sense in which having a sibling is the best practice possible for being *married* one day. Think about it. You live with this person whom you love, but you cannot stand them sometimes—and you both have to work it out! A sibling is the perfect training ground for having a spouse! What siblings love to do, however, is to triangulate you, the parent, into their system, asking you to be judge and jury. Here's how I like to respond.

They're being Itchy and Scratchy in the next room and come to you complaining. You say, "Look, guys, do I look like I'm wearing a striped shirt and a whistle? I'm not the referee! So, here's the deal—either you guys work it out about the Xbox, or I'm shutting it down and nobody gets to play with it."

They will respond, "Yeah, but he ... No ... but he! ..."

Hold your course. Say, "Right. I'm not gonna solve this for you guys. Work it out, or you both pay." What this does is put them in a position where they have to say, in essence, "Well, I hate your guts, and you hate mine, but we gotta work it out or else we both lose." (Like marriage!) And again, the *event* is the bad guy, not you, or either of them.

With my brother and me, our dad would often use a classic technique for conflict resolution. He called it, "One kid cuts/Other kid chooses." Now, if you're not familiar with this technique, it goes something like this. Suppose that there is one piece of pie left and both brothers want it. Well, "Cut 'n Choose" prescribes that one of the brothers will be the one who divides the piece in half, but the *other* brother gets to be the first to pick which side he wants. Get it? Of course, this puts the "Cutter" in the unique position of knowing that if he accidentally cuts one piece bigger than the other, his greedy brother will choose *that* one. The result, of course, is the sort of measured cutting seldom encountered this side of the Midtown Manhattan Diamond District. A jeweler's loop is often employed as well as calipers, graduated to the millimeter. My dad's Solomon-like wisdom at work!

If you have a situation in which one of the siblings is overtly being a bully, then it is obvious that we need to set limits on his assaults on the younger sibling. I recommend that parents tell the bully sibling something like this. "Know that in addition to having consequences for hurting your brother, we will also respond thusly: I'm going to be taking my cue from you as to how kind and generous you want me to be to *you*, based how you treat your brother. To the degree that you are unkind and hurtful to him, then that will give me a vibe for how giving you want me to be to you. In other words, if you are unkind to your brother and then ask me for that new Xbox game, I'll probably say no. I will simply be as kind as you are."

Good limits on the "perp" are a first step. However, don't stop there. A bully/victim dynamic is very complicated and always has two sides! So yes, set limits on the jerk. But also, we need to work to *empower* the victim! A bully can only dump their cruelty on someone who has ears to hear it. The victim is part of the dynamic as well.

One of ours went through a phase in which she was being picked on by her sisters and constantly tattling to us about it. We engaged the aggressive sisters, but our solution wouldn't be complete unless we also challenged the victim. We told her that we were not going to continue rescuing her, and we gave her permission to push back on her siblings by any means necessary to protect herself. This meant that if her sisters took her ball, she had license to wrestle them to the ground and take it back—to take care of herself. (Once she learned how to be strong, by the way, we revoked her "double 0 license to fight") We'll talk more about this in the next chapter when we discuss building strength—but with children, it is the law of the jungle, and bullies need to be stopped by their victims whenever possible. (I know that's not politically correct, but it is *correct*. The fact that we don't believe that is why our country is currently being run by bullies.)

We have children of different ages with different privileges. Furthermore, they are very different people, so we sometimes treat them differently. One of ours is constantly saying, "That's not fair! You let him do everything but you're always telling me No!" What do we do with Mr. Justice?

Great question. First, know that statements like "That's not fair" and, "But you said" aren't pleas motivated out of your child's anguished heart, battered by the unfairness of life. They are a power play. The child is in essence saying, "Yes, beloved parents, indeed you are somewhat of an authority here in our home. But, unfortunately, there is an even higher authority to which I now appeal—the authority of *Fairness*. She is a cruel mistress, yet you must bend the knee to her. She alone gets to decide justice in our home, not a couple of puny parents. So back down from your position and submit to the goddess of Fairness. And let me have what I want."

The response to this, of course, is Love and Limits. I want to say (lovingly), "Gee, I'm really sorry that this all seems so unfair. Unfair things in life really do stink. Nevertheless (limit), if you don't do what we're saying, there will be consequences for you despite the fact that it feels unfair to you." (In other words, we're not backing down to "fairness.")

Another thing I like to add is, "By the way, Shorty, this 'fairness' thing really seems to bother you. I'm not willing to talk with you about it during our conflicts though. However, if you'd like to swing by the kitchen some evening when I'm cooking dinner and have a seat and talk to me about your feelings regarding fairness and unfairness in our home, I'd be glad to have that discussion with you."

Now let me tell you what is going to happen. He is *never* going to have that conversation you. Why? Because he's not really concerned about the issue of fairness! He's just using it as a weapon in the moment to try to get you to do what he wants.

Oh, yeah. We own the night!

What if you put them in timeout and they scream and yell? Or what if they keep coming out?

As I said, timeout is not the only available consequence by any means, but it is one of my favorites. However, the opportunities for tomfoolery there are myriad. There can be banging, yelling, and constant coming out—pick a card. One day, one of ours got sent to the half bath for timeout. On the way, she put a handful of Fruity Pebbles into her pocket.

Once the cell door was closed, she chewed them up, spit them in the toilet, and then started crying, claiming that she had thrown up. Their creativity is actually impressive if you sort of squint your eyes and hold your mouth just right.

With the child who keeps coming out of timeout, the response sort of depends on their age. With three- and four-year-olds, since their sentence isn't very long anyway, I would hold the doorknob when possible. Another option is to let them know that they are welcomed to come out. However, they will receive a spank and then be returned to their "cell." Again, not my fav, but don't dismiss it entirely just because our culture frowns upon it.

With older kids, I might say, "If you come out, your time starts over," or, "You can scream all you want, big guy. Your time in timeout *begins* the moment you are finished screaming. You owe us twenty minutes—so if you scream for thirty minutes, then that's fifty whole minutes! So choose wisely, my friend."

Another response I like (especially with school-age kids) is to simply let them come out of timeout. However, they do not receive any privileges in the home until they have paid their debt to society. Let them come out, comment on it—"Oh, wow, you're just going to blow off my discipline? Interesting!"—and go about your day. But then when they want to watch TV, or eat dinner with the family, or attend that birthday party, respond, "Oh, I'm sorry, you owe me thirty minutes in timeout, remember? You don't get to have anything in our home until you have done your time." It's the casino's rules, and it's their choice—otherwise, we are back in the power struggle.

By the way, I call what we are doing here, "Layering Consequences." In other words, if they refuse to engage consequence number one, or tantrum and rage at us, then we often need to move on to another consequence—for not honoring the first consequence. If you hit your brother, then no TV. If we catch you watching TV on the sly, then no baseball game tomorrow.

If they scream and rage at your discipline, be cool. And spend that time silently *adding to/layering* their consequence in your head, only to announce it later. "Yeah, buddy. Remember how you raged at me about losing TV this morning. I didn't say it at the time, but that cost you your afternoon treat. You can rage all you want, but please choose more wisely. I hate to see you lose things."

By the way, parents who feel defeated by their children's refusals often miss the fact that we make their lives *happen!* They need us for everything! And often, all you have to do is wait until they need you, and you've got them. They refuse timeout. Just wait until the next thing they need from you—maybe tomorrow. Be patient. Tomorrow there's that movie everyone is going to. "Oh, I'm sorry. You aren't going, Spanky. Remember how you wouldn't go to timeout yesterday? Blowing off our discipline will always just cost you later. I'm so sorry. Maybe in the future you'll go to timeout we ask. But that is always your choice."

So many parents talk like they are lost in helplessness

and defeat. "But what do you do if he just refuses?" Like that's the endgame. You own all the power here, parent. Let them refuse. Just wait. They will need you soon. They are just children. You have the power. Lovingly *use* it! This is especially true for teenagers! (Remember Callie and the necklace?)

Another point: I encounter a lot of moms who tell me about a child who acts like a jerk at home after school, and then refuses to go to timeout. Oftentimes the father is key here. I want him to say to that child later, "I am going to do what I need to do to help you learn to choose better regarding how you relate to us. And when I'm gone, your mom is my Kemosabe! If you don't honor her consequences when I'm gone, then when I get home, you and I are going to do the evening together." Two parents who are standing shoulder-to-shoulder are almost impossible to defeat.

(See Q&A appendix for more)

---

[1] *Proverbs 13:24, New International Version.*

[2] *Psalm 85:10, English Standard Version.*

I didn't do it. I mean, nobody saw me do it.

— Bart Simpson

Chapter 3 ¾

But what if I don't want to do what you say?

Chapter-Three-and-Three-Quarters is not one of our original seven questions, but it is very important. That's why we are sandwiching it between Chapters Three and Four, like the hidden platform that leads to Hogwarts. Besides, no parenting book would be complete without at least one moment in which our kids interrupted us and "talked back." If your kids are anything like mine, they hated that last chapter, and they want to weigh in! While we were talking about discipline, they were climbing on the credenza and playing Flying Wallendas in the middle of the living room. Anything to interrupt and distract us from talking about how to regain control of "their" home. So suddenly, here in the middle of our seven questions, they wail in abject protest. "But what if I don't *want* to do what you say!"

Is this a surprise?

News flash: *Your kids are not willing participants in this process.* They don't want us to limit their wackiness, and they don't want to do what we say. And even if you use effective Teaching Discipline, and they learn better behavior, they aren't going to naturally like it. I think it was psychologist Henry Cloud who once said about kids, "They don't want what we're selling!"

Think about it. It's not like your kids posted an ad on Facebook saying, "Immature, self-centered child seeks wise parent to limit and tame him into being a wise loving adult; to teach that child that he can't always have what he wants; to show him that other people matter as much as he. Is anyone interested in being my sponsor?"

No! Even if they are willing to *do* what we say, they still want world domination in their *hearts!* I mean, have you ever met a patient, selfless kid? "Hey Mom, I want a snack, but you've given me so much today, why don't you just put your feet up. I'm fine for now." Or, "Gee, Dad, I've given you so much hassle every time you've asked me to do anything today, I think I'll just quietly obey this time and give you a break." If mine had acted that way, I would have assumed they had been replaced by android replicants.

My real, human kids would have loved to have run the world! They would have elected *That's so Raven* and *Hannah Montana* as president and vice president. Bob Saget from *Full House* would have been youth coordinator at our church (with a Nintendo in every pew). Everyone would live in malls.

Kids don't like this submission thing we've been talking about.

The following interaction between Bonney and me illustrates my point. She was about six at the time.

Bonney: I want to be the boss.

Me: Well, being the boss really isn't that great.

Bonney: I could do it. I'm smarter than you.

Me: If you are smarter than me, then why aren't you already the boss?

Bonney: Because you are bigger than me.

I also peeked in on her once and caught her arguing with a calculator. (I promise I'm not making this up.) I observed her pushing the numbers 2+2=4. And then I heard her saying "Nuh-Uh!"

3+3=6. "No, it's Not!"

You get who we're dealing with here?

So here's our situation: Since you've read Chapter Three, and are certainly now expertly wielding its Jedi-level discipline techniques, your kids might *obey* you—but for the most part, they still don't *like* doing it. Their behavior might get in line, but their hearts can often still resent obeying. We've got to speak to those little hearts! *Having a heart that can be submissive and humble is more important than having obedient behavior.*

And here in our hidden Hogwarts heart chapter, we're gonna talk about that.

We can teach obedience, but I want more than that. God wants more than that. He talks about his own people and says (not just in a voice of judgment but one of sorrow), "These people honor me with lip service, but their hearts are far from me." A loving parent feels the same way.

In other words, so far, all we've talked about is our children's behavior—their external choices. And yes, I want my children to learn to make wise choices in their lives. But I also want them to develop *hearts* that can honor authority, respecting those who are over them and learning the value of making loving choices.

So, how do we help our kids develop the *emotional ability* to bend the knee to authority? How do we soften their hearts to help them learn to value submission and humility? Otherwise, we are just raising little "robot obeyers."

Teaching heart submission

Here's the human condition. Basically, the Bible tells us that we are all born, hold a board meeting, and elect ourselves chairman. Our natural orientation is that we want to run things. Unfortunately, the latest research data is indicating that four-year-olds are not very good at "Universe Running." The planets get out of alignment. *Cap'n Crunch* gets all over the furniture. It's not good. So, in order for our kids to not grow up being entitled little jerks; in order for them to learn to obey; and in order for them to comply with their boss one day, we have to help them learn to get off the throne of their own lives; we have to help them learn *heart submission.*

I remember hearing Dr. John Townsend say something like this: Part of our job as parents is to help our kids *grow up*, right? To handle life, to be strong, to develop wisdom. But, for adulthood and whole living, we also need to help them *grow down.* To learn that they are not special snowflakes—for them to learn to recognize that we are their parents, and they need to respect that—to learn submission.

Parents sometimes say to me, "Our teenager is running our home! He just walks around, living like this big entitled two-year-old. He's such a jerk, it makes me worry—did something *happen* to him when he was younger?"

I tell them, "No, nothing happened to him when he was younger. Actually, the truth is that something *should* have happened to him when he was younger and *didn't!* Namely, for someone to *lovingly alpha* him!"

So how do we teach submission at the heart level? How do we develop kids whose hearts are willing to bend the knee?

Here's how we teach our children's hearts: We help their hearts learn to embrace submission when we *Lovingly Disappoint* them. We *Disappoint* them, but we do it *Lovingly.* Let's take these apart and look at them.

Disappoint

Number one, we do need to disappoint our children. They can't always get their way or get what they want. In other words, step one for a child to learn to submit is for someone to *alpha* them.

Many of us in the last two generations of parents have lived in a position of over-care for our kids. "What is thy bidding, my Mastaaaaah?" Norma and I laugh at how we essentially thought we could teach "servanthood" by *modeling* it. Like, maybe if we sacrificially met all of our children's needs, they would think, "Wow, being a servant to others is really cool. I think I want to do that too." Instead, they just looked to us to serve them more. "Um, Garçon!"

A disturbing number of medical and mental health professionals recommend that discipline that involves negative consequences for a child be abolished in the place of verbal reprimand and positive reinforcement only. As the Colonial Marines say in the movie *Aliens* when their guns are taken away, "What are we supposed to use, harsh language?" If we follow this kind of thinking, we should go ahead and start building the fallout shelters, because the next generation is going to be a doozy!

Instead, I believe that we need to stand our ground and push our kids to recognize that they don't run things. We need to *disappoint*—using all the real consequences and Teaching Discipline that we discussed in the last chapter. We are the parents here; let's act like it. Otherwise, it's *Planet of the Apes* all over again.

One time during the years in which teenage Bonney was home alone (remember the Golden Years?), I was making a cappuccino downstairs. Apparently, Bonney could hear the milk frothing, and she shouted down in her most charming voice, *"Daaaaaady? Would you make me a cappucciiiiiiino?"* I was okay with that, and was reaching up to grab another cup, but then she continued, "... and bring it to me in my bed!"

At that point I walked to the bottom of the stairs and responded, "If for no other reason than that I can one day look your husband in the eye, No, I will not bring you a cappuccino in your bed!" Sanity begins at home!

Two parents of a preteen were in my office recently. They told me that they had tried to take electronics away from their son. He raged at them, aghast. "How dare you!" he literally said. "These are mine, and you cannot take them!"

Blessedly, his parents responded with silence and strength, calmly walking back down the stairs with his phone, iPad, and computer under their arms. He protested for hours, but the next morning apologized to his father. Apology accepted. He'll get the gizmos back in a week—to try again.

So to teach submission, first, we have to disappoint. If you never alpha them, they'll continue to be chairman of the board to the demise of all concerned. If you need more reminders on how to do that, reread Chapter Three.

But we need to do more than just disappoint. If your entire goal with your kids is to *just* demonstrate your authority over them, then go directly to the adolescent unit, do not pass GO, do not collect two-hundred dollars. Not only will it create trouble, there will be a real sense in which you will be missing their hearts, and they will be missing yours. Besides, to most kids (and I've had kids tell me this), when parents sling around authority with justifications like "because I say so," it feels all the world to a child like the parent is saying, "because dad just feels like it," or, "because he's big and I'm small." And that's just sad—sadder than that scene where they lock up Dumbo's mother. We can do better than that, gang.

So next step—let's get *loving*.

Do it lovingly

Secondly, in order to teach submission in a way that changes our children's heart, we have to disappoint *lovingly*.

Here's the psychological secret. Think about it, why is submitting so hard? Why is it painful to bend the knee and submit to someone being in authority over us? The reason is because submission can feel potentially *humiliating*. I mean, *you win* and *I lose*. That's why it's hard. That's why your teen would rather swallow a meteorite sometimes than obey you. It's why some adults still hate authority.

So what heals that humiliation of having to bend the knee? (And if you don't heal it, your child won't "heart learn.") The gift that heals the humiliation of submitting is the fact that we, their parents, are under authority too, and we "get it."

In other words, *we* lose sometimes too.

Think about it, you are under authority too. You have to bend the knee just like your kids. You have to pay taxes. You have to do what your boss says. You have to detour on the interstate when the bridge is being repaired—even if you're in a hurry. And it doesn't matter whether you like it or not! *Don't you hate that?*

So, to prepare our kids *hearts* to learn to submit, we say two things to them; we "Lovingly Disappoint."

First, we say, "I am over you in authority, and you have to do the stuff I say, or your lifestyle around here may change."

And secondly, we add, "But, you know what? I am also someone under authority just like you, and boy it sure is hard sometimes, isn't it? Doesn't it stink? I totally get it."

That's what Loving Disappointment sounds like.

And that loving empathy takes the sting of humiliation out of submission, which makes bending the knee not feel as bad. Now kids can do it!

So with Littles, while we are carrying them screaming back to the car after ending a pleasant trip to the park, we add empathetically, "I know, baby. I know how much you just wanted to stay and play. It is no fun to get dragged away from something that we are enjoying."

This interaction is simple. But deep down, there is magic at work! You are lovingly recognizing the pain your child feels as they are having to submit to your limit. Even just those simple words of kindness are forming a background in your child for experiencing love, even while they are required to submit to authority.

I set a limit on one of the girls when she was about nine-years-old. She responded by saying, "This is so unfair! You just get to make up stuff, and we have to do it!"

Part of me wanted to say, "Duh! Are you just now getting this?"

However, that very same day I had experienced the same dismay my daughter was expressing. It was 1994 and Bill Clinton had just gotten elected. I'd been talking to my accountant that day and had been informed that my taxes were going to increase significantly that year. I was outraged! I didn't even vote for the guy, and I was going to have to do what he said! What a rip off!

Allowing this to sink in, I responded to Katherine. "You

know what? You're right. Nothing feels worse than having someone else just get to decide how we're going to live. It happened to me today. And it really ticked me off. I don't blame you for being angry, and I totally get that it doesn't feel fair. You're still grounded, but I totally get how hard it is. Trust me."

When we "talk with" teenagers (instead of talking at them), we are softening their hearts too. When one of ours was in college and visiting home, I heard her grabbing her keys and purse one night to head over to a friend's house. Only problem was that the whole city was under a tornado warning. You could hear limbs falling in the neighborhood. It was apocalyptic!

I said, "Whoa, sister. You aren't going out in this. It's the end of the world out there."

She responded, "You can't tell me what to do. I'm in college!"

Immediately, I felt that "feeling." Remember the "feeling"? That hot, offended indignation that wanted to "put her in her place." How dare she just thumb her nose at my authority?

Following my own advice, I stopped and thought. (Remember "thinking?") I responded, "So what you're saying is that since you are a college student, I no longer get to speak into your life and choices in any way?"

She paused, taken aback that I didn't walk into her power struggle trap.

"No, I guess not," she responded, and put up her keys.

I added, "Being in college is a weird time. You are doing

your life up there on your own, and you are doing it well. And suddenly you visit home for the weekend and this jakeleg dad still gets to boss you around. Kinda crazy, eh? I get it. I'm sorry. And I so respect you for backing down. Maybe we can get a FEMA truck to take you over to Kelsey's later!"

No amount of rules alone can change the heart, and this submission thing is a heart issue. Our children's hearts only change and grow when we welcome and join their fallenness and immaturity in the context of limits and love. *When our kids see that we "get" the loss and pain of submitting, they soften and learn to recognize the value and kindness of authority.*

Deeper growth

This theme of helping our children's hearts grow by engaging them doesn't just apply to discipline issues. It is the way that all heart growth takes place. Basic psychological/spiritual law: *The only way to change a feeling or an inclination of the heart is for it to be known and understood in the context of limits and love.* Our children's anger, resentment, rebellion, and even sadness are only resolved when we receive them and respond to them with love and limits.

I remember having a conflict with one of my school-age kids. She suddenly whirled around with rage in her eyes and said, "I hate you! You are the meanest daddy in the world!"

Ouch, girl! Do you kiss your doll babies with that mouth?

Now, part of me was indignant and wanted to take her downtown to the Department of Human Services and *introduce* her to the meanest daddy in the world! "Hey, Sweetpea, this is Roscoe. He can be your daddy now!"

But then I remembered this principle of heart growth—her rage would only get resolved if I made room for it in our relationship. (I also remembered that I did indeed have an anger problem.)

So I softened and said to her, "You know what? I know I can be a jerk sometimes. And I know I can be mean. And I totally get it if sometimes it feels like I'm the meanest daddy in the world. I don't want to be that person, and I care that I am sometimes. You're still grounded, but I will take a look at my anger. And in the future, I invite you to just talk to me about it instead of raging at me. But we can talk about that later."

She never said that to me again.

Now, what would have happened if I had raged back at her? "You will *never* speak to me in that tone ever again young lady! I never want to hear those words come out of your mouth again—ever!"

If I had responded like that, there's a real chance that she *wouldn't* have ever said anything like that again—to me or to anyone else. But where would her anger and hurt have gone? Down inside? Never to be heard from again? And never resolved.

The only way we actually *heal* destructive parts of our children's hearts is by lovingly engaging them in relationship.

They say, "I hate my brother." Don't scold and recoil from their nasty thoughts. Engage them. "I know that he makes you real mad sometimes, Zippy. I remember my brother used to make me want to rip my skin off sometimes. I'm glad you are telling me. We all get angry. Now, if you hit him again, you're losing TV, but I so understand." (Love and Limits.)

We can also use this kind of engagement to help our children with their pain.

Your child says, "I wish you and Mommy hadn't gotten a divorce."

Be with them.

"I know, man. I know it's so hard sometimes—moving back and forth on weekends. And you remember those days when we were all together. We both love you so much, and we will all walk through these losses together." (cf Q & A appendix for more on divorced families.)

Just to be balanced, however, if your child is a chronic screamer, habitually berating you, we have to change our recipe a bit. I might want to begin with a kind acknowledgment of what they feel. "I care that you're so angry. ..." But with the chronically disrespectful child, the punchline of this story is going to need to be *limits* on how they are *doing* those feelings. "Hey, Sparky, we care that you are so angry, but if you're committed to talking to us like that, we're going to need to take that phone for a while." Love is not just a group hug, remember? It always dances with limits.

When we encounter our children's destructiveness or immaturity, we can heal it by using love and limits. We welcome and join the bad feelings, and we set limits on what they do with them. For some reason I don't understand, when "badness" is brought into relationship like that, it gets better. It's one of the reasons that the Bible talks about the importance of confession. Bringing our hearts to other humans helps us heal. When we emotionally join our kids in their screwed up fallen feelings and choices, their hearts will heal and grow.

They'll thank you later

Here's one final thought regarding helping our kids learn to value authority. And they won't get it yet, but one day they will.

Think about it. What is the goal of parenting? It's not for your children to behave themselves in Sunday school. *The goal is to prepare them for **adulthood.*** The goal is to send them off after eighteen years or so, equipped with the ability to love well, to choose well, to manage failure well, to have loving relationships, and to basically be a steely-eyed missile man. As I once heard psychologist John Townsend jokingly remind parents, "The goal is to get rid of them!"

One of the best things about Teaching Discipline is that it's not just designed to help your children make wise choices *now.* It's designed to help them learn to make wise choices *period.* Teaching Discipline is designed to help them learn, by the time they are adults, that guiding principle of life: We humans can have anything we want in life, we just have to pay for it. We are free to choose whatever we want. But we can't choose the consequences that might come from those choices. Reality does that for us. Adults who know this secret are cookin' with gas!

Didn't you have those friends in college who, the moment their parents drove off campus, went completely nuts, hanging out of their dorm windows and joining Delta House? Maybe their parents controlled them at home, but no one helped them learn to control *themselves*. They never developed that "internal parent" to help them make choices based on what consequences might be coming down the track. They never learned the principle, "If I do A, then B will happen." Mommy and Dad just controlled or coddled them, so naturally, freshman semester is a countdown to mayhem!

Teaching Discipline helps our kids learn to make wise choices one day when we aren't around. I mean, who "parents" adults? *Reality* does.

Oftentimes I'll have some surly teenager in my office—one of those kids who's been living life on a diet of bourbon and bad choices. He's wearing the requisite Doc Martins and a T-shirt that says something like, "If you're not ticked off, you're not paying attention." And he always says something like, "Man, I can't wait to get out from under these parents … Man. Then I can do anything I want … Man."

And I always say something like, "Yeah, that'll be great. But then you'll have to deal with the Mean Ole Reality Parent. The teen groans and says, "What?"

I continue, "Well, you've got nice (albeit strict) parents now, but you can usually manipulate or sneak around them. But the Reality Parent—he don't take no jive. In Reality, you don't have to show up for work, but then Mean Ole Mr. Employer Parent will 'dock your allowance.' And you don't have to pay your taxes, but Mean Ole Mr. IRS Parent might show up at your house in the black helicopters and put you in 'timeout' for ten to twenty! So it's not that you'll be getting away from parents—it's that you will suddenly be under a *ruthless* parent. Reality!" (At this point, he usually rolls his eyes and groans again.)

Conclusion

So, congratulations! If you're using Teaching Discipline and helping their hearts learn to value submission, you're not just keeping your kids under control at home, you are helping develop hearts that see the value of authority. You are teaching them to think and make wise choices based on the consequences of their actions. More to be desired than gold! And they will thank you for it one day.

I believe that this is how God thinks. God is not about telling people to do a bunch of rules or else he's going to get mad. The way that God calls us to live is not arbitrary. And he doesn't talk a lot about being a good boy versus a bad boy. He more often says stuff like, "Do this that you might live!" Follow this way so that you "may prosper and that your days may be long." Don't do this or "you will die!" God's way is not all about judgey morality like it is often portrayed. His way is much more about *reality* than *morality*. (Like, "Don't eat soap, Goofball! It's bad for you.")

He calls this *wisdom*, and it is about learning to make

choices for our lives based on the consequences that might befall us. Sound familiar?

So, kids, we get it that you don't want to do what the authorities say. Welcome to the party. It's a bummer not getting to be Ozymandias. "Look on my works, ye mighty, and despair!" But there are really only two kinds of people in the world. Those who finally make peace with the fact that life makes some rules that I must follow, and those who live life butting their heads up against reality, living in protest and frustration.

So let us help you learn to be small. To be human. To know our place. Life is bigger than us, and God is the only one who gets to sit in the big chair. But he promises that if we humble ourselves, he will lift us up. Blessed are the poor in spirit, for theirs is the kingdom of Heaven.

And, besides, as I told Bonney that day, "Being the boss isn't really that great after all."

Q&A Time

Hey Doc—All this talk about our kids obeying us out of a consideration of consequences or even rewards is fine, but shouldn't kids obey us simply out of respect for our authority?

Sure they should. Here are a couple of thoughts on that. Number one, obedience because of "authority" *is* very important. But as we said, it is not something to just *require*. It is something that needs to be *taught*. And since children are so concrete and basic in their thinking, motivating them initially with something as lofty and abstract as "honoring authority" is like throwing them in a seminary. They're not gonna get it. So we have to begin teaching authority by using something concrete—consequences, choices, and events. We can then move up to the more abstract "heart" notions later. What happens with good Teaching Discipline is they start to learn to *value* authority; then, when we say "Because I said so" later, it can actually make some sense. So let's *teach* a respect of authority, not *demand* it.

Secondly, submission to authority is great, but I see so many authoritarian parents just stop there, as if good parenting is just about teaching children to obey their elders. I primarily do therapy with adults, and I see adults needing a whole array of abilities to do life well, not just the ability to understand authority. So, sure, let's teach submission, but I hear God and reality calling us to so many other things as well. Wisdom. Values. Love. Forgiveness. Strength. Humility. Not just submission to authority. Don't tunnel-vision your kids' development. We're building a whole operating system here.

Finally, if we're going to err in our parenting (which we will), let's err on the side of teaching them too much love and mattering. It's a lot easier to develop a value of authority later than to develop a sense that I am loved.

We have one child who seems to chronically lie to us. What do we do?

Here's the secret on lying. Primarily, lying is just a subtle form of power struggle. The deceitful child is essentially saying, "I'm not gonna tell you the truth, and I'm betting that you can't catch me." So now the power struggle is, Can you get him to tell you the truth? Can you bust him with his crimes?

Wanna play?

Regarding power struggles—again, they are like global thermonuclear *WarGames*. The only way to win is not to play.

We used to say to ours, "Hey, Pinocchio, we kind of think that you're not telling us the truth, which, number one, makes us sad because it means that we don't really know your heart, and we want to know your heart. Secondly, however, we're not going to play detective and try to catch you. You're pretty smart, and you'll probably get away with it. But this is a small town. Word gets around. So if we do find out that you've been lying to us, your consequences will be *twice* what they would have otherwise been. So ... as Dirty Harry says, 'Feeling lucky, punk?'"

Now the child is in the position to have to *think* about their choice to lie, which is where we want them, rather than just playing cat and mouse with you.

Another thing to consider regarding a child who does not tell the truth: Every now and then, I find a child who is simply afraid. They feel shame and fear about being bad or about getting in trouble. One thing you can do here as a parent is double-check with your spouse to make sure your reactions aren't coming across as shameful or scary. A friend of mine would upset her mother, and the result wasn't just a consequence or discipline. Her mother would loudly disconnect from her—for *days.* "The sun would go behind the clouds," my friend would say. That kind of stuff is scary. Be on the lookout to avoid it. Let's make discipline about learning, not fear.

Also, be sure and read Chapter Five about helping kids learn to deal with shame and badness. A child who feels like they need to deceive their parents and hide their badness may need help learning that, while their failure or rebellion could certainly lead to consequences, they will never lead to shame or the loss of our love. Let's help make it safe for them to tell the truth.

(See Q&A bonus round appendix for more)

Impressive. Most Impressive. Obi-Wan has taught you well.

— Darth Vader

Chapter Four

How do I teach my kids to be strong?

Parents live with a lot of anxiety about how their children are going to function in the face of the difficult, real world. Of course we do! Life in the real world can be a buggy whippin'. Part of feeling free as a parent is having the confidence that we are preparing our kids to be strong and powerful as they face adult life. So if you're asking questions about how to *prepare* your kids for life, I applaud you. Because the question most parents are asking nowadays is how do I *protect* my kids from struggle. In other words, they aren't asking how do I prepare my *child* for the road; they are asking, How do I prepare the *road* for my child? How do I make sure they never suffer?

So, congratulations, if you want resilient kids who turn into resilient adults, you are in the minority, and you are one cool parent. This is gonna look good on your report card.

The world is a tough place. And no matter how many street protests they might stage to change it, life isn't going to smooth out for our kids. They are going to need to be strong in order to face real life. My wife reminded me the other day that my motto as we were raising our kids was, "I want us to help create strong loving adults who are able to function in the twenty-first-century." Little did I know that the twenty-first century would be this difficult.

We just spent a couple of chapters unpacking what it looks like to teach our children to bend the knee—to submit. But think about it, how are the adults who are just *compliant and obedient* doing in life?

One demographic I'm seeing more and more in my practice is the young person who is straight out of college. Since college is the new high school (and high school really doesn't count) these kids are basically walking out of a world in which they have been protected, provided for, and entitled. They have been able to manipulate and milk mommy and daddy into protecting them from all of their problems. But remember the "Mean Ole Reality Parent"? Suddenly they have a boss and a landlord who aren't willing to come rouse them from their bed after they have hit the snooze button for the seventeenth time. They are dealing with reality for the first time—and they are terrified! They feel like a child in a world full of adults (because they *are!*). And they are afraid. They are not prepared to do real life as strong people.

So obviously, raising great kids involves helping them learn something besides just submission and obedience (and how to use our credit card). We are trying to produce adults here. We are setting *you* free, but we are also working to set our kids free too.

One of the ways I like to phrase this is to say that parenting essentially has *two goals*. I like to call them *Roots* and *Wings*. *Roots* is that warm safe grounding in love that we discussed in Chapter Two. Our love for our kids "roots" them in their sense of home. *Wings* on the other hand is the power and freedom to leave the nest (even if we have to kick them out of it!). One of the greatest gifts that we can give our children is the courage and confidence to have the "wings" to manage life on their own. In other words, parenting has two goals not one—Roots *and* Wings. *Teaching our kids to be powerful and resilient is just as important as teaching them nurture and love.* Let's look at how Roots and Wings can help us teach our kids to be strong.

Roots and wings
Building strength with roots

"Roots" is about teaching our kids that they are all nested, safe, and protected under us. We talked in an earlier chapter about how that kind of connection fills their hearts with mattering and belonging, the foundation of feeling loved.

But here's the added bonus: *Roots also form a foundation for helping our kids be strong!*

Remember, love isn't just about making us feel nurtured and cuddly—it also becomes that inner battery pack that allows us to walk out into the world and weather disappointments or deal with jerks. Like we said, once we get those kinds of "Core Questions" answered, we don't need other people's reassurance all the time. That's *strength*, sports fans!

For instance, if I have my Core Questions answered about being a "good enough" writer, then you can tell me that my book stinks (just to use a completely absurd example) and though I might be interested in getting your thoughts on it, my battery pack of love keeps me from feeling wounded or ashamed. Love is the foundation for teaching strength and power.

By the way, if we don't get good answers to those Core Questions early on, we will continue asking them—of *everyone!* We will wander through our lives always asking at some level, "Do you think I'm good? Do you like me?" And we will ask those questions of everybody we encounter. We will ask those questions to our boss and to our spouse. We will ask those questions at our church, and based on the number of "Likes" we get on Facebook. We will ask them on a train. We will ask them in the rain. We will ask them of a fox. We will ask them in a box.

And when we get bad answers from any of these people, we will experience that shame and insecurity that haunts us all way too much. We need to have good answers to our Core Questions to be immune to everyone else's opinions.

So, if you're wanting to build strong kids, answering their Core Questions about roots and love are the blast off launching pad of it all!

Building strength with wings

But we also need to give our kids *Wings*. In other words, in addition to building a foundation of loving nurture, we also need to *overtly teach* our kids be strong—to be *them*. In this section, we're going to look at two parts of building these "wings" of power and teaching resiliency. I'm going to call them *Identity* and *Strength*.

Identity

One of the things humans need in order to be strong enough to do life in the real world is a sense of *Identity*, or what we shrinks call a "Sense of Self." This doesn't mean selfishness or self-centeredness (our kids don't need any help with that!). Having "identity" simply refers to the ability to know who I am—not needing to always be asking, "What is everyone else doing?"

After Joshua leads the people into the Promised Land, he invites them to consider a question. He says, "Choose *ye* this day whom *ye* will serve."[1] All we are talking about here is having a "Ye." That inner sense that puts a finger on our pulse and asks, "What do I believe. What do I value?" This is the spiritual quality we call "stewardship." What am I going to do with the mind and heart and gifts that I have been given? We gotta have a "ye."

So this isn't about giving our kids license to matter more than everyone else, because they are "special." We're just talking about helping our kids get a seat at the table in their lives—be a player; have a sense of who they are. About half of you are married to someone, who, if you ask them where they want to go eat dinner, responds, "Oh, anywhere's fine." Drives you crazy, right? In order to do life, to have a job, to pick out your clothes—we need to have a sense of who we are and what we value.

I see adult clients all the time who tell me, "I don't even feel like I know who I am." One guy told me once, "I live life as a 'sponge,' absorbing the color of anyone around me. If I am in 'purple water.' I am purple. If I am in 'green water,' I am green." Living as this kind of chameleon is often the result of never having answered these identity questions. I have found that one of the reasons that adults might end up not knowing who they are, is simply because they were never *asked*—or no one ever showed them. Instead of having the freedom, space, and safety to ask and learn, "Who am I?" their childhoods were too busy asking other questions, like, "How do I keep Dad from getting angry?" or, "How do I make Mom proud of me?"

I want you to be aware that one of the tasks in which your child is engaging is the lifelong project of answering these questions of, "Who am I?"; "What do I like?"; "What do I believe and value?" And I want you to be helping them answer these questions.

God made humans to naturally do this. Remember toddlers? If given the option to remain a tiny little baby or be big, most toddlers will buck out of your arms in their Spiderman pull-ups and try to get away. They are built for autonomy. Congratulations, toddler independence is the first sprout of this sense of identity.

Think about it, their favorite new words are "No" and "Me" and "Mine"! (Who am I?) My daughter told me that my eighteen-month-old grandson should have vocabulary of a hundred words by the time he is two. I asked her, "Does saying 'No' seventy-five times a day count as part of that one hundred?"

So suddenly, Captain Underpants starts walking around, saying words, throwing tantrums, and basically making your life more difficult. Welcome to the Terrible Two's! (Though more and more this seems to be happening during the "Three's"! One of my therapist friends calls it "The Therrible Three's"!) Anyway, all of this upheaval is normal. Billion Dollar Government studies have revealed the following: Relationships are always more difficult with *two people* in them! And with toddlers, you have the birth of another person!

Now, the authoritarian parent types sometimes respond to this independence thing as if toddlers are these little self-centered Sandinistas, shaking their fist at God and parent. And they say that this self-centered little will needs to be brought under parental authority. And that is kind-a/sort-a, one-half true. But we shouldn't miss the fact that one of the things that is happening here is the development of a *Person*— the development of *Identity*. I see "doormats" in therapy who never learned this.

I met once with a guy whose wife had cheated on him. I asked him how he was feeling since finding out about the affair. He said, "I just feel really bad for her. She feels so guilty and is so scared that I will leave her."

I replied, "No—I don't think you understand. I'm asking how *you* feel about this."

He didn't know. Down underneath, he had a very diffuse sense of self. He never learned to ask these questions about who he was and what he needed. Let's help our kids develop Identity!

How do we help?
If you want your kids to be ready for real life in the real world, there's a lot you can do to help—at every age. Just like we *taught* Love and Submission, we can *teach* Identity and Strength. We do this by looking for opportunities where we can inquire, make room, and give permission for our kids to be asking who they are.

When we say things to a preschooler like, "Here are two outfits; you get to pick," we are making room for their early little opinions. I made up a silly nickname for Callie when she was about three. Considering myself clever and funny, I continued to use it. After a couple of days, and already tiring of my "dad joke," she said, "Not call me that!" I immediately stopped, wanting to honor her little preschooler sense of self.

With older kids, we can give them more overt choices. They don't get to choose whether they do their homework, but maybe they can choose whether to do it now or have a snack first. They can choose whether to focus on music or baseball. They are learning what they like.

We can also teach Identity by asking questions and being a "mirror." "What did you *think* about that?" "How did you *feel* about that?" "You really love soccer, don't you?" When you talk to your kids like this, you are being a kind of mirror to help them literally learn who they are. We are saying in essence, "This is *you!*"

At the other end of the spectrum, be careful about telling them kooky confusing things about who they are and what they experience. Don't be a "funhouse mirror." I remember playing with my kids once at a public park. Suddenly we heard screaming. Some kid had slipped and totally busted his mouth on the monkey bars. His dad picked him up and despite his mouthful of blood said, "Aw come on, that didn't hurt!"

Now, let me ask you—what's that kid supposed to do with that? He's experiencing searing bolts of pain and spitting out blood, but the person to whom he looks to help him define reality tells him that it doesn't hurt! This stuff keeps me in business.

Instead, let's look for opportunities to help them *explore* who they are. I was talking to a mother the other day whose eight-year-old son had had some conflict at school. She told me that she decided to ask him how *he* would like to handle the conflict. And he *told* her. And he *handled* it! I was really struck by that—the opportunity to ask himself, even at eight-years-old, *"Hmmm—how do I want to deal with this situation?"* That's *Identity* happening right there, folks!

Now, of course, unless she wants her own personal little

Kim Jung Un on her hands, she will also have to teach him that what *she* wants matters too. This isn't just, "Tell me who you are, Johnny, and we will let you run the world." But it is, "Tell me who you are, Johnny, so you can *function* in the world!" Even as we teach them that other people also matter, we are helping them form a sense of self. I matter and so do other people.

So at the same time that we are laying down limits and discipline like we talked about in the last chapter, we are also fostering an atmosphere that welcomes their sense of self— so we have a lot of plates spinning here. But look for those times in which we can make room for their little opinions to emerge. This is identity forming right before your very eyes— the same identity that will help them be powerful adults.

When Bonney was little, she had very definite opinions about clothes—albeit strange ones. She went through a season in preschool in which she only wanted to wear *orange* clothes! And then another season in which she only wanted to wear a little cheerleader outfit—every day. This was a harmless way in which we could let her express her identity. I still smile when I see her school picture from that year. You guessed it; she's dressed as a cheerleader. And her birthday cake from the previous year—orange!

Callie's real name is Norma. She is named after her mother, who was named after her mother, who was named after her mother, etc. Callie was actually the fifth Norma. (It's a Southern thing). We ended up calling her "Norma Callie" just to distinguish her from everyone else! Around the time she was in second grade, however, she approached us and asked if her name could just be "Callie." "I don't want to be named Norma like everyone else," she said. (Finally, some healthy individuation bloomed in the South!) She was asking us if she could be *her!* We, of course, agreed, and she has been Callie ever sense. We had a ringside seat to watch her identity forming. Of course, my buddies gave me a lot of grief about this decision—"The shrink let his kid change her name! If she had wanted to be named Dora the Explorer, would you have let her do that too?"

This is why I have trust issues.

Blindspots

Now, some kids don't want to step out and declare who they are. This is an opportunity too. Perhaps you have a child who just wants to please mommy and daddy (You wish, right?). Counterintuitively, it's important to push back on those compliant little "follower" kids. They are missing the opportunity to explore who they are.

One of our children went through a season in which she seemed to take on the responsibility of being the family "Pleaser"—the Peacemaker. If anyone was unhappy, she was quick to lay down her own needs and please someone else. Now, of course a child showing compassion and selflessness is wonderful, but if you see one of your kids habitually compromising their own needs to keep everyone happy, they are walking the tight rope toward doormat-hood. (Good identity and stewardship always work to make *both* people matter.)

In this case, I felt like she was taking on too much responsibility for being the "good child." As I came in from work one day, she walked up to me and asked, "How was your day at work today, Daddy?"

I replied, "Well, it was tough actually. I saw a full load of clients, and I am kind of braindead."

She turned around to her sisters who were playing in the den. "Okay y'all," she announced, "Dad has had a hard day, so y'all be really quiet and turn down the TV."

I turned to her and said, "No, no, no, darling! I love you and you are sweet, but I don't need you to take care of me. I can take care of myself, and I have your mom to help me. You need to go be a kid! Go watch a dumb cartoon and fight with your sisters or something."

I wanted to "fire" her from this job of being a compliant child caretaker. (Years later I wonder if I had done *too* good of a job.)

The next level

In the teenage years, this identity thing goes viral! Just like that toddler, the teenager is asking questions about identity. I mean, have you *talked* to your teenager lately? What do they say? "No, me, mine … Man!" Just like a feisty little toddler, only with earbuds.

Being a teenager is sort of like unscrewing the top of your head and dumping all of the contents out on the table and going through them, trying to decide what you want to throw away and what you want to keep. Adolescence is the proving ground for adulthood. They are working to build the identity and individuality necessary to function in the world. Which we want, right? #Goalistogetridofthem. We want them to be powerful, insightful, and thoughtful as they hit the real world. We want them to be ready to chart a course for adventure—to pull up a groove and get fabulous. Of course they often use this newfound sense of identity just to be surly, arrogant, and irresponsible. When that happens, simply put down your Love Potion and pick back up your Limits Gun. It's time to bring the consequences. Just like that toddler, we *welcome* their strength and we *set limits* on it—at the same time!

Now for today's Bad News Moment.

To build identity and power, teens will have to push back from you.

This pursuit of identity is why your teenager will come out with bizarre comments like, "I don't think I want to have a regular job like Dad. I think I just want to be in a band." They are asking questions about who they are; who they want to be. The parent who doesn't understand this is going to jump up and freak out and say, "Oh my gosh, then you're going to end up living in a TRAILER down by the RIVER!" But what they're doing is experimenting. Trying to find their sense of identity. If we can make room for some of these proclamations rather than freaking out, they will usually experiment, learn, and come back to a more grounded position.

I remember one of our teens hated every decorating decision we made when we remodeled our house. We would be talking to the decorator, and she would roll her eyes and groan, "Oh my Gosh! I'm going to be too embarrassed to have any of my friends over—for the rest of my life!" Years later, when she was an adult living in Nashville, she brought friends home for the weekend. One of them said, "Oh my gosh, Callie, I see where you got your sense of design. Your house is decorated just like your parents."

Teenagers are all about getting wings (i.e. away from *you!*). This is why when you ask about their day, they only give you a monosyllabic answer or maybe just a grunt. Wings are why they disappear up to their room and rarely speak. One of ours remained so distant during one season that she asked if we could start a family newsletter and slide it under her door so she could keep up with current events. "Wait!—Mom got a job?"

Wings are why they want to spend so much time with their friends. They're working on their identity, apart from us. Some of you have experienced the "Teenage Girl Spend the Night Party." It's like someone dumps a whole box of cats out in the middle of the house. We would try to smile, bake some cookies, put in our earplugs. and lock ourselves in our room.

I see parents get all wigged out about their child's distance, and affection for friends (instead of for their parents) and start a power struggle, trying to make them come downstairs and spend time with family. But healthy teens are in some ways becoming more connected to the opinion and the "family" of their peers, than they are to you. That's why peer rejection is so devastating to them.

Again, don't let this make you go postal. They're forming the model for adult life. I mean, *we* are all each other's best friends, right? I mean, if I told you, "Y'all, I'm fifty-nine years old—and my mom is my best friend! We talk every day, and she's who I go to when I need a buddy. Sometimes we just go on vacations together," you'd say, *"Riiiight!* We've read Tennessee Williams, Dr. Cox—Thank you very much."

So sure, set some limits and require them to join you for some meals or maybe an event here or there. But manage that loss and fear you have and create space for them to be separate. We are *de-parenting*, remember? As we said in Chapter Two, this is very loving to them, but it also is building their sense of who they are apart from their family. This is identity forming, and it is a core foundation for being able to be strong in the world one day.

One model I like for thinking about de-parenting a teenager is the image of a kite. The goal with a kite is to get it to fly, right? But we don't just let all the string out at once. We help it catch a breeze and then let out a little string. Once we are sure it is flying well, we let out a little more string. But *your* goal is same as the *kite's* goal—for it to fly higher. Of course, being a kite comes with consequences for the knuckle-headed choices it might make while flying—but we still foster the flying.

Prepare and protect

Good teenage parenting always dances along the continuum of, "How much should we let them go and possibly make mistakes?" and "How much should be set limits and protect them from all the trouble out there?" I call this dance, *"Prepare and Protect."* We want to prepare them for real life, but they are still kids, so we also need to protect them.

So do we let them go to that party or not? Where do we land?

To be honest, in the ambiguous world of adolescent parenting, we are never fully sure. (We are learning too!) But it's the parents who can live with the ambiguity, uncertainty, and anxiety of the teenage world, who make the best parents of teenagers. The parents I worry about are the ones who *are* completely sure! "There's no way you are going to that party or any party, so I don't want to hear another word about it." That parent is not living with the uncertain, ambiguous nature of the teenage universe, and that child will go compliant, rebel, or sneak—lickety split!

So, maybe you don't want them to go to that party. (Remember what happened at that party last year!) But on the other hand, maybe you *do* want them to go—and maybe even make some mistakes, and certainly have consequences because of those mistakes. *And Learn!*

I would much rather them learn now than later in college— much less in the real world. Let me put it this way: If college is the first time your child starts making choices on their own, those choices will certainly be unfortunate ones.

Instead, let's make room for them to choose poorly while they are younger (especially on the innumerable "smaller issues,") and learn from their choices—and be there for them when they fall.

If we give them the freedom to learn who they are, there is a *chance* that they can have problems because of the choices that they make. But if we control them, there is not a *chance* that they will have problems, there is a *certainty* they will have problems! So we walk that vulnerable line between Protecting and Preparing. Between holding them back and letting them go.

This is scary

Obviously, managing our parental anxiety at this point is crucial. A package arrived at our house one day addressed to teenage Katherine. It was from Victoria's Secret. She arrived home from school, tucked it under her arm, and disappeared into her room. The next day, Norma could not stand the curiosity any longer and began digging through Katherine's garbage. All she found was an empty box and a receipt. It said that Katherine had ordered a "black leather thong." Norma freaked out! She came to me with the receipt. "What in the world is a 'black leather thong'?" Norma exclaimed. "Is this some kind of kinky S&M thing? I mean, who wears 'black leather thongs'?"

That evening, Norma went upstairs to "confront" Katherine with this aberrant purchase. "Katherine, I found out what you ordered from Victoria's Secret. A black leather thong? What in the world, honey? We are worried about who you are becoming!"

Katherine looked at her mother and rolled her eyes. "Mom—it was flip-flops."

Here's a more poignant story about identity. The parents of one of my teenage clients came in for a parent consult session one day. They were in a complete swivet. Their son had announced that he wanted to get a tattoo. "The only tattoo I'll let him get is the one from the Marines!" said his dad, "... because that's where he's headed if he keeps up this foolishness!"

I encouraged them, "I don't think he's becoming a whacko here, guys. Have you really talked with him about what he wants and why?" They had not.

Playing a hunch (since I knew him), I continued, "Why don't you chill on your anxiety for a bit and go ask him why he wants this tattoo so badly?"

They returned the next week, softened. What he had wanted was a tattoo of his family name. You see, he was adopted. And all he was wanting to do was to underline his identity as *really* their child. They warmly embraced this need to permanently affirm his status as theirs in this teenage way. If we can get our fear out of the way, beautiful things can happen.

Now, of course, just because we are managing our anxiety doesn't mean that we aren't going to remain *vigilant*. They can become morons at any moment, and we will need to swing in hard regarding overt rebellion or bad choices. But to help *teach identity*, we must never forget the importance of managing our anxiety and stretching to embrace their separateness.

Blindspots again

Teenagers are usually itching to get away. Snuggly closeness with their parents is "not their bag, Baby!" However, I sometimes encounter a teenager who is one of those "homebody children"—the ones who are more comfortable with adults than their peers. They often claim that their mother still *is* their best friend. That's sweet and all, but I often see these kids struggle with significant anxiety regarding peers, school, and life challenges. Their fearfulness is often directly related to the fact that they are not practicing their independence and strength apart from their parents. We have to be on the lookout for these dependent, home-loving kids. Sometimes they need pushing.

Look for ways to help them discover their heart—their identity apart from you. Push them a little. When they proudly say, "I liked that sermon at church today, Daddy," I might say, "Cool, tell me something about it you disagreed with." Challenge them. If they say, "You're awesome, Dad," say, "I doubt it. Tell me something about me that drives you crazy!" They need us to not buy into their little homebody fantasy.

Push them in real life too! If they need car insurance, make them go with you and do most of the talking. If you make them get a job, then you get to move to the head of the class.

But if our goal is to help teach them to be strong adults in the real world, we need to be pushing them out of their comfort zone and stretching them find their own strength and identity.

Strength

Part of preparing our kids for life and resiliency happens when we help them develop their identity and sense of self. But we can also overtly teach them about *strength*. Lots of kids need to be taught to be strong.

Life is difficult. And about twenty years after you first hold that squally little baby in your arms, you're going to send them out into a difficult world. And maybe you haven't been keeping up with current events, but in order to not get steamrolled by death, taxes, and infomercials, your kids are going to have to be strong.

I see adult clients all the time who never learned to be strong and resilient. They are picked on by their boss; they are anxious about what tomorrow may bring; and they are bullied by their spouse. I had one guy tell me, "You won't believe what 'she' did to me last night! She just stood there and berated me for like three hours!" In response, I just stared at his feet. He asked me what I was doing. I said, "I just wanted to make sure you had *feet*, because I was wondering why you sat there and listened to her for *three hours!* Where was your power? Where was the part of you that needed to say, 'Wow, if you're going to talk to me like that, I don't think I'm willing to interact with you, Babycakes!'?"

In order to do adult life, our kids are going to need to be strong. So how do we teach them about Power and Strength?

Face it, if you could just protect your children from all suffering, you would. We all would. Overprotective parents have gotten hammered a lot in the last decade or so. They have articles written about them—other parents shake their heads in disapproval (She's *sooo* overprotective!), and they are always being compared to some annoying machine. First it was helicopters, then it was lawnmowers, now they are snowplows—"Snowplow parents"! Can't we give these poor guys a break? They're just afraid. They just hurt inside when their children suffer. So they think that maybe if they could shelter their child from all of the dangers out there, then little Nathan Junior wouldn't have to hurt in life.

Unfortunately, I get it. My children went through a lot of suffering, and I still cringe when I think about it. I don't know if there is any greater pain in life than watching our children hurt. So, helicopters, lawnmowers, hoverboards—I get it. You aren't crazy, just loving. That's the good news. The bad news is you cannot ultimately succeed in protecting your children. Instead, we need to pack their lunch satchel full of all sorts of love—but also a heapin' helping of *power* and *strength*.

Power and littles
If you are the parent of an infant or toddler, you can play on your iPhone during this part of class. Babies just need nurture, and the last thing any of us need to do with a

toddler is *empower* them! Heavens! They are already *fearless!* They'll stick their hand up in the Shark Vacuum if you aren't watching.

One Saturday, I turned by back on one of mine while visiting the mall. Suddenly I turned around, and she was gone. Fear flooded over me. I frantically scanned the atrium, calling her name. Suddenly, I spotted the top of this little blonde head, descending the escalator. Other parents were looking and pointing like, "Where is your negligent father, little girl?" Like most preschoolers she was oblivious to any danger—headed to the Disney Store, I guess.

Toddlers don't need empowerment.

When one of my nephews was about two-years-old, his brother, his father, and I were hanging out in the front yard. Mark, the two-year-old, suddenly spotted a large stick lying on the ground. Curious, he picked it up and examined it. Then he tapped it in the dirt. Then he swung it harder against the ground with a curious look on his face. Then he hit the ground again, causing another stick to fly up in the air. He swung again harder—breaking sticks and creating clouds of dust and destruction, like that monkey at the beginning of *2001: A Space Odyssey.* Then, walking across the yard with his new discovery ------ he hit his brother with it. The dawn of Man.

Though we don't want to embolden toddlers, we can help them develop some mastery in learning to manage their little worlds. One place we can do this is by joining them in their emerging *separation from mom.* A baby says, "Mommy and I are One." A toddler starts saying, "Mommy and I are *Two!*" Toddlers are beginning to explore their emerging independence. As we said, this is the birth of identity, but this is also a major strength builder.

Mine used to love leaving the house for intrepid exploits with me. We would put on boots and a coat, and head out into the world for an "adventure." As we left the house, they would look over their shoulders at mother and boastfully say, "Bye, Mom!" as if to declare, "I don't need you anymore. I'm big and independent." Dads are super key figures in this process because we are a safe *parent,* but we're not *Mom,* from whom little Speed Racer is working to separate! Later, the adventurers get to return victorious to an excited mother who says, "Oh my gosh! Was it *so* fun?" Mom and dad are both working here to help their toddler learn to separate and be strong.

A second way we can give toddlers tools to better manage their topsy turvy little world is by helping them learn to manage and understand their feelings. As we said in the love chapter, Littles have no idea how to deal with their floods of emotion. We can help them by working to keep our cool during their outbursts, helping them soothe and settle down when upset, and also by swinging in and helping them learn to "mentalize" their feelings. As we said, helping them develop words for their emotions (make them mental not physical) begins to give them "hooks" for understanding what they are feeling. This is deeply empowering to a toddler.

I remember taking three-year-old Callie to the grocery

store during the year I was interning in Memphis. As we got to the checkout counter, an imposing, over-dressed woman (all lipstick and big hair) leaned over tiny Callie and said to her in a Memphis drawl, "Well, you *are* a little cute one, aren't you!" Callie's eyes grew as wide as saucers (as did mine). She scampered up into my arms like a spider monkey, and buried her face in my neck. I leaned my mouth down to her ear and whispered, "That lady scared you, didn't she?"

When we arrived back home from the store, Norma asked, "Well, how was the grocery store?"

Callie replied, "A big 'yady' *scared* me!"

I did a total fist pump in my mind, hearing my daughter begin to use mental categories to make sense of her feelings.

School-age strength

School-age kids take the need for strength-building to the next level. Remember how school-agers are engaging the world alone for the first time? In the love chapter, we talked about how nurturing it feels to them when our hearts join them in these obstacles and adventures. Now we are also going to use this challenging time to begin their education in *power and strength*. Your kids will help you know when you need to start doing this.

For example, about the time kids turn nine or ten years old, they will start to encounter problems in their lives that you will find difficult to solve. Some kid is being mean to them at school. They develop a fear about weather or you dying. They keep forgetting things. They're afraid they won't be able to go to sleep.

And you will attempt to comfort them and reassure them about these problems—and it won't help. Perhaps you've encountered this phenomenon.

For instance, if a five-year-old says, "Mommy, I'm afraid a tornado is going to hit the house," you can simply comfort her and reassure her. "No honey, you don't need to be afraid. A tornado is not going to hit the house." She will then return to her *Daniel Tiger* reruns, quite content. But if a nine-year-old tells you he is afraid that a tornado is going to hit the house—*after your reassurance*—he will respond completely *not reassured!* He will say something like, "Well I just saw Jim Cantori on the Weather Channel, and he was standing *in front of* a house that had just been hit by a tornado."

What are you supposed to say now?

The reason you will find these problems hard to solve with more Roots and Love and Reassurance is that you *can't* solve them with more Roots and Love and Reassurance. You have to solve them with *Wings—Strength.* In other words, when you experience this realistic helplessness, (no matter what I say, he's still anxious), that's your sign to *stop* reassuring and *start* building strength—teaching them about their own ability to solve problems. "Yeah, weather is kind of scary. But I know that you are strong and can push back on that fear. Let's not let it win. You know we love you, and that God loves you. I know that you're scared, but you can do this!"

Just like kids need to be taught about love or discipline, lots of kids also need to be *taught* things about strength. Covering them in a frosty coating of nurture and rescue is fine when they are small. But by school age we need to be working to help them also learn a wonderful new fact—They are *strong*.

The eyes of a parent

Remember this Secret of the Solar System from Chapter Two? *Children get their view of themselves and of their world from the eyes of their parents.* Children don't know the truth about themselves. They are learning. Constantly. And one of the most powerful places they learn about who they are is by "looking into our eyes."

So, what are our eyes telling them if we are always rushing to the rescue to fix their problems and bail them out? What are our eyes saying about who they are? "You are just little and fragile and pitiful, and you need your mommy to rescue you. We're gonna buy you a special weather radio." Is that what we want to be teaching them?

I was a camp counselor one summer in the seventies. We had cabins full of kids, and counselors who were there to guide them. One little boy in my cabin didn't ride the bus to camp with the other kids. Instead, his mother brought him. As we were unloading his trunk and duffel bag, she pulled me aside and said, "Stephen is going to have some trouble with homesickness. I just want you to be aware." Now, nineteen-year-old me didn't have a doctorate in psychology yet, but who needs a doctorate? This smelled fishy to me!

A few nights later, Stephen woke me in the middle of the night crying. You guessed it, he was homesick. We stepped out to the front steps of the cabin and sat together in the dark.

He looked up at me and said, "My mom said I was going to get homesick."

I thought—"Well, you certainly did not disappoint her, amigo."

I see a lot of kids who have been "helped" or "protected" so much that they have no idea that they are able to solve their own problems. Almost like if you could protect your children from all bacteria, they would never develop an immune system. In fact, medical professionals are starting to condemn all those antibacterial sanitizer goos because they are literally preventing kids from developing immunities—they never encounter germs. Doctors are saying kids need to go eat dirt—or that gum from underneath the table at Applebee's. They need to develop the defenses to deal with all those varmints out there. Same principle applies to their hearts. Sometimes our eyes need to be saying, "Dude, you have entered the big bad world and guess what—you can do this! We can do this!"

I was guilty of this rescuing/overprotection sometimes. When Bonney was a senior in high school, she had the most challenging English teacher in the school. One night she was up late working on a paper that was due the next day. Now, for all of Bonney's charms, I must add this: she was a terrible writer. I was an English major—4.0—and as I sat down to help her with her paper, I had to manage my horror. As we say in the South, this paper was a "dog rug"—I wouldn't let my dog sleep on this paper. But with my English background, and having previously read the book, I offered to help Bonney with this catastrophe.

However, after hours of frustration and tears (from both of us), I finally told her in exasperation, "Just go to bed! I am going to write your stupid paper. Just go!" (Yes, I really did this—I guess today is sharing day) So I stayed up late and knocked out the paper!

Days later, Bonney came in from school and marched straight over to me with a bit of a smirk on her face. "I got *your* English paper back, Pops. He gave you a C!"

"A *C?*', I screamed in outrage! Give me the phone! I'm calling that moron! I've never made a C in English in my life! This is ridiculous!"

And to add one last insult to injury, Norma was mad at *me* because Bonney needed a good grade!

So, overprotection!—biohazard for all concerned.

Instead, how do we *teach strength?*

Challenge and celebrate

Here are my two favorite ingredients in the recipe for teaching kids that they are strong. We are going to *Challenge* them, and we are going to *Celebrate* them. Like everything else we've talked about, the most powerful place that kids learn is through what they experience. And the classroom for teaching strength is going to be the difficult world—where we are going to challenge them to engage obstacles and difficulties, with us at their side. Together we are going to help them learn that they are stronger than they think. We are going to push and challenge them to stretch outside of their comfort zone. And then we are going to get a big fat fist bump ready once they do it. Challenge and Celebrate—our latest manifestation of Limits and Love.

Let's look at them.

Back when I used to do play therapy with children, I had a large dry-erase board with markers in my therapy room. The kids love to draw big scenes on the flat white space. And on many occasions, the following interaction would occur: I would be seeing a child who had been brought to me because of chronic anxiety. Maybe they were afraid of school or refused to spend the night away from home. We would talk about their fears in the play therapy, and maybe play games together and draw pictures, (one of my little clients told his mom once, "I want to do what Dr. Cox does when I grow up. He just plays with toys!")

Anyway, invariably, during one of my drawing sessions with an anxious child, they would struggle pulling the top off one of the markers—like it was stuck. They would then wordlessly offer the marker to me. I would always respond by asking, "Are you asking me to take the top off this marker?" The child would nod shyly, looking up at me with needy eyes. I would respond, "Well, ya know, I would love to do that. But if I did, I would be *lying* to you. So, I don't think that's the best plan."

The child would then look at me with a confused expression.

I would continue, "What I mean is that you think that you are weak and small and not able to solve your problems—

even little problems like figuring out how to get the top off a marker. Now, I know that's *not true*. I know you are strong enough and clever enough to figure out how to solve this problem. So if I took the top off the marker, it would be like agreeing with the lie. Agreeing that you are too small and weak to fix this problem. I think you can solve it. In fact, I know you can."

And at that point, I would hand the marker back to them.

Every single one of those children would then take the marker in their hands, look into my eyes, and pop the top off of it. We would then high-five and elbow slap as we celebrated their awakening to the *Truth*. They are stronger than they think. This is school, and they are learning that they are strong. Challenge and Celebrate!

When one of my nephews was about eight-years-old, he was afraid of going in the ocean. We were on a family trip to Florida, and he would stand on the shore unable to get in the water. I decided to hang out with him. As we talked, he told me that he was afraid of sharks—that's why he didn't want to go in the water. Now, like the "tornado boy" that we spoke of earlier, I knew that reassuring him that there was no danger would go nowhere. Instead, I decided to address his *fear*.

I told him, "You are right. There *are* sharks in the ocean. But the secret is that what is keeping you out of the water is not the *sharks,* it is your *fear.* Your fear is making up a story about what might happen and whispering it to you. And when he does that, he takes away all of your fun. I say we push back on him. He's a bully. You see me windsurfing in the ocean, right? Well, I get afraid all the time, but I refuse to let "Mean Ole Mr. Fear" take good things from me. Come on, let's you and me walk out into the water together and see what really happens, rather than listen to what Fear tells us will happen."

(I like to "objectify" fear for kids. Children just think, "That's scary!" I want to teach them, "No, what is happening is that you are feeling a *feeling* of fear. And we can push back on that! Together!" Now we have a common enemy and can work together to help the child be strong.)

Looking into my eyes, he agreed to this adventure, and we walked out into the water. When we were about waist deep, I asked him, "You doing okay? So far, so good? Is anything bad happening?"

"No—nothing bad so far," he replied.

"See? Fear is wrong!" I said.

There was a shallow sandbar about thirty yards offshore that was filled with shells. I said, "Let's make it to the sandbar and get some treasure. I'm with you, and we are doing this together. You are really being strong and brave."

Soon we made it to the sandbar and were quickly joined by my daughters on their floats. I commented to him, "This is what happens when you thumb your nose at Fear. You get all the goodies and the shells and the treasure, and then fun girls show up, and you have a great time. You just conquered your fear, Capt'n!" *Challenge and Celebrate!*

He now designs and builds nuclear submarines for the U.S. Navy. I kid you not.

Stretching and strengthening

Look for opportunities to stretch and challenge your kids about their power. That's where they learn! If that seven-year-old wants more Polynesian sauce at Chick-fil-A, say, "Cool! Go up there and ask the lady yourself." If he's afraid, then offer to go up there with him as he talks to her. If he is still afraid, then invite him to go with you, and watch *you* ask the lady for Polynesian sauce—and then next time, it's *his turn*! Building strength is like weaning them off their dependence on you and *teaching* them the skill of being powerful.

Building strength is a great place for dads to swing in. In our culture, the role of dad is often relegated to pitching baseball or being the "heavy" in discipline. But a father can have a powerful role of being a "broker of strength" in their children's lives.

I've encountered so many dads who respond to their child's anxiety with comments like, "Come on, son, toughen up! Be a man!" For real? That's a bunch of malarkey! When we talk like this, we are actually creating *more* fear and anxiety in that child. We are essentially saying, "I'm big and you're small. So—Be Big!"

Ton of help there!

Instead, I encourage you dads to come alongside that child and *teach* them about the world of power. "I totally get it that you're scared, man. I get scared too sometimes. Let me teach you how to be powerful—you and me! We can do this!" That kid is going to be a dynamo!

School work is another place to build strength. When our oldest was in fourth grade, we decided that she had the capability of managing her own schoolwork. (Most children aren't ready for this kind of autonomy in fourth grade, but we felt that she was.) So we told her, "You're in charge of keeping up with your own homework now. And we want you to begin learning to manage your own assignments and knowing when you need to start studying for tests. We will totally be your assistants in this process, but this is your ball game now. So ask for all the help you need, but you're the quarterback—just like Hingle McKreengleberry, San Diego State University!"

As might be expected, her grades dropped for a little while as she worked to get her feet under her. Around the same time, we had a meeting with her teacher. The teacher expressed some concern about the drop in Callie's grades. We explained to her what we had done. "We put her in charge of her grades. So it's okay if she struggles a little bit at first." The teacher looked at us like we were crazy. However, six years later, Callie was diagnosed with juvenile diabetes. Suddenly she was in charge of keeping up with what she ate and managing her own blood sugar. We were glad that we had begun early teaching her strength, independence, and managing her own life.

Speaking of teachers ...

Bonney went through a phase in high school in which she constantly complained to anyone who would listen about how much she hated school and how impossibly difficult it was to her. "I can't do it!" she would groan.

Gratefully, she had a wonderful teacher in eleventh grade who loved her dearly and wanted to playfully challenge Bonney's despondency. She made a little sign with a string on it that displayed a Wonder Woman character flying through the air. Underneath it, it said, "I'm Bonney, and I can DO IT!" Whenever Bonney whined in class about the difficulty of an assignment, the teacher required her to wear the sign around her neck.

Bonney found her power. She's now an OB nurse in Charleston. She saved the life of a mother and child as I was writing this book last night. And in her little girl room at our house, the "I can do it" placard still sits propped up on her bedside table. Talk about celebrating!

One of my clients has a college-age daughter who lives constantly frightened, panicking about every challenge. The mom actually came to see me because of her own depression. It turned out that she was living her entire life as the caretaker of everyone else. The result was, her own soul was dying on the vine. Who was taking care of her? Growth for her has involved withdrawing some of her tentacles of care, requiring the people around her to learn to manage their own lives. Obviously, this has had application to her anxious daughter. We've been working to teach Mom to empower her daughter. Instead of swooping in and rescuing her, we have taught her to use, Roots and Wings, Challenge and Celebrate. "I know you get so scared of these things, Babe, but I also know that you are strong. I know that you can do this. I'll be waiting on the other end of the phone, and I want you to call me when you have succeeded."

Initially, of course, her daughter panicked and begged for rescue, frightened by her mother's "abandonment." But over and over again, this young lady has managed her problems and succeeded. Her mother told me the other day that the daughter had called in tears, but tears of joy this time—joyful at her success. The mom responded, "Look at you! This is who you are! You are strong and powerful and able to handle your life. I bet that feels so good to you." Children of all ages need challenging and celebrating as they learn how to be powerful adults.

Expect Strength

One last form of empowering to consider: I don't want to be too far out for you here but, we can build strength in our kids by *expecting something from them*. I know this goes against our current culture in which childhood is supposed to be a Club Med Resort, but I believe we also teach kids strength by requiring some significant participation from them in the upkeep of the home. I don't even want to call this "chores," any more than when dad keeps the kids, you would call that "babysitting." Helping out around the house isn't "chores," it's part of being a family—it's part of living.

I was thinking about this the other day as I walked back into the house after cleaning the gutters. I was elbow-deep in slimy grime and exhausted. I reflected on how, if my parents had told me that I was going to have to spend two hours on a

Saturday morning cleaning the gutters instead of doing what I wanted—and, by the way, you aren't even going to get paid anything for doing it—I would scream in protest at the unfair slavery into which I had been sold.

Nowadays, that kind of thing is just *life* for me—it's what needs to be done. I think we should engage our children in such duties. Find appropriate jobs for your children and require their participation—with consequences if they don't. Pay them a salary if you want, but begin early expecting your children to engage in the upkeep of your home. Setting the table. Feeding the dog. Keeping their room clean. Helping with yard work.

I realize I'm inviting you to swim against the raging current of our culture here, but go ahead, live on the edge! Make them part of the home workforce and show them you are working with them. By the way, this kind of thing also falls under the category of "parent self-care." We shouldn't be folding laundry all afternoon while our kids play. They are strong enough to help. And we are stressed enough to need it.

I read something the other day that was talking about the "culture of low expectations" that now surrounds teenagers. It sets them up to flounder in the real world that awaits. A lot of our goal as parents is to prepare our kids to be strong enough to do adult life. Yet, I see so many kids who were so waited on as children that they have no category for being responsible for their lives when they grow up. Challenge, celebrate and teach your kids strength.

This is still scary

Now, I'm figuring after this much talk about challenging, empowering, and not rescuing your kids, some of you are thinking, "Yeah, this all sounds great. But you are asking me to essentially let my child risk and fail and possibly suffer? Forgive me for not putting out the bunting, Cox, but that sounds terrible!"

Touche' You are correct. Everything I'm telling you to do to prepare your kids for the world, does require you to step back sometimes and expose them to failure, hurt and even danger. It requires you to watch them struggle with problems on their own—even watch them fail. I'm asking a lot of you here. Nevertheless, managing our own anxiety and sorrow as our kids learn strength is one of the greatest gifts we'll ever give them—and one of the most painful.

But it is true love.

I worked with some parents years ago whose child was frightened and bullied and fearful of everything. It quickly became apparent to me that this mother's own fear of seeing him suffer in any way had kept him shielded, like an eight-year-old baby bird—now pummeled by life and school and peers. As I pushed her to back off and let him learn to be strong (and let his dad's voice speak more into his life), she resisted and eventually stopped therapy. I've sometimes wondered how that now-teenaged "baby bird" is doing —and wished his mother had loved him more than she loved her own anxiety.

All of us can fall into this trap. I remember Callie's first tricycle. We lived in a little apartment at the time, and there was no real space for her to learn to ride, so I took her to a church parking lot. I pulled the trike out of the truck and placed her on it. She immediately peddled into a pothole, tumbling on the ground in tears. I picked her up, dusted her off, and said, "You're doing great, honey. Let's try again."

She got back on the trike, and as I watched, she immediately began peddling toward the *same pothole*. I rushed to her side, bent over her, arms at the ready, prepared to snatch her off the trike in case she wrecked again. Suddenly I caught myself. I was literally "hovering" over her. Literally! I thought, "Is this a position I want to maintain as I walk through life with my daughter—literally hovering over her to protect her from the 'potholes' of life?" I forced myself to withdraw. It hurt. I cringed. And she rode into the pothole again.

But she didn't the third time.

Learn to become aware of how much your own fear and need might be governing your protection of your children. As I said, nothing hurts worse than seeing our children hurt. But a wise, loving parent shepherds their child through the "smallish" hurts of childhood, knowing that they are the "practice field" for the big game to come. Few gifts are greater than having a parent who is brave enough to walk through difficulty with their child, so that that child can dominate life later on.

Yet more blindspots

Now, some of you are thinking, "My child needs no training in empowerment, Doc, thank you very much! He's the head of the local fifth grade Yakuza Clan, and is upstairs as we speak, terrorizing his siblings." Indeed, some kids are naturals at this Identity/Strength bit. They *are* Kim Jung Un. They don't need more power for goodness sake!

I was working once with the parents of a teenage girl who was terrorizing her home and her parents. ("Oh my gosh! You guys are *soooo* retarded!") I was teaching them how to push back on her and set limits, informing her that it would significantly cost her to continue to treat them like this. In response, they looked at me with fear in their eyes. "Oh my! We could never say that to her!" they replied. "She would never speak to us again!" (Like, that's a bad thing?)

The mom continued, "We just want to be sure she knows that we love her." I thought to myself, "I want to be sure she knows where 'juvie' is!" But I kept my mouth shut.

This child did not need any more empowerment. She needed someone to take away her glittery pink cell phone until she stopped rolling her eyes in five languages. Refer back to Chapter Three as necessary.

Conclusion

Children get their view of themselves and their world from the eyes of their parents. I have the privilege of having an acquaintance with the Pulitzer Prize winning author, Rick Bragg. One day he told me a story which illustrates this principle. As a child, he remembered riding in the backseat of the family car as his father barreled down the road, "driving that car like he was mad at it." His mother, sitting in the passenger seat turned to his father and exclaimed, "Jimmy! You're going to kill us all!" "Which," Rick said, "scared me to death—given that I had never known my mother to lie!" Kids get their view of themselves and the world from the eyes of their parents.

Just like children sometimes need us to engage, welcome, and embrace their *vulnerabilities and needs*—sometimes they need us to focus and attend to their *strength*. "Empowering kids" sounds like the worst kind of psychobabble, but actually it just means what it says—participating in the process of helping our kids learn to be powerful. "Resiliency" is a big, new word nowadays in parenting, and I'm glad it is. Building confidence and power into our kids is as important a gift as filling their tummies with love. In other words, there's more to parenting than, to paraphrase Wes Mantooth from *Anchorman*, "rubbing Vaseline on their hiney and telling them it's special and different from everyone else's." We also want to challenge our kids to be powerful agents in their own lives. (He said hiney!)

I like mastery and adventure. A friend of mine reminded me the other day of one of my personal mottos: "Every man needs to have a sport he could die doing!" Now, please do not apply this principle to your children, but I want you to get the point. I want to teach my children to be smart and strong and savvy. I want them to learn that you need to downshift a sports car into second gear as you swing into a turn so you can accelerate out of it. I want them to learn that failure is the prize possession of a risk taker—she holds it close to her breast and does not share it with the coward. I want them to learn that if they find a world that they love, be it dancing or nursing or cooking or psychology, they can pour their hearts into it and master it. I want them to boldly go where no man has gone before. And I say to you, parents, hold this book in your hands and know that you are good enough, and that you can give a strength and power to your children that will never leave their souls.

Q&A Time

Hey Doc—What about a child who is getting picked on by other kids? How do we help them be strong enough to deal with bullies?

Great question! And a great time to ask it, since our topic is empowering kids. Dealing with bullies is a nuanced and complex issue, but let me give you some principles that maybe you can apply in your situation.

Number One Bully Secret of the Universe: *The only way to lose with a bully is not to fight.* If you fight with a bully and *win*—you win. If you fight with a bully and *lose*—you win. Bullies are looking for people who do not fight.

The bully/victim dynamic is an interesting one. The bully's goal is to unload all of their own feelings of smallness, fear, and shame onto another person. If he can frighten and humiliate you, he feels better. And through some mystical psychological magic, they can smell exactly the type of person who will be Velcro for those kinds of feelings. That person is called a "victim," and typically they have a personality style that is overly vulnerable and "underly" aggressive. Bullies smell that like a shark smells blood. A bully is overly aggressive. A victim is underly aggressive. It takes both dynamics to create this dance. Two to Tango, so to speak. So we need to address both parties. People who just try to *contain* the bully miss the fact that the victim needs to be likewise *empowered*.

So, firstly—a bully needs to be responded to with powerful limit setting aggression. In the days of Opie and *Mayberry*, this was simple. A firm knuckle sandwich planted in the nose of the bully would typically make him move on to a victim who wouldn't fight back.

In our culture, however, dealing with bullies takes a village. I want parents powerfully engaging with their victim child, assuring them that, "We are going to conquer this together!" I want the child feeling that advocacy. It feels safe to them, but it also models the very aggression that child needs to learn. "We don't play this game!"

I also want parents engaging the school. I want the school engaging the bully. I want parents and school engaging the bully's parents. And I even want you all thinking together about how the victim herself can push back on the bully personally. We're gonna get medieval on this kid.

When I was bullied once as a child, I mustered a gang of the bully's other victims together. We then initiated a confrontation against the bully on *our terms*—he turned a corner and there we all were, fists clenched and waiting for him. Faced with the mass power of his collected victims, he ran home crying. That day changed my life. Get creative, be strong, but mostly work together. Bullies are cowards. It is essential that we not be.

(Tune in for more Q&A in the Bonus Round Appendix)

---

[1] *Joshua 24:15, King James Version.*

You plunge your hand in and draw it back scorched. Beneath, it's shining like gold but better.

— Bruce Cockburn

Chapter Five

How do I help my kids deal with pain in life?

It was like one of our kids was cursed. When all of her friends got the best teacher and the best class, invariably she would get the oddball teacher—in a class by herself (not in a good way). When we finally let our kids have smart phones, it was Christmas morning and three little brown boxes lay wrapped under the tree. Her iPhone did not work—and as the other two pranced around loading apps, she just cried. When she tried out for cheerleader, you guessed it—all of her friends made it and she did not. When she finally did get cheerleader, she fell on her head and got a concussion.

Do I need to keep going? I don't mean to be Johnny Raincloud or anything, but our children's lives are going to hurt.

One of the places I see parents experience the deepest burden is in the haunting fear that they will not successfully protect their children from pain. They live constantly on guard to shield their child from any loss or suffering. Fear is their parenting guide, fear of their child hurting. Their motto: "A good parent wouldn't let their child hurt like that." What a burdensome way to live!

In this chapter, I want to help you understand how to deal with your children's pain. I want to help you learn how to walk with them in their suffering, and how you can help them heal. And last but not least, I want to cut you loose from the guilt that says, "If only I were a better parent, my children's lives would be lollipops and Now & Laters."

We just spent a chapter talking about helping our children learn to be strong in the face of life's challenges. But how do we help them, heal them, comfort them, when life *hurts*? How do we teach them to deal with pain? Just like love, submission and strength, *suffering well* is a skill our kids need to be *taught*.

Life is going to hurt

Whenever my in-laws were visiting, my father-in-law would greet me with the same question as I walked in the door from work. "How was the rat race today? Did the rats win?" Sometimes, no matter how strong we are, the rats win. Life stinks! And it will hurt our children. Parents disagree about a hundred different things in the parenting world—Should you spank? Should you breast-feed? Should you give them an allowance or make them earn their own money? But one thing that unifies all of us parents is that nothing hurts us worse than seeing our children suffer.

One of our children had to have significant surgery as a four-month-old infant. At one point, in order to diagnose her illness, she had to have an infant spinal tap. The medical staff would not even let us be in the room with her during the procedure. We handed that tiny baby over to a nurse who disappeared behind a door. We stood in the hall together crying as we heard our baby screaming. It hurts me to even write this.

Our children are going to suffer. How in the world are we supposed to respond to that?

We discovered Callie's diabetes because, at age thirteen, she almost lapsed into a coma. We took her to the emergency room and called her pediatrician. This woman had been one of the greatest things that had ever happened to our family. She was smart, kind, and tough as a pine knot. But when I looked into her eyes in that emergency room, I saw fear—and my legs almost collapsed under me.

Dr. Ray stabilized Callie and, in effect, saved her life. Later, as we were learning about insulin shots, the nurse looked at us and said, "Would one of you like to give her first shot?" Being the father of this group, I stepped forward, hoping to plant a flag of courage—to lead the way in this new lifestyle we were facing. Only problem was, needles, blood, and medical stuff have always made me weak in the knees. (That's one of the reasons I'm not a "real" doctor.) So as I injected Callie with the insulin, I became overcome with the heebie-jeebies and literally *let go* of the syringe! (So much for being her Captain America.) Callie looked down at her arm in horror as the little syringe sort of bounced up and down, sticking out of the skin. She reached down, pulled it out, and said to the nurse, "Can I just learn to do this myself?"

I could go on, and I know that you could too. Be it anything from having a special needs child to simply comforting that kid who didn't make the team, one of the biggest parts of being a parent is knowing how to suffer with our children. And notice I said suffer *with*. I considered naming this chapter: "How do I *protect* my children from suffering," but then it would be a very short chapter—two words in fact: *You Can't.*

So in the face of a world that is full of pain, and our precious children who are going to live in that world, let's ask instead how can we best care for them *in* the pain? Psychologist Henry Cloud once said something like this: *The goal is not to protect our children from suffering. The goal is to teach them to suffer well, in the context of love.* Like everything else, we must teach our kids the ability to deal with the pain in life.

We have to *learn* to deal with pain

Now the ultimate culprit here is the Universe. It's *way* messed up. It is not how it should be, and it's not the way that God wanted it to be. People talk in movie theaters —death, taxes, robo-calls. Life Stinks! And *we* do too! How much do you enjoy failing or hurting people? We are as messed up as the universe we live in!

Now, in case you haven't noticed, no one prepared your children for this development. They start to encounter the pain and deprivation in the world (not to mention their own failures), and they start hollerin'!—"I don't like this Sam I Am! I think I got off the wrong planet. This place stinks. There's no dessert before supper, I have too much homework, and Mom won't buy me a Kylo Ren light saber! Lemme outa here!"

Our kids aren't alone in this. All humans have trouble with the fallen world.

We weren't created with the ability to deal with pain! If you think about it, we were designed to live in a Garden where there was no suffering at all. So we are fish out of water here. In fact, of all the things we are talking about in this book, this is the only one that we were not designed to have to learn. We are created to learn about love and wisdom and strength and submission. But we weren't meant to have to make sense of pain and shame. That's why everyone struggles with it. No one does this well.

In fact, the basic position that most people assume when they encounter pain in life is some kind of position of *protest*—trying to stop the suffering in some way.

Sometimes we do this by *attacking others*. We say things like, "This is inexcusable!" "What were you thinking?" This is the guy going off at the desk clerk for losing his hotel reservation. This is also what your kids are doing when they throw a tantrum. They are protesting how painful all this disappointment and suffering is. We can also attack others passively, by inflicting the dreaded silent treatment, sulking like Achilles in his tent, hoping the offending party will feel amply punished.

We can also deal with pain by *attacking ourselves*, living filled with shame and perfectionism. "If only I was better/prettier/smarter/not such a screwup—then perhaps the world would not hurt so bad." Maybe you have that child who lives discouraged and self-critical. They are attacking *themselves* to try to make sense of their losses. We will talk about how to help them momentarily.

A third way we can deal with pain is by trying to *escape it*. We feel pain, so we pop smoke and emotionally disconnect. One of the reasons that people run to sex, drugs, and rock and roll is to anesthetize pain, right? This one is popular with teenagers. Teenagers tend to go one of two directions with their pain. They "Act Out" or they "Act In." With Acting *In*, they push their pain inside, creating anxiety or depression. *Acting out*, of course, involves their *doing* kooky behaviors to escape their hurt. So many of the whacky things that we all do in life are actually ways we are trying to cope with things hurting! So we take pain, do kooky stuff to escape it, and thereby create more pain. Humans are brilliant!

A more brutal kind of escape can also come in the form of depression—when people feel ultimately crushed under the weight of their pain. One of the ways depression works is that our pain becomes so intense or chronic that something in our hearts throws a breaker switch. We disconnect. Now we are no longer feeling the pain—but we are also no longer feeling *anything else*. Presto—depression.

Given the rainbow of destructive ways that we often deal with pain, I'm thinking it won't come as a surprise to you to hear that we (and our children) actually have to be *taught* the ability to metabolize the yuck and pain in life. Someone needs to come along side of us and help us find peace in our pain as opposed to protest. How do we help our kids with this?

Let's look at two different sides of pain, and talk about how we can help our kids.

- There is **Pain in the World**—Suffering, loss, sorrow.
- There is the **Pain of being Us**—The shame and loss we feel about our own failures.

We're going to have to teach our kids with both of these Let's think about how.

Pain in the world

As parents, we are given the opportunity to stand at our children's sides as they begin to encounter how painful life can be. What a gift! They get to go through the suffering of life for the first time—*with us!* The way we respond to this opportunity is crucial. If our children's pain is dealt with well, it can be a wonderful opportunity for *connection*. What binds people together more than walking through difficulty together? Like a band of brothers.

Walking with our kids through pain can also be the matrix to create *strength* in their hearts—the strength to live powerfully in the sorrows of life rather than feeling like a victim.

Finally, engaging our children in the midst of their hurts actually helps those hurts *heal*. Loving connection helps our sorrows soften and melt. Let's look at some ingredients in this recipe for helping our children walk through pain in the world.

Resist Rescue

Step one in helping our children face pain is that we need to *be very careful about rescuing our kids from the manageable pains in life.* (This ought to be a walk in the park for you after having read Chapter Four.)

I don't want to go too fast for ya, but our children will never learn to deal with pain—if they *never - experience - pain!* Of course, you have my complete permission to rescue them from the real disasters of life. If they fall in the river, don't wait for Lassie, jump in and save them! That's not what I'm talking about. What I mean is, just like we build those calluses of *strength* in our kids by allowing them to struggle, we help them learn to manage disappointment, loss, and failure by not swooping in there to make it all better when they experience pain.

When they don't get that part in the school play, don't run out to get them a surprise gift. When they are sad about leaving the playground, don't rush to promising them Popsicles when they get home. When they are crying and overwhelmed with the process of moving out of the dorm, don't swoop in there like "Super Dad" with a moving van and flowers. When their sister seems to have all the friends and they don't—be very careful about rescuing them.

This is where we begin. These inevitable and ubiquitous losses of childhood are *vaccinations*—little doses of the toxins of life. How we help our children manage these losses will be the foundation for how they learn to deal with suffering as they grow up.

Now, I realize that this is one-hundred-percent counter-intuitive for us parents, and maybe one of the most difficult things I will ask you to do. But I promise you, this will not *harm* your children.

Here is a Secret of the Multiverse I want you to get tatted on your arm—*Pain itself does not harm children. Unresolved pain harms children.* Tears, sorrow, and loss, in themselves will not harm our kids. (Pain that is brought into relationship and love actually makes us stronger. Read Romans 5:3, 4.) In fact, I rarely see people become noble, wise, loving individuals without living though significant pain.

So as we begin thinking about how to help our kids survive the pains of life, remember to be careful about our reflex to protect them from all disappointment and loss. Let's not be rescue rangers.

But if they suffer alone, it *will* harm them. Which leads us to step number two.

Be *with*

Pop quiz, Cadets—If "Unresolved Pain" harms our children, then what is Unresolved Pain? Well, here's your answer: Unresolved pain is pain that no one *joins* me in. Pain that no one *helps* me with. I am alone. Pain Mathematics 101: *Pain with someone else is halved. Pain alone is doubled.*

For some reason that I don't understand, if I'm hurting and I bring that pain into relationship with you—and you don't try to fix it, or look on the bright side, or give me cheerful Bible verses; instead, if you just are *with* me and *love* me—something about that connection will somehow make my pain metabolize, soften, and heal. I'm not even sure why, but *pain heals in relationship.* So, step two in walking with our kids through pain is that we have to walk it *with* them—so they are not alone in it.

Let's put some legs on this principle. Here's a model that I like to use when trying to explain the best way to respond to our loved ones' pain. (And this can apply to your friends, your spouse—anyone—but it's a great model to use with kids.)

Three ways we can respond to pain

There are three places we can be when we encounter the pain of others. We are going to call them **Blow off, Fix it, and Being With.**

Blow off

One thing we can do when our kids encounter pain and difficulty is to *blow it off.* This is where we minimize their feelings—not engage them. *Blow Off* is where we say things like, "Aw come on, you can't cry about everything!" or, "In ten years you won't even remember that game." One of my clients told me he brought a painful story to his dad recently. His dad's response? "It's in the past; forget about it."

So, *Blow Off* is your basic "Starving kids in Africa" approach to pain.

Now, not only is this a really jerky way to treat anybody, *Blow Off* implicitly denies to our kids that there is real pain in life. We're acting like their pain is *not painful!* And not only is that mean, it's psycho! Besides, our kids are going to face pain at some point in their lives, right? And when they do, it's gonna feel bad to them. Wouldn't it be great if the first time through, they got to go through it with us? So, number one, don't deny their struggle and don't push them away— don't *Blow it Off.* "Aloneness" makes pain worse, remember! Let's get in there with them.

Fix it

Let's look at the other extreme. Sometimes we don't blow off our kid's emotions; we do the opposite. We try to Fix their problems. Fix is where we swoop in there like that Superhero Mom and Dad and "Make it all better, baby!" *Nobody is going to hurt my little Angel!"* In other words, we act to "Fix" any problem they have.

They are in pain, so we *do* something to get them out of it. We solve all of their homework problems. We run off to Walmart at 9:30 p.m. to buy Styrofoam planets and poster board for that "forgot about it" science project. Or all their friends are spending the night out and your kid doesn't get invited. So we say, "Well, we're just going to pack up and take you to Atlanta for the weekend! We'll show those goobers what fun looks like. We're going to go to the Aquarium and a Falcons game and the Coke museum. We'll show them!" (Please tell me you did this kind of nonsense, too.)

This is where we find the parents who, when their child doesn't make the team, they're calling the coach—or donating a million dollars to buy a new gymnasium—(now their child *has* to be on the team)! This parent lives "head on a swivel" looking for anything that might hurt their child. Heaven forbid!

I was amused to hear that a couple years ago the Pez Candy Co. had to cancel its annual Easter egg hunt because parents were literally pushing down *other children* so that their children could gather the eggs. We parents can be as crazy as road lizards! This is where the "every kid gets a trophy" nonsense started. Nobody wants a child to feel sad. This is a grave injustice to them.

Here's a little rule of thumb to help us temper our reactions to our kids' pain: *We, their parents, cannot be any more than X-1 as upset about a problem as our children are.* (X being the integer that defines how upset *our child* is.) If they are forty-four percent upset, we cannot be any more than forty-three percent freaked out ourselves. (This is hard to do. It's one of the reasons I got my own therapist!)

So they don't make cheerleader. Typically, it's the *parents* who are freaking out! The child is upset and will probably cry on her bed all evening. But mom is going OFF! She's calling the cheerleader sponsor and rallying the other moms. They are going to change this policy—blow up Facebook! So now the child has *two problems:* they didn't make cheerleader, *and* they have mom who is losing her marbles. (This is often why children don't tell their parents about their struggles. They've already got their hands full managing the cheerleader issue. The last thing they need is to have to manage Mom too!)

So *Fix* doesn't blow them off, rather *Fix* prevents them from ever having to engage the yuck in life. Someone has always swooped in and made it all better. (And maybe created *more* yuck by our overreaction!) Either way, when they hit real life, they don't have those calluses for handling pain. So fixing a child's problems might give temporary relief to both of you, but ultimately it will handicap them regarding reality.

Be with

I'm about to introduce you to one of the most powerful prepositions in the English language—the word "With." *With* means that you are not alone. *With* means that someone is at your side. It means that someone hears your pain and cares. *With* does not fix. *With* does not blow off. *With* connects and loves in the *midst of pain.*

"With" is God's favorite preposition. Look it up. He says, "Yea, though I walk through the valley of the shadow of death, I will fear no evil for thou (*art going to make it all better?)"* No! "... for thou art with me."[1] Immanuel means God *with* us. Jesus says, "... and lo I am *with* you always, even to the end of the age."[2] He loves *With*!

My brother died suddenly as a young man at the age of

twenty-seven, more than thirty years ago. Our family was shattered. But one of my most comforting memories was a time after his funeral when everyone came back to my parent's house. Four or five of my oldest and closest friends were there, and somehow, we all ended up back in my old little boy room. We didn't even say very much. Someone might offer a story about Mark here or there—but mostly they were just *with* me. (Want to know why you don't know what to say at a funeral? Because there's *nothing to say* at a funeral! Just be *with*.)

A few years later, one of those friends called me and told me that his mother had been admitted to the hospital. I rushed up to be with him. As the evening rolled on, we ended up sitting in the dark hall of the hospital until late at night. As we sat there, he said, "Remember when you talked about how meaningful it was to you that we all just sat with you after Mark's death? I didn't really understand that. I mean, we didn't do anything but *sit there*. But I understand it now. Thank you for being with me."

For some mysterious reason, if we bring our pain into a relationship with someone who cares, somehow that pain softens and metabolizes. (It's one of the reasons therapy works.) God made us in such a way that, "It is not good for the man to be alone."[3] We need someone with us.

We parents would do anything to protect our children from pain. I can't help you there. But what if I could give you access to something that could actually *heal* your children's pain? Worth the price of admission, eh? Well, here ya go.

If you sit *with* your child and hear their story—and do not minimize it or try to fix it; If you hold them close and say, "You are hurting, and I care. I cannot make it go away, but I love you and we will walk through this together"—*You will heal your child's pain.* They will feel loved and understood and not alone, even in the midst of this painful world.

At one point during Callie's hospitalization for diabetes, the initial ordeal was over, and Callie, Norma, and I found ourselves alone in her hospital room. All of us were scared and hurting. But I remember Norma and me sitting on Callie's bed and saying to her, "We don't know what all this means yet, but we do know this: You will never walk through this alone. We will live it with you and walk it with you—the three of us. We love you and you will never be by yourself."

We could not fix that problem. But we all needed to be "with" each other. And she needed us with her. We still walk it with her to this day. Unfortunately, life will give you opportunities like this. Walk that kind of sadness *with* your children.

What does "With" sound like?

Let's put some legs on what it sounds like to be *with*. With Littles, we can do something as simple as put words on their little feelings. You know when they've reached that breaking point where they needed a nap (like two hours ago), and they are just fragmenting. We manage our anger and frustration and say, "I know, I know baby, you are so tired. I know! It's been a long day." Just that empathy and "withness" is someone engaging them in their pain. When you do this basic thing, you aren't just hushing them up; you are literally helping metabolize how much life is hurting for them. You are creating that soft landing spot in their hearts that they will take with them through life.

And you will see them internalize this—have it inside. I used to love to hear our girls talk to their doll babies. They would hold them close and say, "It's all right, baby. I love you. You don't need to cry. It's gonna be all right." I had to fight tears every time! Think about it! Where were those words coming from? They were the very words that they had heard us speak to *them*, now flowing back out of their hearts. Now we're haulin' the mail!

With older kids we put that reflex to "fix" their struggles or "blow them off" in a tight little box and we be *with*. We say, "Oh, Sweetheart! Every kid got a hit but you!" or, "Your new best friend has a new best friend, and they're being mean to you! Oh, dear one, I remember that feeling. There is nothing worse. We love you so much and are so with you. Hang out with us tonight. Let's watch a movie together or something." And suddenly they are not alone, and we are teaching them that pain can soften if it is met with love.

Remember how we talked about how our children's *sinfulness or hurtfulness* is healed in the context of love and limits? Well, *shame, loss, suffering,* and *pain* are also healed by our loving presence with our children.

Remember the "Three Hs" from Chapter Two?—*Hearing Heals Hurt!* Well, here's another way of saying it: *Pain Hurts. Pain Alone Harms. Pain Together Heals.*

The gift of sadness

One of the things that will happen if we don't run away from pain is that our children (and us) will feel *sad*. Sadness is a very interesting and misunderstood emotion. Everybody wants to avoid it, but it's not just some painful feeling to run away from. Sadness is actually quite powerful, almost magical in fact.

Sadness is unique in that it is what I call a "progressive emotion." You can be angry forever. You can be anxious forever. You can be depressed forever. But if you feel genuine sadness about your losses (especially "with" another person), you will *move*. You will *progress*. Your pain will *transform*. Feeling sad changes and heals us. I don't even know how it works; it just does.

I was just talking to you about my brother. Thirty years ago, I would not have been able to do that without sobbing. But now, the sadness and grief that I worked through has transformed that horrifying pain into something that feels sweeter, warmly heartbreaking, even loving. Why did that transformation take place? Do I love him less? Do I miss him less? No—that sharp pain has been softened by grief and sadness.

This is why the Bible talks so much about "mourning." It is one of God's most powerful tools to heal us. Don't be afraid of your children feeling sad. In fact, I want to teach them *how to be sad*. Remember, the goal is not to protect them from suffering. It is to help them learn to suffer well. Sadness in the context of love is suffering well. In fact, the best of us was called "a man of sorrows ... acquainted with grief."[4] As we engage the sadness of life, eyes wide open with our children, we are creating an atmosphere where the sad can be sad, and the wounded can heal.

Be cool

Look, gang, I'm just going to go ahead and apologize for this next step right from the start. I already know that I was a colossal failure at this one, so I'm assuming you will be too. But let's just count to three and rip off the Band-Aid.

Ready?

*The most powerful way in which we teach our children about how to deal with the painful world is by letting them see and experience how **we** deal with pain, disappointment, and loss.*

In other words, can we *keep our poise*, manage our own frustration and anger? Can we be cool—like two little Fonzies? Can we stay loving in the face of their losses and ours, or do we act like Mommie Dearest? (See, this is why I went ahead and apologized.)

Remember those Core Questions that we talked about? Kids spend their lives implicitly asking us questions about how the world and relationships work. And, unfortunately, they are getting answers all the time from us, mostly from how we *relate* to them. Well, one of their Core Questions is, "How big a deal it is if things are screwed up. If I screw up. If the world is a mess. Can you gimme a vibe for that?"

So if we are the uptight, white-glove type, carrying on all the time about how their teacher isn't good again this year, or the guy next door won't shut his dog up, or how they aren't going to grandma's house with a dirty face, or we're freaking out and defensive if anyone points out our own flaws—then that is sending a pretty loud message to our kids about whether pain and loss are manageable or not. Unfortunately, *this* is where they learn that *gut sense* of how big a deal it is that things are fallen. "Wow, Dad is acting like a complete maniac. I guess Mom's mistake really *was* a big deal!" So, unfortunately they need to see us face disappointment, loss, embarrassment, and our kindness and poise stay intact. I told you it was bad news.

I have a client who has struggled with significant anxiety in his life. He is afraid of taking risks and facing failure. Some of his loudest memories are of his father's intense protests when things did not go the way he wanted. He has memories of watching his father chew out the Delta Airlines gate agent. He remembers he and his siblings slinking down in their chairs with embarrassment as their father marched back to the kitchen when a restaurant was not bringing the food quickly enough. I asked him if his father ever treated *him* this way. Not really. But as a boy, he was constantly watching his father "teach him" that when things were screwed up it was intolerable—unacceptable.

Here's another example—about me. Perhaps you can learn from my skillful and kind heart. One year, the girls got infatuated with their little plastic buckets, shovels, and sand toys after a trip to the beach. Problem was, they loved playing with them in the garage, exactly where I parked my car. Not having had the benefit of an enchanting parenting book such as this one to guide me, I fumed, scolded, complained, and badgered them to stop leaving their little plastic toys where I parked my car. One day, after an especially unpleasant day at work, I turned the corner to pull into the garage. Again, my spot was littered with little plastic toys. I flew into a rage! I put the car in park, got out, and started kicking and throwing the toys across the garage—punctuating my display with salty language. Finally, I stood there, surveying my destruction, huffing and puffing with satisfaction. Surely now, my wise justice had been accomplished. However, as I looked up at the back-door window, there silently stood Norma and the girls watching me. The girls had concerned looks on their faces, almost as if they were thinking, "Who's that crazy man, Mommy?" They still tease me about it to this day.

"I'm John, and I was a moronic parent."

"Hi, John."

Point being, *our children are watching, learning, and asking— "Is pain something I can handle, or is it something that handles me?"*

One of my friends who has a four-year-old did a better job at this. You know how with little ones everything is a catastrophe, devastating? They're not just thirsty. They don't just ask for something to drink. All of a sudden they fall apart in a heap, potentially on the verge of dying from dehydration, begging for a drink like they need the antidote to a quick-acting poison.

This mom worked out a great response to these sorts of

histrionics. She calls it "No Biggie—No Prob!" When her little one discovers that his brother has eaten the last cookie and starts his meltdown, her response is "No Biggie, No Prob!—We can handle this!" She is literally teaching him that pain and difficulty are things we can manage together. Now he walks around the house chirping "No Biggie—No Prob." He is taking that freedom inside of his heart.

Here's a Jedi at work: When I was about twelve-years-old, my mother's mother died. My mother was only about forty-two the time, and I watched her grieve. It was a shocking, devastating loss. Sometime not long after that, on a rainy day with nothing to do, I occupied myself by throwing a rubber ball against the wall of the kitchen. (Visions of Steve McQueen in the *Great Escape* danced in my head)

Hanging on that kitchen wall, however, was a classic old Southern Rose Medallion plate. It had belonged to my mother's grandmother and was a treasure to her. Not surprisingly, my mother told me to quit throwing the ball against the wall. But like any self-respecting child, I waited until she was out of sight and continued throwing. About five minutes later, I watched my ball crash directly into the plate, dislodging it from the wall and crashing it to the floor—shattering it into pieces. I could hear my mother approaching and I braced for impact. I saw her enter the room, survey the scene—and I watched as her eyes fell when she saw the broken keepsake. I knew that my end was near. "Those who are about to die salute you." But suddenly, to my amazement, I saw her eyes soften and even fill with tears. She looked at me and said, "It's okay, John. It's just a thing."

Even at twelve-years-old, I realized that my mother was deeply feeling the loss of something she loved, but a deeper feeling that the *people* she loved were more important and more irreplaceable to her than a plate.

What was she teaching me about how to engage sorrow and loss? She taught me *experientially* that love is bigger than the bad! That we don't have to run to protests, anesthesia, and anger to face life and loss. Love is where we run. That's God's answer, and it's ours too.

Good enough freedom

Now, again, if you're like me, this story makes you depressed. I mean, who can actually live that way? (My mom confesses that she rarely did either.)

So the good news! Let's get free! Let's remember our good enough theme song. *The only thing better than a perfect parent is a humble parent!* So when we mess up, overreact, shame, and scold, what do we do? We swing back in! "Man, I made way too big of a deal about that! I acted like that was the end of the world and took it out on you. That was a really jerky thing to do. And I hurt you by doing it. That's just really not okay. "

In other words, here is the *best* Secret of the Universe of all: *We can teach grace and love by **needing** grace and love!* Grace (the love that says it's safe to fail) gets wrapped into our home when we *give forgiveness* to our kids, *but also* when we *need forgiveness from them!* In other words, I'm not telling you that you *have* to handle all of the pain of life with poise and grace. I'm *announcing to you that you **can***!

I want my kids learning about failure and pain by watching an expert at work—*me*! I want them learning through *my model* that it is safe to fail. I want them to see me and learn that if they take risks, engage other people and pour themselves into real life, they will often stumble and fall flat on their faces. And that will come as no surprise to them, because they have watched their parents do it all their lives.

If we do not rescue them, and if we are "with" them, we are teaching them that even though life hurts, love does not stop. Life hurts but love stays. Somehow, love survived the Fall. And if love stays, then even in the midst of pain our kids have something that doesn't go away. They have their parents and their God who love them—even if they are struggling in school, or are left out of that group, or suffer a painful physical injury. They live in a home where love (and those who love them) are bigger than the bad. This is how we all learn to deal with the pain in life.

Pain about being me

Unfortunately, pain and sorrow do not just assault us from outside of ourselves—the painful world. We also have to make sense of pain and shame *inside*—the ways in which *we* fall sort of what we want. Disappointment and loss are not just *outside*, they are *inside* as well.

You know that feeling when you wake up the morning after a party and you think, "Oh my gosh, I can't believe I said that! (or *danced* like that!)"? How about that face-hot feeling you get when you find out people have been talking about you? Or that awful feeling when you've done something truly wrong? That feeling is called s*hame*, and it is one of the most common poisons that I deal with in my office.

Shame is a technical term. It isn't the same as guilt. Guilt says, I *did* something bad. Shame says I *am* something bad. Shame is not the same as repentant sorrow. It doesn't think, "I'm *sad and convicted* because of my wrongdoing." Shame says, "I am *despicable* because of my wrongdoing. No one else is as bad as me."

Should we feel *bad* about our wrongdoing? Absolutely. But that bad feeling should be g*odly conviction*, "the sorrow that leads unto repentance"[5]—not shame.

Technically speaking, shame is the emotion that humans experience when their brokenness, fallenness, or failure are exposed apart from the context of love—and every one of us experiences it. Including our children.

Remember the old Seinfeld routine? He says he read somewhere that the number one phobia in the world was public speaking. He goes on to say that the second most prevalent fear is death! In other words, he says, "Given any funeral, most people would rather be in the casket than giving the eulogy!" Funny, right? But there's a grain of truth here. Most people are more afraid of shame than *anything*— and public speaking puts us on display where we might look like an idiot. (I already know that I am an idiot, so I rarely experience this anxiety when speaking.)

But shame is our enemy. It is the enemy of relationship, and it is the enemy of growth. It is self-condemnation. It is that feeling that I am an imposter. "If you really knew me, what would you think?" It's that sense that I am *uniquely* bad, defective. "No one else would have done something as bad as I did."

We've just been talking about how to help our kids deal with pain in life—and much of that pain is located out in the sorrow-filled world in which we live. But another kind of pain that assaults us comes from *within*. I see client after client who live their lives held hostage by their terror of being seen as bad. They are unable to take risks, or stand up to jerks, or allow themselves to be intimate in relationships— all because of their fear of the shame that they would feel if their inadequacy was seen.

Our children are no different. It is innate in human beings to compare ourselves to some sense of what we "ought" to be—and then feel shame when we fall short of it. How can we help our children with this enemy?

We all have this problem.
Firstly, I believe that shame is an inborn part of being a human on this planet. Everyone has it, whether they had good enough parents are not. It's part of what it means to be born "Under the Law." We all have a background sense of condemnation and shame.

Of course, Littles have no shame at first. They scamper out of your hands before bath time and run around the house for a little "Nekkid Time"! But once a child develops consciousness, around age five or six, they also begin to develop an awareness of shame. Their face falls when they fail. They hide and feel embarrassed when they are discovered doing something wrong—Shame is innate.

The folks who believe that children are just born as innocent little blank slates, and only learn shame from their external world, don't seem to notice the ubiquity of shame. My wife has always poked fun at me and the field of psychology. "You guys are always looking for these sophisticated diagnoses. The problem is just that everyone is 'insecure.'" And there's a sense in which she's right. Have you ever met anyone who is not burdened at some level with a fear of rejection, insecurity, or shame? In thirty years of doing therapy, I haven't.

Contrary to conventional wisdom, the most advanced psychological theories recognize that children are not born as innocents. They're born with a natural bent toward self-centeredness and its mirror image, shame. Consequently, if we parents are going to help our children with this problem, we need to recognize that shame comes as the "standard equipment" of our child's heart. In other words, we don't just need to be careful about not putting shame *in*—we need to be working to get that shame *out*! Just being careful to not *inflict* shame on our children is not enough.

So sure, avoid phrases like, "I'm surprised at you!" and, "I thought we raised you better than that." But to really help our children with shame, we need to *Un-shame* them. We need to listen for and engage the shame that will naturally bubble out of them, and heal it.

Remember the old joke where the little chick pecks his way out of his shell? He looks up at his mother, and she says, "Now look what you've done!" Let's not be a mother hen. But in addition, let's learn how to spot the shame our kids already have in their hearts and stomp it out with love and strength. Let's look at some ways we can do that.

Un-shaming our kids

We had told one of ours that the consequence of not doing her chores would be a loss of all electronics. After having blown off her chores (again), she was offline. I remember walking past her that afternoon. She was sitting in the kitchen, despondent, dejected. I asked her what was up. She said, "I'm just an idiot! I'm so stupid. I forgot to do my chores again, and now I don't get TV."

I said, "Wow, you're really hammering yourself for this one! It is indeed a hard thing to deal with—how we all do dumb stuff. But, if you want to know my opinion, you were just doing your job."

She looked at me a little confused, "What do you mean? I made y'all mad again."

I replied, "Well, you didn't make us mad, you just lost TV. What I mean is this: I have a job—I go to the office and see clients, right? Well, your job is to be a kid and to *learn*. And the best way that we all learn is by screwing up and making mistakes. It's part of your job. You're a kid. Your job is to learn. You screwed up, so *good job!*

I was wanting to reach in there and "welcome her to the club" of all of us who fail. I wanted to normalize her screw up. I wanted to assault the shame that was condemning her. Like psychologist Phil Sutherland's paradoxical quote early in this book announced —"Anything worth doing is worth doing poorly." *Take that,* shame!

Remember what I used to say to my children—"The only difference between you and me is that I was born twenty something years before you, and God put me in authority over you? Other than that, I'm just a guy who is screwed up and still learning—just like you." We heal our children's shame by joining them, as fellow screwed up people. Shame researcher and author, Brenee Brown, talks about how the two words that heal shame are, "Me too."

Shame only works its harmful magic when we think that our badness is unique—when we feel alone in it. And we conquer shame when we show our kids that they live in a family full of broken people. They are not alone. "Me too." We are *all* only good enough.

So, we love them even in their shame and badness because we are full of badness too. To paraphrase what we said in Chapter Two, We *all* matter more than what we are like. And if God (or us) marked iniquities, then which of us could stand?

Your own failures can help!
Since normalizing failure helps kids fight shame, don't be afraid of your children seeing your goof ups and mistakes.

Nothing bonds humans together like the fact that we are all screwed up. I wanted to set that stage in my family by showing that I was not afraid to be "bad." I remember shuttling my kids to a party once. As we drove, they insisted that I had the location wrong. I kept brushing away their feedback, boasting that I was certain! (This was in the days before cell phones.) As we pulled up to the country club, where I was *sure* the party was to be held, it was a ghost town! Empty. No one in sight. The girls dissolved into peels of jeering playful laughter. "We told you! We told you!" they chanted. I had a delightful time being the brunt of their teasing, dramatically banging the steering wheel and slapping my hand to my forehead. "You guys were so right! Oh my Gosh! I need y'all to come help me pick out my stock portfolio!"

One of the reasons I talk so much about the importance of being a "humble parent" is that living out of our humility can be an incredibly powerful way to show our children how to respond to shame—I thumb my nose at it. In God's universe, I will fight any force that tries to still condemn me, and it will *lose*—guaranteed. Christ took our shame on the cross. It is finished. And it will not be a part of my family. To the degree we live this way, we are creating an atmosphere of grace and freedom from condemnation in our home—and our children will catch that like a cold. And be freed.

Now let's flip that over.

Shame cuts both ways

In our child-centered culture, I encounter more and more parents who live being judged by their *children*. I had a mother tell me the other day that she had picked her child up from a friend's house. Upon getting in the car, her son accusingly said to her, "I was having a great time, and then you showed up and just ruined it!" Foolishly, this mother bit. She started trying to defend herself and justify how it was "time for the party to be over anyway." This is basically saying to her child, "Wow, good point. It is legitimate to demand that your mother 'dance monkey dance ' and be held accountable by you in a shamey way. And here are my justifications for my behavior." Now, I don't know about you, but I don't want to jump on that grenade. Instead, let's take this youngster to school!

I want you to respond, "Wow, Skippy—sounds like you are not only really sad that I picked you up, but you need to *scold* me for it! Well, there's a new sheriff in town, and she don't take kindly to people in our family shaming one another. If you're unhappy, you can talk to me about that, but if you need to keep beating me up about it, I think I see a little time-out in your future."

In other words, we use "Love and Limits" again. "I have room for you to feel bad feelings, however, I'm not willing to let you *do* shame to me (or anyone else) because of those feelings."

The same principle applies to siblings. I remember one year in which Katherine was struggling in school. We were discussing it at the dinner table, and one of her sisters piped up and jeeringly said, "Katherine, I think there's something wrong with your brain!" It is essential that we put the quietus on that kind of talk. Shame is not something that is permitted in our home—from parents or siblings. Boys especially love to trash talk to one another. You are the sheriff. Don't allow shame to be part of your family currency.

Conclusion

As parents, we live as sort of a bridge between our children and the world. We meet their needs, we protect them from harm, and we act as mentors, teaching them the skills necessary to function in life. Well, some toxic enemies lurk in that world—and they are pain and shame—things that God told us would happen if we didn't follow him. Despite the fact that our deepest longing would be to protect our children from yuck, the ultimately loving (and empowering) thing to do is to begin *teaching* them to have the skills and resources to manage that pain, not to escape it.

God has this problem too. He loves us, his children, and he longs to deliver us from the bondage of sin and of death. His solution? To be *with* us in it. His solution to the suffering in our world was to literally join us here. To come down and become one us and to suffer more than any of us, that he might ultimately defeat death and suffering and bring us to himself.

His position with us regarding our pain is beautifully illustrated in Aslan's relationship with Digory in C.S. Lewis's *The Magician's Nephew* in *The Chronicles of Narnia*.

Digory's mother is dying, and Digory pleads with Aslan to save her—to rescue him from his pain. Lewis tells us that as Digory looked up at Aslan, that "great shining tears stood in the Lion's eyes. They were such big, bright tears compared with Digory's own that for a moment he felt as if the Lion must really be sorrier about his Mother than he was himself. 'My son, my son,' said Aslan. 'I know. Grief is great. Only you and I in this land know that yet. Let us be good to one another'."

God will redeem the pain. In the meantime, he is *with* us in it—Sovereign God and yet also Fellow Sufferer. This is our model with our children. Our deepest healing of them is not to frantically try to protect them from all suffering. It is to have great shining tears as we look into their eyes. And be good to one another.

Q&A Time

Hey Doc—We have a child who seems to be chronically burdened with self-condemnation. She gets so down on herself when she doesn't do things perfectly. How can we help her?

That's a very common question. Here are a couple of thoughts. Step one, sit down together as parents and do a little bit of a personal inventory. Do either of you sense any perfectionistic vibe in your parenting. I doubt that's the problem, but we need to check that box. All of us have some perfectionistic parts. I mean, who doesn't want life to go just the way they want? Do a little honest check with one another that none of that is contaminating your parenting. Especially with perfectionistic younger children (five- through eight-year-olds), I want to look for ways that parents can create a safer, more grace-filled, atmosphere.

Secondly, with older children, (eight-year-olds, until), we are going to have to involve them more in the process of conquering their perfectionism. Remember when we talked about building strength and de-parenting, we said that your child will reach an age at which nothing you do to comfort them will allay their anxiety. The same dynamic is taking place here with your child's perfectionism. You've probably noticed that no matter how many times you try to reassure them that it's "really okay, honey. You don't have to be perfect," that nothing seems to help? That's because you cannot solve this problem with nurture alone. You have to solve this problem by coming along side your child and helping her find the strength in herself to fight her self-condemnation.

The first step in helping her find mastery over her perfectionism is to lovingly hold it up and look at it together. "Oh my gosh! It breaks my heart to see how much pressure you put on yourself. It's like no matter what you do, there's a voice inside of you telling you that it's not good enough. She's so mean!" When we do this, we are sort of objectifying her perfectionism, like we did with fear in an earlier chapter. "Look at how much that shame and perfectionism beats you up! Let's fight her!"

Secondly, I want to empower her as the primary warrior

against her perfectionism. "You know, darling, every one of us has to make sense of how much we fall short of what we wish we were. And you're going to have to make sense of that too. We know that you are strong, and we know that you are loved, and we will stand at your side as you learn to push back on that condemnation! We know you can do it!"

Whenever children live mastered by emotion (be it fear or anger or perfectionism), they need us to lovingly be with them, but also to help build the structure and power for them to learn to push back on those feelings—to not let them control their lives. Emotions are like cravings. Just because I crave a bag of Cheetos right now, doesn't mean I should allow myself to act on that craving. Instead, we learn to see the craving (or feeling), master it, and choose well.

Our teenage daughter just broke up with her boyfriend. She says that it has hurt her so much that she thinks that she will "never be able to trust anyone again." How do we help her?

There's a lot going on in this situation. Number one, remember that most teens are "histrionic." That is, they lead with their emotional foot. When they *feel*—they feel *big*! We are going to engage her feelings in a moment; but first, remember that managing your own anxiety about her intense reaction is key. Remember that teenage girls are deeply dramatic. They will often initially spiral or despair in the face of losses and wounds, but most of them tend to settle soon. She needs to "look in your eyes" and see that you are not panicking too.

Secondly, she needs us to be *with her* in her pain. Remember that what heals pain is connection to those we love. She is suffering what in her world is a devastating loss. She needs the understanding and the kindness from parents who remember the devastation of that first breakup. Show her you "get it" by talking to her about her loss. This will also help her "mentalize" her swirling emotions. Your tender and wise heart toward her will help her heal.

Thirdly, the notion of "trust" is a complex one. The secret to making sense of "trusting again" lies in remembering that trust has two sides, not one. Sure, part one is, "Can I believe that others will not hurt me again?" That takes experience and time.

But if we stop there, we will always live in the victim position of wondering when the next blow with fall. How could we ever "trust" that much again? We can't. Which is why we have the other side of trust as well.

The second part of trust is the "trust" that *I know I am strong enough* to manage and resolve any future pain that may befall me. The trust I have in *me*! Most people who have "trust issues" are lacking this second part of trust. So in addition to nurture and empathy, swing into her regarding her strength and power. Speak to her about her identity—who she is regardless of how relationships might hurt. That will be the key to her "learning to trust" again.

We've just been through a family tragedy. How can we make sure our kids are okay as they face this loss?

Great question. So often parents approach me, concerned about their child after having encountered "big pain." Maybe there has been a death in the family, or an ugly divorce, or maybe your child has been uprooted from their home and school and moved to an unfamiliar new city. How do we help our children deal with traumatic pain?

Sometimes I sense that parents believe that these kids of painful circumstances will *necessarily* harm their child in some way. So let's begin by remembering our primary pain principle—*pain itself does not harm children.* Pain experienced *alone* is what hurt our kids. So whatever loss your family is walking through, work to keep open communication with your child about what they are experiencing. Help your family become a place where your child can talk with you about how difficult the journey is. Walking through their pain *with you* is what resolves it, remember?

But recognize that children often need to process loss at their own pace—on their own terms. Don't rush them to have to talk about a loss just because you are concerned about how they are handling it. God made us to naturally grieve, and your child will do so.

"But what if he is not processing the loss like he should?" parents ask.

The best way to determine if there is a glitch in your child's grieving process is to look look for "fruit" or symptoms.

Discerning emotional problems in children is typically easy. If they are struggling to metabolize their pain, they will usually produce a relatively overt symptom. It's like asking, "How do you know when shrimp are done cooking?" They turn pink! It's obvious. And if a child is struggling with managing pain, there will usually be some fruit of it in the child's behavior. You might see their anger level increase or their school work unravel. Some kids might regress to wetting the bed again. If you see these kinds of symptoms, begin pushing harder for opportunities to talk to your child about their emotional world.

Suppose he becomes more aggressive with his siblings. While he's in timeout for "acting out," join him and say, "I noticed that you have been more angry since we moved. I know that this has been a really hard transition, and you had to leave all of your friends. A lot of times when we are hurting, it is so much easier to be angry." At this point, a lot of kids will deny that they are struggling. That's fine. Back off and let it go for now. But look for times to bring it up again in the future.

I saw a pre-teen once whose mother brought him to therapy after the death of his father. As I spoke with him, he vehemently claimed that he was doing okay and didn't need to talk. I wanted to honor that, so we talked about his favorite video games for a while. I then talked to his mother, coaching her a bit about how to listen for his pain, and I sent them both home. A few months later *he asked her* if he could come back to see me. As he sat down, he thanked me for not pushing him harder about his father's death. "I was not ready to deal with it back then, but I am now."

Your *availability* to help your child metabolize pain is the key, not your pushing them to talk about it. Just like they will let you know when they are hungry, they will let you know when they need to process loss with you. I had a mother tell me the other day that her daughter refused to discuss the recent family divorce. However, on so many evenings, the little girl opens up and processes her sadness and confusion when her mom is putting her to bed. There is your opening! If we can manage our fear of their pain, and keep our ears open, they will let us know what they need.

(See appendix for more Q&A)

[1] *Psalm 23:4, King James Version.*

[2] *Matthew 28:20, King James Version.*

[3] *Genesis 2:18, New International Version.*

[4] *Isaiah 53:3, English Standard Version.*

[5] *II Corinthians 7:10, King James Version.*

I think all Christians would agree with me if I said that though Christianity seems at the first to be all about morality, all about duties and rules and guilt and virtue, yet it leads you on, out of all that, into something beyond. One has a glimpse of a country where they do not talk of those things, except perhaps as a joke. Every one there is filled full with what we should call goodness as a mirror is filled with light. But they do not call it goodness. They do not call it anything. They are not thinking of it. They are too busy looking at the source from which it comes. But this is near the stage where the road passes over the rim of our world. No one's eyes can see very far beyond that: lots of people's eyes can see further than mine.

— **C. S. Lewis**

Chapter Six

How do I teach good values to my kids?

While answering the "Proust Questionnaire" in *Vanity Fair* magazine, Melinda Gates responded that her "greatest achievement" was raising her kids with "good values."[1] Tall words from someone who, with her husband, Bill, helped change the world. All good enough parents are asking this question.

One of the most confusing and disturbing things about our current culture is that its purveyors maintain more and more that there is nothing that is ultimately *true*—nothing that is ultimately *right*. (However, if you offend their sensibilities regarding this belief, they suddenly become overwhelmingly "righteous" and indignant at your naive provincialism!) I believe one of the greatest gifts we can give our children is the treasure of teaching them that there is something bigger than ourselves. Something to which we all bend the knee. That there is a *way* that is life-giving and right—things that really matter, whether we agree with them or not. They are called Values.

Part of what it means to be a fallen, screwed-up human (is that a redundancy?) is that it is our natural inclination to see God's *way* as some sort of arbitrary set of rules: God, the party-pooper wants us to act "right" instead of acting "wrong"—Do this because you're "supposed to"—God's gonna be mad at you if you don't obey.

That's scary and all, but that's not what I hear God saying. The Bible doesn't seem to talk so much about being a "Good Boy" or "Bad Boy." God's way is not about just "doing the right thing." It is far richer than that.

One of the most interesting things about having done therapy for the majority of my life is that I have learned through experience what kinds of things are life-giving to human beings. I have learned what heals depression or anxiety—what makes marriages work; what makes businesses excel; what helps kids grow. One of the most fascinating parts about that discovery process has been looking at these things that good "psychology" has discovered, and realizing that they are the same values that God has been calling us to all along: justice, relationship, love, integrity, forgiveness, responsibility for ones actions, power, and humility. God's *way* is about what leads to wholeness. It is the way that is *right* for life. As we have said, God's way is not so much about *morality* as it is about *reality*.

The Greek word for "righteousness" in the new Testament literally means "accuracy." Blessed are those who hunger and thirst to live "accurately." There is a way that is ultimately true and ultimately right and ultimately matters—and we don't get to make that up. So, one of the greatest gifts we can give our children is to teach them about that *way*—the way that leads to life.

Many people in our culture propose that, if left to their own devices, children would naturally assume a civilized posture. Please contact me if you know of such a person—I have a bridge I would like to sell them. I mean, have you hung around your children much? It's the *Lord of the Flies* out there! If we do not engage and teach our children about selflessness, humility, and love, their natural orientation will be to become that bald James Bond villain who sits in his lair and strokes his cat. They will live out of their impulses and never look back. One mother told me once, "We named our son Billy because the name Attila the Hun was already taken." We need to teach our children about values—the way of wisdom and compassion and strength—what really matters. We have to teach them or else!

On the other hand, if you try to teach values by lining up your kids "bootcamp-style" and lecturing about the "values we hold in this family," you are going to be about as helpful as a roto-virus. They'll go "compliant, rebel, or sneak" and ultimately all their values will go out the window. I've seen so many Christian adults who have either blown off their family's values (or are still imprisoned by them) after a childhood of rigid beliefs. Lecturing your kids about values is like buying them a train—not much use on its own. But the kind of "heart growth" we've been teaching all along is like building the *tracks* for that train first. Now when you teach values, they've got a good heart to "run" them on! So how can we teach rich heart values?

Let's look at three different aspects of this journey. Let's ask:
— *What* are life-giving values?
— *Why* should we live by these values?
— *How* do we teach those values?

What are life-giving values?

What values do we want to instill in our kids? Most books that talk about teaching values to kids tend to begin a *list* at this point—kind of like something out of the Boy Scout manual: "Teach your children integrity, honesty, industriousness, thriftiness, self-control, and walking old ladies across the street." And that's Kool and the Gang, but the focus of this book has been more about helping develop the *heart* of our children. We've been talking about developing "heart stuff" like Love and Mattering, Wisdom and Obedience, Identity and Strength, Pain and Forgiveness. And here's the surprise—as we've done that, we've *already* been teaching our kids about values. If you really want to teach your children values, first build *hearts that value good things*, then the "list" of virtues will be an easy sprint.

Another way of saying this is: If you've been working to teach your kids *heart values* like love, wisdom, strength, and forgiveness, now can be a great time to teach them an *overt value system*. But if you haven't been teaching these heart things, and just want to swoop in there, line them up, and preach right and wrong, you are missing the point. You cannot teach real values outside of the context of everything else we've been talking about.

A client of mine grew up in a strict "value-heavy" home. Every night the kids were expected to read the Bible and confess their sins. But their home was a scary, angry place. The result: Her siblings went off their rockers as they grew older, and she was saddled with a bundle of anxiety. Unfortunately, we can't just "talk" values—we have to live them in the lives of our children. But fortunately, we've been doing that since page one! Let's look at what we've already been teaching our kids about values—from the *inside out*.

We've been teaching them about love.
Let's go back to Chapter Two. When you live a life with your children that says, "You *matter* and you are *loved*," you are building the deepest foundation for the value system we ultimately want to teach our children. What is the right thing to do? The right thing is to *love* people and remember that they are *hurt* if we don't treat them with kindness, mercy, and compassion. We love our neighbor as ourselves. Morality is not about ethics; it's about how other people *matter*.

So what values does love promote? Kindness, gentleness, compassion, patience with one another, even humility. As we've been teaching our kids that they and other people *matter*, we've been building the foundation for all of these values. We've been teaching that people matter more than things or money or prestige—that kindness is important because other people can get hurt, just like me. Contemporary corporate culture has even begun to focus on how, in the workplace, *relationships* matter most. Check mark! We've been teaching that too.

One of our kids went through a season in which she was scared to go to sleep at night. We, of course, pushed her to stretch and be strong and try it anyway. (cf. Chapter Four) However, one night we peeked in and found her big sister asleep on the floor next to her bed. We woke her and asked what was happening. She replied, "Bonney was scared, so I told her I would lie in here with her until she went to sleep." You can't teach that value out of the *Book of Virtues*, gang. You teach those kinds of values by teaching love and compassion at the heart level.

See my point? We've been teaching this all along. If we are building the grounding that people matter, then teaching values like selflessness, sharing, and kindness will be a cinch.

Here's a thought. I wonder sometimes whether it's the best idea to make our kids just say, "I'm sorry." I see these situations in which a couple of kids are fighting. Then Mom says something like, "Tell him you're sorry." So we end up with this angry kid, huffing and puffing, and parroting back meaninglessly, "I'm sorry." Gives me the warm fuzzies.

I wonder if a better way would be to invite the child to talk some (maybe while they're in timeout) about how it would have *felt* to the other person to have been hurt. "How would it have felt to Billy that you took his toy?" And we help them, in a non-shamey way, to touch the fact that he would feel *bad*—"He wanted to play, just like you! We don't take someone's toy because they hurt *just like us!*" In other words, the empathy involved in "loving your neighbor as yourself" feels like the best apology ever—at least to me.

So with love, we teach the "value" that people matter. We show our kids that we are willing to sacrifice and suffer because *they* matter. We correct their jerky behavior by saying, "That *hurt* your brother." We tell that sassy teenager, "I can't let you talk to me in that way. That hurts me and we aren't going to talk to one another in unkind ways." We watch our scolding and shaminess in discipline. Hear how we are teaching the "list" of values here, but we are doing it as we *relate to our children's hearts?* Love teaches values.

We've been teaching them wisdom and obedience.
Secondly, we've talked about loving, powerful discipline. We have been teaching our kids that you can have anything you want in life—you just have to pay for it. We can choose any action we want, but we cannot choose the consequences of those actions. This is also a foundation for ultimate values.

As we've engaged in Teaching Discipline, we've been teaching our kids the value of pushing back on our impulses because we know that they will cost us. This is the essence of *self-control*—what the Old-Schoolers called *temperance* and *moderation*. We've also been teaching *patience*—the ability to sit with the tension of not getting what I want *right now* in order to get something *better later*. In other words, we've been teaching them to "Look before you leap!"

Remember how kids come into the world? They might as well be wearing superhero tights that say, "Impulse Man! I take what I want! To infinity and beyond." Yet some of the deepest values we teach our kids involve learning to resist our impulses and choose out of wisdom and love. As our kids learn to choose wisely in discipline, they are learning to *delay gratification*—to push back on their impulses.

My wife said something to me the other night that irritated me. However, I knew that I was braindead from a hard day of clients and probably wasn't at my best. My *impulses* said, "Let her have it, Six-gun Pete!" My *values* said, "Just because you feel ikky doesn't mean that lashing out is the best plan." There is a sense in which you could say that the *ability to not live out of our impulses* is the essence of having good values. This is what we are teaching our kids when we teach discipline and consequences.

I am always a little cautious about people who say they do things just because they are "the right thing to do." I once heard someone express this same question with a story. They said something like, "If I see a guy holding a baseball bat, I might say, 'Gee, Altuve, I'm kind of afraid you might to hit me with that bat!' If he responds by saying, 'No, that would be *wrong!*', I'm probably going to *duck*. However, if he responds by saying, 'No, that would *hurt you* so badly!', I'd pitch him a ball!" Love and consequences are a powerful grounding for good values.

So, one of the richest ways that we have been teaching

values is by helping our kids learn that loving values lead to *consequences* that are life-giving. Selfish values, on the other hand, lead to consequences that hurt us and other people. A fundamental human value is the wisdom that remembers that our choices have consequences to us and to other people. We should therefore choose wisely.

Sometimes, I would even go so far with my children as to say, "Wow, you really chose *wisely!*" when they obeyed me. Not, "Oh my gosh, you are so *good!*" I wanted to teach them to think about the fruits of their choices, not just to "be good." Life-giving values teach us that when we choose poorly, the consequences cost us and other people. A thousand hurtful, destructive things could be avoided if we learned that simple truth. God calls the person who never learns that a "fool." Consequences guide values.

We've been teaching them about strength and power. Choosing well is hard!

Part of that is because following life-giving values often goes against our nature. Don't you think it's interesting how doing what is *bad for us* is always easier than doing what is *good for us?* It's easier to gain weight than it is to lose it. It's easier to spend money than it is to earn it. Welcome to the fallen world. The "Fall of Man at Eden" sounds like a fancy theological concept, but you feel it every time you would rather binge Netflix than work out. So in order to follow the values we treasure, we must be *strong.*

Lucky, us! We've been teaching our kids grit and resiliency

since Chapter Four! I worked with a family once who's college-age kid came home for the summer and all he wanted to do was to sleep until 2 p.m. (after staying up until 2 a.m. playing video games!). His parents wanted him to get a job—to learn the "value" of hard work.

"I'm too tired," he would moan.

So they moaned back, "I thought we had taught him better than this. We wanted to teach him the values of industriousness and self-discipline. What happened?"

Nothing happened.

He just simply needed to be pushed to be *strong*—probably with consequences. "We understand that you are tired, but if you don't get a job, we get your car." Suddenly our work teaching resiliency (with a pinch of consequences) is teaching the *value* of hard work.

By teaching our kids the character abilities of strength and identity, we've been building values—the knowledge that some things are worth sweating for. "No pain no gain." And for you workaholics, even the strength to say, "Enough work! Now it's time to play!"

We say to kids, "Thank you for telling us the truth. It's a hard thing to fess up. You were very strong to do that. Good for you, pal!" When they complain about having to take the garbage out in the rain, we empathetically say, "Yeah, work stinks. It's a hard thing to have to fulfill your responsibilities. But you are strong, dude. I'll grab your raincoat." Doing what needs to be done requires strength.

You can have good intentions to act rightly until the cows

come home. As we've been helping our kids develop the resiliency to actually *do* it, we've been teaching values!

We've been teaching them about pain and forgiveness. In Chapter Five we talked about helping our kids learn to be grounded enough to deal with pain. Life is not just hard, it *hurts!* Here's the Secret of the Universe regarding choosing well according to our values: *The options in life are pain now or pain later.* (Think happy thoughts.)

In other words, one of the most important principles for living out our values is understanding that living according to what is most life-giving is going to *hurt*—but not as much as it would *hurt later* to not do so. As we've been working to teach our children the ability to "suffer well," we are giving them a heart that can endure practicing good values. If we can't face pain, the values of humility and selflessness can feel out of reach. Instead, we've been teaching them *courage*, the ability to face pain and fear and choose well anyway.

A woman asked me the other day if I could hypnotize her into not wanting to eat—that way she could lose weight and not mind doing it! I told her that I could not, but I would be glad to give her the secret to weight loss. "Learn to be comfortable living with deprivation and pain. Presto! Weight Loss!" (The famous "John Cox Diet Plan"—I'll make millions!)

We can talk about lofty values all night long. But the primary reason that my adult clients do not live with integrity or selflessness or temperance or responsibility is not because they are "bad" people with sketchy values. They *want* to live well and love well. But most of them cannot endure the loss or the suffering that living according to their values requires. It *hurts* too much to work out. It *hurts* too much to not flirt with the secretary. They are *too scared* to give money to the church. And they have never learned to manage that pain. But once we do some smokin' hot therapy work together, they suddenly find themselves able to choose what they've wanted to choose all along. Bingo—they have "good values"! Why? Because now they can face pain with integrity.

So the work we are doing to engage our children's pain with love and strength is building the software for godly, strong values. A heart that can face the suffering that choosing well requires, can choose good things.

What about shame (the other side of the painful world)? Aren't forgiveness and humility values we want to instill?

One of the things that Jesus most deeply calls us to is *humility*. He says unless you get the log out of your own eye, you can't even *see* to find the speck in your neighbors'. How true. I often ask judgmental people to consider the following challenge. Which are you a greater expert on, *your own* badness or your spouse's? If asked to give a presentation, which would be longer—your brief comments about your own fallenness, or your PowerPoint presentation about theirs (with handouts and small group discussion)?

The value of humility comes as we learn that is it safe to be a fallen, imperfect person. In this book, I am wanting to free you, but helping you find freedom as a parent is not just to provide comfort. As we feel the room to just be good enough, we are also modeling and teaching the core value of humility to our children. When we teach our kids that it is safe to be screwed up, we are building the grounding for the values of humility and forgiveness. What a gift to free our children by teaching them that they can be just good enough kids!

So love, wisdom, strength, forgiveness. We are teaching values all along—at the heart level and the relational level. And the heart is the wellspring of loving values.

When we imagine sending our kids out into the world one day, ready to practice good values in contemporary culture, remember—the first culture within which our kids live is our home. As we create a culture in our home that is built on loving values, our kids will absorb that through their skin and take it with them as they go.

Why should I live by these values?

"Great, Mom and Dad. These values sound super. Now, why should I live this way? I mean, being slovenly is so much fun!"

Values are *developmental* just like everything else in kids. A child's understanding of what "ultimately matters," and why they should follow it, progresses from the *simple* to the *nuanced*—from the *self-focused* to the *love-focused*. I like to look at three different stages of maturing values in kids. I call them:

— Only I Matter
— Rules and Laws Matter
— God and Other People Matter (and me too)

Only I matter.

We start out as babies, remember?

And basically, as we said, all of us are born and begin looking around for how we can take over this operation. Our natural orientation is to get what we want when we want it. Of course, for infants, that's a matter of survival. But as kids get older it can become more of an issue of selfishness and entitlement. Self-centeredness is in our factory specs—it's our operating system. We humans are a naturally self-focused bunch, who tend to live for what pleases us. In other words, meet our *first* human value—*"Only I Matter."*

It's our life principle. I mean, have you ever met a patient infant?

When one of our kids was little, she approached me in the Kwik-E-Mart and held out a candy bar for me to see.

"Can I get this, Daddy?" she asked.

I had told them that they could each get one treat, so I replied, "Of course, Babe."

But smelling shenanigans, I leaned down. Underneath the candy bar was another candy bar just like it, camouflaged beneath its twin—a "two for one sale" of her own making. Kids need us to teach them values.

I remember my brother and I being taken to visit the home of one of my grandmother's friends. The nice lady offered us a jar of candy, saying we could have all we wanted. My little brother pushed ahead and reached inside the jar, grabbing the biggest handful of candy he could—so big in fact that he couldn't get his hand out! He pulled and tugged at the jar, but he was trapped. The more he wanted to take, the more stuck he became. I think this is actually how they trap monkeys in the Philippines. But welcome to early childhood values. We start life as shysters, grifters, and conmen. We all do. One of the reasons that civilization was invented was to set some limits on this kind of law of the jungle. Otherwise, everyone would live out of the "Only I Matter" value system, and the world would be *Thunderdome*! "Two men enter. One man leaves."

Rules and laws matter.

So into this picture enters the *second* human value, *"Rules and Laws Matter."*

Rules and Laws Matter is how young children begin to see values. Young kids are concrete. Life is black and white. These are the "Good Guys" and those are the "Bad Guys." And when you're a kid, it's good to think like that. It's *simple* but it's good. At least we aren't just living "every man for himself" anymore.

Children need the structure and the direction of simple rules and regulations when they are young. When we tell them things like, "You have to pick up your toys," or "Stealing is not okay," we are building a "paint by the numbers" picture of what living by good values looks like. We are giving them concrete practice at living rightly. They need us to take them by the hand like this and walk them into the world of living well.

When I was about ten years old, I wanted a new bike.

When I asked my dad for one, he told me that it would be better if I bought it myself, and that he would help me earn the money. This was news to me. I had been under the impression that just getting things for free was the pinnacle of happiness. My dad disagreed. He began giving me chores to do; cutting the grass, raking leaves, etc., and paying me for my work. It took several months, but I still remember the Saturday morning that I had finally earned enough money for the bike. I remember my dad taking me downtown to the bicycle store. I remember how it smelled. I remember the *tick-tick-tick* of that three-speed bike as the store owner wheeled it toward me, candy apple red and shining under the store lights. My dad taught me a value I've never forgotten—that the things that require work and sacrifice yield us more than just a bike. They continue to give us the joy and satisfaction of hard work and its rich rewards.

One final thing about rules and laws. Not only do concrete values build a sense of right and wrong in children, they create security for them. It feels safe to kids for their parents to communicate right and wrong in a clear, shame-free manner.

Remember that old story about the kids at the inner-city playground? The children always played huddled in the center, keeping their distance from the edges of the play area. Then some smart person decided to build a fence around the perimeter of the playground. Suddenly the children began using every inch of the block to play. The structure of the fence boundary made them feel safe, resulting in a playtime that was even better! Clear structure and rules feel safe to young kids.

God and other people matter (and me too).

This *rule* thing, however, is limited. Ultimately, it can incline people to believe that what is most important is the *rule itself*—that doing what is "right" is what matters most. So as children grow up, their motivation for values needs to grow up too. You know those legalistic types (conservative or liberal) who get stuck here with rules and law? They run around being the Barney Fifes of the world, pointing at other people and proclaiming, "Citizens arrest! Citizens arrest!" Their ultimate value is that "this is the rule, and if you violate it you must bad." I believe that Jesus's message to the pharisees was that loving "Law" like that misses the heart of true goodness. So it's time to grow up some more, and move from *rules* to values that are more *heart-based.*

When Jesus comes, he tells us that he didn't come to do away with the rules. He came to say that there is something *bigger* than the rules. The story is *more* than "Rules and Law Matter," and it's certainly more than "Only I Matter." His message is that we do what is right because *"God and Other People Matter (as well as me)."* And suddenly, *love* is what compels our values—love, and the life that it creates. In other words, as we said, we do what is right because it is *loving.*

Teaching our kids to make choices because "God and Other People Matter (and me too)" is going to be their ultimate guide as they mature into adult values.

When I was a young teen, my friends and I would still trick-or-treat on some Halloweens. We would dress like "hobos" and follow the little kids around. "Trick or Treat, Man. Gimmie some candy or somethin'."

One year, my little brother wanted to join us. At one point during the evening, however, someone threw an egg and it hit him in the face. He ran home crying, dropped his trick-or-treat bag at the front door and disappeared inside. Then true disaster struck. At some point while Mom was tending his injuries, someone stole his whole bag of candy. Now as you know, in a kid universe, this feels about the same as an adult losing their entire stock portfolio. He was devastated.

My parents pulled me inside and said, "Hey John, Mark's really hurting. Would you and your friends help him out. Would y'all share your candy with him?" They were creating a response of love to my brother, the casualty of this heinous crime. Even as a young guy, I found this solution quite moving. So I grabbed an empty bag and started going around to all my hobo friends and asking them to donate candy to help my brother's cause. They all generously poured tons of candy into Mark's new bag. He ended up with more than us! My friends loved Mark, and so did I. Presto, heartbreakingly good values.

So be aware that your children are gradually *developing* in their understanding of values and why we follow them. Initially they are just about "taking." As we begin teaching our kids about right and wrong, they develop simple categories—these things are "bad" and these things are "good."

Later we can begin weaving in the more abstract principles of love and empathy as road signs toward godly living. Remember this developmental process and walk with them along the way.

How do we teach values?

Let's get practical. How do we actually instill these values? The key word here being "instill." Basically, what we mean when we talk about "having a conscience" is the *internalized* values that we have been shown—values that have now been folded into our hearts. How do we help our kids develop a conscience that holds deep heart values—a conscience that they can take with them through life? Let's look at some ways we do that—and as we did with love, we teach it *differently at different ages.*

With **babies**, we tuck the beginning foundations of values inside their hearts simply by *nurturing* them well. Babies only have two questions in life: Am I going to be alone, and am I in distress? And as we said in the love chapter, when we comfort, soothe, and bond with them, we are scripting the motherboard for understanding love and empathy and security—things that will become the bedrock of a value system later on.

With **toddlers** we can began to teach overt values, but in a very concrete way. As we've said, values always move from the external to the internal—from the concrete to the abstract. So we begin teaching values to toddlers in very concrete ways. "You can't run in the street." "If you hit mommy, I'm going to express my disapproval and possibly put you in your Pack 'n Play for a little timeout." "Running off when Dad calls you is not okay." Toddlers and preschoolers live in that world of black and white. Something is right or something is wrong. Mommy is pleased. Mommy is displeased.

Our grandson, Whit, picked up a little pinecone from a decoration that his grandmother had placed on a table. We both inspected it, running our fingers along the jaggedy texture of the cone. But then he just threw it on the floor and started to walk away. Par for the course with a toddler, right? Nevertheless, I picked it up and added, "Hey, amigo, if we take Nonnie's things, she would want us to put them back." Though that is simple for us, it's integral calculus for them. With toddlers, we are beginning to imprint the basic categories for right and wrong—kindness and unkindness.

With **school-age kids** we can begin to become more verbal and direct about what it is that we believe. "You have chores for which you are responsible." "You are in charge of your allowance—and when you spend it there is no more." "Lying is not okay." (Which reminds me of the old joke: The dad lectures his son, "Come on now boy, you know that honesty is the best policy." To which the guilt-ridden son replies, "Well, what's the second-best policy?")

With school-age kids, we can also begin to give more *relational* reasons for our values as opposed to just, "That's wrong." Now we are beginning to teach that "God and other people matter!"

We start saying things like, "We don't go into brother's room and take his stuff. That is *unkind*." (As opposed to just saying, "Stealing is *wrong!*") When some kid at school is unkind to them, we comfort them, but throw in, "This is why we talk about kindness to one another. It really hurts us when people are mean."

We also teach values by *modeling* them. When we live good values around our kids, they learn them experientially. "Monkey see, monkey do!" We say, "I'm taking you guys to the park because Mom is really tired, and I want to give her a break—because I *love* her." Hear how we are beginning to teach them values, but also the *loving reasons* behind the values?

Norma was good at modeling values. One of our adult kids told her recently that she had always noticed how Norma had shown respect and kindness to the people who "served" her. The bank teller, the pharmacy guy, the girl who did her hair—all became friends who were shown respect and kindness. I guess the girls were observing this all along and seeing the power of it. Sometimes you don't know it's getting through, but it is.

Here's another idea for teaching values as your kids engage the world. Norma and the girls used to play what they called the "what would you do if…" game. You know how when you're playing outfield in baseball, you think, "Okay, if the ball gets hit to me, where do I throw it? The bases are loaded, so I'm throwing it home!" You are playing the "what would I do if" game in baseball—anticipating what you might do in a given situation.

Norma would play the "what would you do if" game with *values*. She would ask the girls "what would you do if …" you saw one of your friends being left out? What would you do if someone invited you to cheat in school? What would you do if you saw someone being unkind to your sister? And the four of them would discuss the situation. As they got older, the questions became more about "what would you do if …" people started passing a joint around at a party? Or one of your friends was sending topless photos? Norma was practicing practical values with the girls all along.

Another practical way that we reinforce values with school-age kids is when we can pull off *non-angry discipline*. (Wishing us all luck there!) As we have said, anger and shame (I'm surprised at you!) ultimately create fear and hiding instead of wisdom and love. Shame destroys loving values.

As Paul tells us in Romans 7, the fear and shame that are the language of "Law" are actually *obstacles* to our hearts becoming more godly. Jesus's message throughout was that love is what compels us. It drives us to a deeper, wilder obedience than fear and shame ever could. To the degree that we can relate without anger and shame, we are actually *freeing* our kids to live better. "It is the kindness of God leads us to repentance."[2]

I worked with a client once who had spent her life

burdened with shame and guilt. In her family, missteps did not result in discipline, they resulted in cold rage from her father. The message was terrifying—"Mess up and you are cast out." Consequently, she never thought about learning to do what was *life-giving*. Instead, all she learned was to be *afraid of her dad.* Keeping anger and shame out of our discipline teaches values based on wisdom and love rather than fear and shame.

By the way (an interesting aside), as my client began to find freedom from her shame and fear, she went through a brief crisis. She said, "I'm not sure how to act now. If I'm not controlled by my fear of doing something wrong, then why should I do right?" It took her a little season to discover that once she was free, the desire to be *loving and wise* would govern her choices—not fear.

What about **Teenagers**? Well, again, welcome back to the puzzle factory! Go ahead and expect it; teenagers are going to question your values. It's maddening! You've spent more than a decade carefully working to craft your child's heart, and suddenly they slope through the room mumbling about how they're not sure they agree with your position on abortion!

As we said in the love chapter, it's important that we not freak out at this point! Teenagers are stretching their wings and trying on every stupid belief they can find to see what fits. Of course, we will set limits on hurtful or destructive *behavior*, but remember that our secret weapon regarding their *hearts* is to talk *with* them.

Your teen says, "I don't understand why people feel like they need to get married. I mean it's dumb." And you're thinking, "Great! Hello, Square One, we meet again! I thought we had taught them better than this. Family, Marriage, Fidelity! It's all down the tubes!"

No, Catastrophe-breath, chill a minute and talk *with* them. Say, "Really, Speedy? What bugs you about marriage? Why are you all in a wad about matrimony?" One of my clients said this to his son, and the boy began to really talk with his father about his fears regarding his *parent's marriage!* He saw them frequently conflicting and had been worried about it. He opened his heart, because his Dad *asked!* Solid Gold! (People who say your teenager never talks to you—listen up!)

To the degree that we try to force our thinking about values on teens, they will either shut down or get even crazier. The trick here is to manage your anxiety, hold your ground, and be patient. Instant gratification is not the friend of a values teacher. (Oh, and bring the whirlwind if they *act* on their stupid values!)

On the other hand, lots of teens need our help in navigating the crazy world of adolescence. The values they encounter in their world often scare them. Our's expressed concern about what to do if a party got out of bounds. Our answer to that "what-if game" was that we would always be glad to come pick them up, or offer them a "my parents are so strict" excuse to have to leave. That way they get to roll their eyes, groan, and save face as their "jerky parents" demand that they come home. As they got older, they would call each other for rescue. Family is a refuge for safe values in an unsafe world.

Let's get free

Now, we can't leave this topic without at least dipping into one more "Bad News Moment." As you know by now, the most powerful way in which children learn anything is through what they *experience*. This means, sadly, that they're going to get a very core sense of values through watching how we relate to them and other people. Yet again, if you're anything like me, you want to throw in the towel at this point.

Sometimes our kids will see us act without integrity, being rude to a waiter or acting like a maniac in traffic. One mom told me that after fighting traffic all the way home, she finally pulled up in the carport. From the back seat her little girl asked, "Mommy, what *is* an 'ash hole'?"

On the other end of the spectrum, some parents act with *harsh judgmental* "integrity." I think about the innumerable clients I've had whose parents acted like they loved "right and wrong" more than they loved their kids.

So what does being free look like when we drop the ball with our own values? Well, think about it, what was the *value* that Jesus *valued* the most? It was a repentant and a humble heart. He looked at the worst of sinners and said, "Neither do I condemn you." The *deepest value* is being that "humble parent" we talked about.

When I do conferences for singles about marriage and dating, I talk about the sort of character traits that we need in order to do marriage well. Just like in this book, we talk about things like intimacy, identity, forgiveness, and strength.

Invariably, someone asks me, "So where am I supposed to find someone who has all of those wonderful character traits?" Point taken. (There really is only one, and he lives in Montana somewhere—and I think he's engaged now. Sorry, ladies.)

Otherwise I tell them to find somebody who has only *one* trait. Repentance—a humble heart that is open to growing. I mean, maybe he's a Neanderthal emotionally, but he *knows* he's a Neanderthal! Marry that Neanderthal! That person can grow.

Christians cannot talk about values without also talking about what to do when we screw them up. That's the point of the Bible. Here is God's way, and here is where to run when you fail. This needs to be at the top of your list when teaching your kids about values. "We long to live by life-giving values, but since every one of us in this family will fail, we will love each other well in our failure. There may be consequences, but love never goes away." If the only value you can instill in your children is that it is safe to be fallen and to talk about it, then you've taken your first step into a larger world. And you teaching good enough values.

Q&A Time

Hey Doc—Since we're talking about preparing our kids for real life, do you have any thoughts on how we should manage their exposure to values we disagree with out in the world—like in the media or even crazy stuff they hear from their friends?

My entire practice, I've had parents ask me questions about where to land on this issue. "What movies should we let them watch?" "They have a friend who uses inappropriate language. Should we allow them to play together?"

And I've seen parents land at either extreme. Some parents shut down the television altogether, covering their children's eyes during the tampon ads. And I've seen others who seem to be oblivious to the fact that their seven-year-old boys are watching *Scarface* in the next room.

The answer is neither of these extremes. The answer is to ebb and flow between the lines of *Prepare and Protect,* as we talked about in Chapter Four. In other words, there's no way to know exactly where to land on all of these issues. I want you struggling somewhere between *protecting them* from the pollution that they will often encounter in our culture, and *walking* with them to understanding the junk they *do encounter.*

We always wanted to be vigilant to shield our children from the worst that our culture has to offer. But, on the other hand, we did not want to become cultural Mennonites. One day our children will encounter all of the junk in the world. We wanted them to walk through at least some of it the first time *with us!*

One family I know somehow created a beautifully welcoming atmosphere in their home in which their school-age kids could come to them and ask about any phrase that the rude kids at school had been using. "Mom, what does @$%&* mean?" The mom would never act shocked, but would give an age-appropriate response to their question, adding, "But that's not a word that we use in our family. It's actually kind of an ugly word that hurts people."

If you're watching a movie with your kids and suddenly the screen is filled with violence, racism, or sexuality—keep your cool. Don't somersault to the remote control and flip it to the Hallmark Channel, acting as if nothing had happened. Be cool, but talk to your children about it. "That part of our movie disturbed me. What did you think about it?"

This harkens back to our primary principle of parenting. Good enough parenting is not about always doing it right or being a perfect parent. It's about living in relationship with your kids. We encounter the gross stuff in the world *with* them! As we said in an earlier chapter regarding pain, walking through difficult things with our children is what heals them and makes them strong. So Protect and Prepare. Give your children a safe, pure home, but help them build the muscles to deal with the wildness. It's a jungle out there.

We have a child who seems super-anxious about doing anything wrong. It's like she has a hypersensitive conscience. How can we help her better understand grace?

Like we said with the perfectionistic child, begin by doing a crosscheck together as parents to determine whether anyone in your home is sending out any scary vibes, laden with shame or anxiety. I remember taking one of my children to the pediatrician once. I could hear the child in the next room crying and telling her mother that she was scared. The mother angrily told the child to quit crying, and finally left the examination room, closing the door and leaving the child alone. I could hear the mother say through the door, "When you can quit your crying, I will come back in." Ultimately, the doctor arrived, and to my dismay, I heard the mother say to him, "Doctor, I don't understand. She is only three, and she has so much anxiety." It was all I could do to not go next door and "assist" the doctor in his diagnosis!

So step one, sweep the house for any messages that would incline your child to believe that being "bad" is scary. This is especially relevant for a preschooler who is already struggling with that level anxiety. She's catching that somewhere.

Secondly, remember that we un-shame children. With an older child who has an overactive conscience, I want to *under*-react. Even play with her. When she is self-flagellating because of her iniquities, I want to poke her in the shoulder and say, "Oh my gosh, Babe. It really sounds like your mistake is freaking you out. Let's play a game. Let's all go around the table and talk about something each of us has messed up today. Let's play the "Messed-Up Family" game! You don't get to be the bad guy all by yourself! We want to be bad, too!" Games and play help kids objectify their pain and conquer it—and normalizing failure is a great shame cure.

With a pre-teen or teen, I want to talk to them like a person—a person who is entering the adult world of having to deal with shame. I want to say, "Ya know, man—Lemme teach ya somethin' big! One of the things that we all have to make sense of is that awful feeling we feel when we mess up. It seems like you are really letting that feeling beat you up lately! Now, at some point, you need to decide how much power you are going to let that shame have. Let me help you. Nobody gets to tell my son he's a moron but *me*! Let me help you tell that condemning voice to jump in the lake. He doesn't get to bully my son! I love you, Slick!"

I like this question because we as parents need to be Shame Busters in the lives of our children. Lock and Load.

You talk about how we should teach our kids to be kind because if they aren't, it hurts people. My mom used that as a weapon. When we were being jerky kids, she would act hurt and pitiful—"That's fine. Go ahead and act that way. Just know that it hurts your mother." How do we teach values based on kindness without guilt-tripping our kids?

Great question. The lynchpin of the answer lies in the degree to which you are taking responsibility for your hurt, versus dumping it on your kids. Your mom laid all the responsibility for her pain on you guys, which is whacky. It's quite a different thing to inform your kids that they are being hurtful—without dumping the responsibility for your wellbeing on them. It sounds like this: "You guys are being hurtful, and I can't allow that. If you can't get a handle on the snark, I'm going to need to *help* you do that—maybe with some extra chores around the house. I can't let you hurt other people."

By speaking to them that way, you are informing them about their hurtfulness, and letting it cost them. And you are taking responsibility for protecting yourself instead of guilt-tripping them. Then go to your spouse or your friends for help if your kids have left you with any real injuries. We shouldn't bring our emotional needs to our kids to fix.

By relating to them in these ways, you are taking responsibility for challenging their behavior and caring for yourself, but you are still teaching them about values based on kindness and love.

(More Q&A awaits in the appendix)

[1] *Vanity Fair, May, 2019.*

[2] *Romans 2:4, New American Standard Version.*

[3] *John 8:11, New International Version.*

Why so many forms? Why not just that one hydrogen atom? The creator goes off on one wild, specific tangent after another, or millions simultaneously, with an exuberance that would seem to be unwarranted, and with an abandoned energy sprung from an unfathomable font. What is going on here? The point of the dragonfly's terrible lip, the giant water bug, birdsong, or the beautiful dazzle and flash of sunlighted minnows, is not that it all fits together like clockwork—for it doesn't particularly, not even inside of a goldfish bowl—but that it all flows so freely wild, like the creek, that it all surges in such a free, fringed tangle. Freedom is the world's water and weather, the world's nourishment freely given, its soil and sap: and the creator loves pizzazz.

— **Annie Dillard**

Chapter Seven

How do I teach my kids about God?

I was a child of the sixties. My heroes weren't Han Solo and Chewie, they were John Glenn and Neil Armstrong—*real* space men! I remember getting to stay up late to watch the first steps on the moon in July of 1969—and in the blink of an eye it was July 1994, twenty-five years later to the month. The kids and I were all going somewhere in the car, and one of them pointed through the sunroof and said, "Look Daddy! The moon!"

Indeed, a sunny daytime moon hung in the crystal blue sky. The moon landing had been on my mind that month, given the anniversary of the event, so I turned to them and said, "You guys want to hear a really crazy story? When I was a little boy, three men got in a rocket ship—and they blasted off the earth and flew all the way to the moon! And when they got there, they landed on it. And after they landed, they got out and *walked around on it!*"

"No WAY!" they exclaimed. "You're making that up!"

I'll never forget how much fun it was to tell them about an event that had been so deeply important to me. That's why I love this chapter. As I hope you can tell, I enjoyed being a parent, and I enjoyed teaching my kids about love and strength and forgiveness. But now we get to tell them about the most exciting thing in the universe! I've never understood why church can sometimes be so boring. I remember going to a Springsteen concert years back and watching thousands and thousands of people explode with absolute joy. I thought, "Bruce Springsteen is just a small image-bearer of the One who *owns* joy and wonder and excitement. Why doesn't worshiping God feel like this?"

I believe that to the degree that we know who he really is, it *can* feel like that!

Think about it—what is he like? Here's an example: We've talked a lot in this book about how it is possible to be free. But why do we get to be *set free?* Why do we just get to declare that "the only thing better than a perfect parent is a humble parent"? I didn't just make that up! I don't get to make those kinds of calls in the universe. None of us do. So why is good enough, good enough? Because Christ died to make it safe to be fallen! The love and grace and forgiveness that Christ wrought don't just give us eternal hope in our future, they give us hope *now*. His grace in our hearts and relationships has the bizarre effect of enabling our brokenness, fallenness, and failure to draw us *closer together* rather than *further apart*—closer to him rather than further from him. (Remember the "Grace Effect"?) Instead of running to shame and defensiveness, this "grace to the humble" gives us the wonderful gift of being fallen *together!*

As we said earlier, those who are free to be broken get to say to one another, "You too? I thought I was the only one!"

As someone who lives his career in the relational world, I am dazzled by this solution. It is brilliant. It is genius. And it is heartbreakingly beautiful. Only him! Only he could have come up with something like this! He is the "author and perfecter" of every gift we've been wanting to give our children. This is what he is like! And he is the capstone of our book on parenting.

If we can live with a glorious celebration of who he is in our own hearts, it's going to be contagious for our kids. We get to help build their faith life. Let's enjoy talking about the wonderful privilege of teaching our kids about a relationship with the One who makes all thing wondrous.

We're ahead of the game here.

First, let me say this. Like we said about Values, we've already been talking throughout this entire book about helping our kids develop a relationship with God. It's not like we're suddenly switching to the "religious segment" of our program. Think about it. We've been working to teach our children about love and limits and submission and strength and forgiveness and grace. Basically, we've already been teaching them the basic software of a relationship with God all along. We've been giving them the "ears to hear" his voice throughout. It's not like it's suddenly "Bible time."

By teaching them godly character "software," we've been creating a context wherein, when they learn *content* about

God later on, it's going to be easier for them to plug it into the categories that we've already built. In fact, a huge reason people have problems in their "spiritual" lives is not because they are "bad people" or that they like sinning. It's because they have blindspots in some of this software we've been talking about. I mean, how is your obedience to God going to go if no one ever taught you to submit? How is your understanding of grace going to go if you never resolved the issue of badness or shame? Our character (our heart) is the tool with which we relate to everyone, including God. When we grow in our character (as we have been discussing in this book), we grow as a Christian. There aren't "psychological" parts of life and "religious" parts of life. If you really want to infuse your children's hearts with the heart of God, it's important that you remember that these are not separate things.

But, specifically, how can we teach our kids about God?

I like to think about two ways: I call them **Content** and **Experience**.

Content

God is an individual—a person. Just like you. There are things that are true about him, and things that are not true. He loves love. He hates the destructive cruel alienating choices he calls sin. He hates it enough that he would die to get rid of it. He made families. He made the miracle of children born from the love of their parents. And he made Jupiter as big as one-thousand-three-hundred Earths. This is who he is. We have a lot to tell our kids—a lot of content. Let's get busy.

The spiritual community

The Body of Christ itself is, of course, a powerful resource for teaching our kids about God. In our church when a child is baptized, the congregation is part of the sacrament and is asked to acknowledge their own commitment to be part of this covenant family—to raise these children together in the way of God. Church, Christian schools, Christian friends are all great resources for learning content about God.

I still remember sitting on the floor of a Sunday school class as a child, listening to Miss Mary Jane tell us Bible stories. Those stories have always stayed with me. Decades later, I visited her in the retirement home. I introduced myself. "Miss Mary Jane," I said. "I'm John Cox. You taught me Sunday school when I was about five years old, and I still remember your stories." She responded to me in a classic elderly Southern drawl, "John, you were *fowah*. And you always listened so well."

The Body of Christ that surrounds us is an invaluable resource for teaching our kids about God, but let's not leave it to the spiritual institutions to introduce our kids to him. You're the quarterback here; let's drive this ball downfield ourselves too. How can *we parents* teach our kids about their Savior?

Time with your family

The time you spend with your family engaging God is a real sweet spot for introducing kids to him—despite the fact that our family devotion time would often degenerate into something like, "You will sit down, and you will worship as you are told!" Nevertheless, work to have time together where you can pray and talk about God's heart.

Developmentally, young children learn the best teaching about God from **stories**. (Miss Mary Jane knew this!) I think that's one of the reasons that God made the Bible so much of a storybook. He wanted to speak his heart to children (of all ages). His stories are a great way for your family to spend time together spiritually. Even let your kids help tell them.

With little kids, a challenge to overt teaching about God is their concrete thinking. One of mine asked me once, "How do you get to heaven, Daddy? In an airplane or school bus?" Part of our job is to "translate" God's world into terms that little ears can understand.

One of my six-year-old friends told his parents that he was afraid of going to Heaven because he didn't want to be away from them. They translated the lofty concept of Heaven into categories that he could understand. They told him, "Heaven really isn't like that, buddy. It's not about leaving anybody! God promises that in Heaven, we will all finally get to be the *most* together! It's going to be like the best holiday, with all of your family and everyone who loves you. Heaven means that God made sure that little boys like you will *never* have to be away from their mommies and daddies. And he sent Jesus like a soldier and a protector, to make sure that none of us ever have to be apart from the people we love. That's one of the reasons we go to church and worship him—because we are thanking him for making it so we never have to be apart. So you can be sure that Daddy and God and me will be with you and rock you to sleep every night forever. That's what Heaven is." Just like Christ is an advocate between us and the Father, we are the bridge between our kids and God, teaching them what he is like in their language.

However, as you have probably picked up by now, my best plans often failed. Once I was telling our kids the story of the little children being brought to Jesus. I told them about how the disciples were annoyed, but Jesus called the little kids to his side anyway.

That night I paraphrased: "And pulling one of the kids to himself...," I said, reaching out to little Bonney in her nightgown, and pulling her next to me, "Jesus said, 'Unless you become like one of these, you will not see the Kingdom of Heaven. For the greatest of you will be the least, and the least of you (like one of these) shall be the greatest.'"

At that point, Bonney strutted into the center of the room and threw her arms over her head, saying, "That's right! *I* am the greatest!" Sometimes I just shook my head in futility.

Another thought—teach them to **pray**, preferably by *modeling* it. Here's a pointer for helping your children develop a more genuine relationship with God. When you pray, pray like you're really *talking* to someone. Because you *are*.

You know those people who put on a "prayer voice"—
"Lord, we beseech thee to anoint us with thine unction."
What the heck does that mean? Our children will learn a lot
about God from hearing someone talk to him. Throughout
this book I've been encouraging you to be *people* with your
children, not just parents. Nowhere is this more important
than in helping your kids develop spiritually. I want them
to hear a real person talk to a real God about real problems.
I want them to hear you stumble, and not use "God words,"
and even to not be sure what to say. (You know, like you do
in every *other* conversation you have?) If we want to teach
our kids that God is a person, then let's talk to him like one!

Also, let them hear you pray about *them*! One of the most
moving things to me about the High Priestly Prayer in the
Book of John, is seeing that, when Jesus could have prayed
about anything on the night before he was going to die, what
he prayed about was *us*. The disciples (and us) get to sit and
listen to him talk to his Father about *us*.

I want our kids to hear us say things like, "Father, I want to
ask especially that you help Jimbo with that test tomorrow.
He's been working really hard (and so have his parents!).
Help him out, Lord. And Sally has been having to deal with
those catty friends. We pray for the friends, but also that you
would be with Sally as she makes sense of how people can
be jerks." Instructing our children about God is not some
separate time that we tack on to our day. It is as much a part
of our relationship with our kids as everything else we've
been talking about.

How we **live life** with our kids is going to teach them a lot about God as well. This is going to become more relevant as they get older. Because, as our children grow up, we will have to shift our approach. When ours began asking if they could just text their prayers onto the family thread instead of having family devotions, we realized we had crossed some sort of line. At this point, if you turn family devotion time into some sort of a "required attendance" power struggle, I promise you you'll be shooting yourself in your spiritual foot. Instead, let's get smarter.

God is everywhere

Overt teaching is great. I always loved it—but then again, I'm a teacher. The most powerful place that we teach kids about God, however, is not with overt teaching. The real rocket ride happens someplace entirely different. Now we finally get to knock this ball to Neptune!

When God was asked how to teach kids about him, he didn't say, "Go do family devotions." He said, teach them "… when you sit in your house and when you walk along the way and when you lie down and when you rise up."[1] In other words, he said make your *life* a "family devotion." Do it. Show it. Walk it. Live it.

In other words, if you really want to teach your kids about God, bring him up—all the time. (He's there all the time anyway!—Hello!)

I really had fun with this one as a parent. Get creative. It's Candyland!

Your child says, "Look at the rainbow, Daddy."

I used to say stuff like, "Oh my Gosh! How crazy is that! You know how you color in a coloring book—and you use a crayon? Well, God colors the *sky*. And uses *light itself!* He uses raindrops to splash tons of colors out of the sunlight! He's a crazy artist! And we get to watch!"

The heavens declare the glory of God, and now you do too. He's everywhere!

You know how saying the blessing at dinner can become this meaningless rote habit. ("forthisthybountyweareabouttoreceiveohlordwearegrateful" Gives me warm fuzzies, right?)

Anyway, I wanted to shake that up a little bit. So we used to play a game in which everyone had to taste the food first before we said the blessing. That way we could determine exactly *how* thankful we were! I mean, the food might *stink!* And we really wouldn't be that thankful after all. On the other hand, it might be pizza! And we would need to have a celebratory festival with burnt offerings! God is real! This is not a bunch of religious activities.

Your child shows you an art project—"Look at my picture, Daddy." I told one of mine, "Wow, that's beautiful, baby! I bet you feel so proud of your amazing work. It reminds me of how every time God would make something in the book of Genesis, he would stop and say, 'It was good.' When he said that, he was literally backing up and saying, 'I so killed this! The sun, the moon, the stars! This is good stuff! Dynamite!' He's an artist like you, kiddo, and now *you* know what it feels like to do good art just like him."

God masterminded this whole show, Space Rangers. Everything is the way it is because he made it that way. And he loves for us to celebrate his world and his heart for us in that world. How could we not want to tell our kids about it all the time?

Did you know that if you squeeze an egg in your palm with just your fingers (not your thumb) you will not be able to break it—something about the structure of the shell? I would often let the girls cook with me, and of course "who got to crack the eggs" was a highly coveted opportunity. One time, I challenged them to break an egg by squeezing it in their palm and fingers. Of course, they were unsuccessful. "See? God made eggshells to protect little chickens from goobers like you guys."

He's everywhere!

Here's my mike-drop story. (I only have one, so read it slowly.) In 1996, the Nintendo 64 was released. Of course, our kids wanted one for Christmas—but *every* kid wanted one for Christmas, so the stores were sold out. (When we read somewhere that even Steven Spielberg had been unable to find one for his kids, we gave up.) I promised them, however, that the day the stores restocked, I would get them one (and it wasn't just because I wanted to play *Goldeneye!*).

Anyway, a few weeks into January, I saw in the paper that Toys 'R' Us had gotten a new shipment of Nintendos. I corralled the kids from various activities around the house and yard, announcing that the day had come! Nintendo 64 had returned to the stores, and they should pile in the car to join me in retrieving the prize!

With much cheering and adulation, they jumped in my truck and off we went. We bought the Nintendo and tumbled back out of the store, the girls taking turns carrying the box and already talking smack about who was going to win at Mario Kart. Suddenly, I saw the big picture—and an opportunity to teach the kids something about what God is like. I had a beat-up old Bible in the back of my truck, and I told Callie, "Grab that Bible back there, honey, and turn to Matthew 7—verse nine or ten or something—and read it to us."

She began, "What man is there among you, if his son will ask him for bread, will give him a stone? Or also if you will ask for a fish, will he give him a snake? Therefore, if you, being evil fathers, know how to give good gifts to your children, how much more will your father who is in heaven give good gifts to those who ask him."[2]

I said to them, "You guys had forgotten about the Nintendo 64. You weren't even thinking about it today. But I made you a promise that I would get it for you. So even when *you* had forgotten that promise, *I* had not. I was thinking about what you long for, even when you were not. And I am just a knuckle-headed, old sinful screwed-up father. How much more will God, your heavenly father, never forget his promises to you? And he's got better stuff in store for you than a video game!"

Of course, sometimes this also backfired on me. One

of ours had lost a baby tooth and was looking forward to putting it under her pillow and receiving a visit from the tooth fairy.

(By the way, some parents get uptight about fostering beliefs in imaginary characters like Santa Claus or the Tooth Fairy. Don't get too squirrelly about this sort of thing—you are not teaching theology here. This sort of "playing" fits into the same category as your children having imaginary friends or playing make-believe. Kids create emotional categories through play. Then they outgrow them. That's all it is.)

Anyway, as bedtime drew near, she suddenly realized that she had misplaced the tooth. She panicked, devastated that she would not receive her money under the pillow. I wondered if this couldn't be an oblique opportunity to teach grace. I told her, "Perhaps if we write the Tooth Fairy a letter, explaining that you screwed up, she would be willing to give you a dollar anyway."

We had a sweet time together writing a note, explaining Katherine's mistake, and placed it under her pillow instead of the tooth. A dollar was discovered the next morning, and there was much jubilation.

However, the next evening, Katherine joyfully reappeared in our room holding the missing tooth victoriously aloft. "I found it! Now I can put it under my pillow and get *another* dollar!" she exclaimed. That's right, gang—she was going to pull some kind of Ponzi scam on the tooth fairy, milking her for more dough! That night the lesson had more to do with justice, and less about grace.

Basic principle: everything is the way it is because God created it that way. Just show that to your kids. That's the best content.

Experience

Unfortunately (yet again), the most powerful way that we teach our kids about what God is like is through how we *treat* them. Have you ever wondered about that phenomenon in which you can *know* something about God, but *feel* something completely different? "I *know* that God forgives me, but I don't *feel* forgiven." "I know God is in control, but I still feel anxious."

Here's the reason that happens. We learn the things that we know in our *brain* through content—reading, teaching, listening. But we get that *sense* of what God is like, that *feeling*—from relationships—from how we are treated.

Think about it. Don't you encounter those individuals who were raised in a "Christian home" but then later blow off their family's faith? What is it that you hear them say? "All those Christians—they're just hypocrites. It's just all a bunch of rules and judgment!" Now, where do you think they learned that? So often, these people were raised in homes where there was a lot of "God talk" but what they *experienced* in their relationships was not the character of God.

I always ask that person who says they don't "feel forgiven" whether they have ever really screwed up but had someone look them in the eye and pull them close and say, "Welcome to the club, Ringo. I screw up all the time. And I *so* forgive you!" They always roll their eyes and say, "No way, man! When we messed up our dad became Mussolini, and we learned our lesson quick!"

No wonder they don't feel forgiven. They've never experienced it from a human.

The deepest way in which we teach our children who God is, is by how we *live like him* in their lives.

Now, don't panic yet. This is not as hard as it may sound. For instance, when you are cuddling that little one before bedtime, you may not know it, but you are teaching them about God—his love; his presence. God even uses that mother-child connection as a reference point—"... a mother may forget her nursing child, ... but I will not forget you."[3]

That eight-year-old runs to see you when you come home from work. Your eyes look delighted to see him and you tousle his hair and pick him up, pulling him to you. You don't know it, but you're building a gut core sense in him for how God welcomes us every time we run to him You are doing this *experientially*. That's where we get our gut.

When you manage your anger and shaminess during discipline, you're not just parenting well, you are literally showing them how God disciplines us. I mean, God never says, "I'm so disappointed in you."

The same principle works for teaching about God's justice and righteousness. One of the reasons that I never refer to "punishment "in this book is because for the Christian, punishment is irrelevant. Christ took our punishment—the just retaliation due us because of God's righteousness.

However, God continues to love what is right, and he disciplines those he loves—not in anger, but in a careful crafting of our hearts to become more and more like his. So when you use Teaching Discipline like we've talked about in Chapter Three—with a powerful loving heart that brings consequences without a threat to your relationship—you are mirroring how God approaches us in his righteous teaching.

Though I can barely remember a time in my life in which I didn't welcome and value God's merciful forgiveness, I must confess that I used to wonder why it was necessary for Jesus to die. Why not just forgive? Why all that justice? Then one day, something happened with my kids that made the light bulb come on for me.

I was minding my own business in the den one day as Katherine and Callie were playing on the floor. Suddenly, as I looked up, Katherine just reared back and slapped Callie in the face. I saw it happen! Callie began crying, and I said to Katherine, "Oh my Gosh! You just hammered your sister! I want you in timeout now!"

Katherine immediately softened and looked at me and asked, "But Daddy, can't you just forgive me?"

I paused. Perhaps this could be an opportunity to teach grace. After all, I do this to God all the time. I run around sinning, and then touch back in, "Will you forgive me, Lord? (Again?) That's our deal, right? I like sinning. You like forgiving. It's a great setup." But then I looked at Callie's face as she saw me considering this question. Her eyes and mouth were open and pleading, with a look of betrayal and disbelief flooding over her. As if to say, "She just hit me, and you are just going to let that *not matter?*"

Think about it. What would it have said about the dignity of Callie and her injury were I to have just let Katherine "off the hook"? Callie would matter so little that someone could assault her, and there would be no consequence whatsoever? Everything *just* in the world would feel violated. Now, imagine what sort of payment it would require for an offense to God, (a slap in his face) to be justified. It would take the horrifying death of the very son of God himself.

We teach about God's justice and righteousness as we hold our kids accountable for their choices, but in a loving, non-angry manner. When I *did* send Katherine to timeout without anger (well maybe just a little anger), I was teaching her about loving justice that brings consequences to our hurtfulness. And I was teaching Callie about God's advocacy on her behalf. He defends the weak and inclines his ear to the oppressed. We get to *show* these things to our children.

God rarely speaks directly to humans. Even in the Bible, a burning bush sighting is rare. For some reason, God likes to use *mediators*—people who speak on his behalf. He doesn't go to Pharaoh; he sends Moses. He doesn't confront his people; he sends the prophets. And likewise, he won't appear to our kids—he sends us! I had a parent tell me once, "I just want my child to feel like they can just crawl up in Jesus's lap." I said, "Cool, then let them start in *yours*! Show them what a loving 'lap' feels like."

Maybe you're like Moses and feel like you are not equipped

to speak for God. Maybe you feel more like Balaam's Ass! That hasn't stopped God before. We really are "Ambassadors of Christ." Bring him to your kids! I mean, "loaves and fishes" were "good enough" for Jesus to use. So are you.

Let's stay free

Now, again, this role of representing God to our kids makes me feel overwhelmed yet again. Who can carry this kind of burden? My children are going to get their "heart index" for God's character from hanging out with me? Check, please!

But don't let this bum you out quite yet. Yes, option one, we need to make our *walk match our talk.* Have your spouse and your friends hold you accountable to be a more life-giving parent. Heck, you're reading a parenting book right now! Yay, you! You're working to be a better parent!

Nevertheless, we will all fail. So, blessedly, there is option number two: As we have been saying all along, the only thing better than a perfect parent is a humble, good enough parent. So, if you can't make your walk match your talk, then let your *talk match your walk!* In other words, quit talking like you've got it together, since you *don't.* "Hey kid, I need grace as much as you! *I* ought to go to time out!" (I hope this stuff is starting to sound familiar by now.)

Remember, we teach grace by *needing* grace! The most beautiful way to show God to our kids is through our own repentant heart. Then, when someone teaches them content about God and his mercy later on, they have a reference point. "Hey, that's how Mom used to ask for our forgiveness when she would screw up." That is living free, and that is Christian parenting—the Gospel at home.

As we said, we've been teaching our kids about God all along as we've been engaging them with love and truth and forgiveness. But enjoy the opportunity to teach them directly about their Creator and Savior. We can speak content to them about him through his stories and our prayers. And we give the greatest spiritual education to our children as we live both reflecting his character, and showing our kids our own need for his mercy and grace.

Q&A Time

Hey Doc—Our teenage son says he doesn't believe in God anymore. We tried to raise all of our kids to be believers, but now our son seems to be losing his faith. What can we do?

I've talked to so many parents who have faced this same heartbreak. It is so frightening and so helpless. I am glad you are bringing it as a question. In so many ways, we are powerless to change someone's heart, but let's at least think about a couple of principles we can bring to this vulnerable situation.

First, remember, he is a teenager. As we have said over and over, this is the age at which kids often question everything! Especially things that are near and dear to their parents.

However, take heart. I've seen so many of these kids grow up and come back, hat in hand to their families and their faith, saying things like, "Thank y'all for putting up with me back then. I was just mad at everybody, including God." So like everything a teen does, manage your fear and remain strong and loving.

Secondly, after hearing your question, I wonder if your son is angry? What often lies behind a blatant rejection of one's parent's beliefs is a real anger at *them*, not God. Get someone to help you do a little digging for any unresolved issues (especially involving authority) that might be clogging the pipes of your relationship with your son.

Related to that, you can still be teaching and giving God to your wayward teen, even as he rejects the notion of God. We've been teaching our kids about God all along through how we relate to them, remember? Well, we can still use those loving, powerful ways of *relating* as a way to bring God's heart to our kids, regardless of how open they seem. For example, I recommend that you live with him and be with him in the most respectful *"talk with"* manner possible. I would want to prop my feet up and talk *with* him about his thoughts. If he says, "I mean, the Bible is just a bunch of stories that a bunch of guys wrote. And there are a ton of contradictions." Don't start doing apologetics! Talk *with* him. "Yeah, it *is* an incredibly challenging book, man. And so much of it is so confusing. I have so many questions myself! Wanna hear them? By the way, what got you thinking about all of this?"

For some reason I don't understand, Christ was impossibly attractive to the people who usually run from religion. To the degree that we continue to relate with his kind of patience and courage, we are secretly wooing our child back to the warmth of God's love.

(See Bonus Appendix for more!)

---

[1] *Deuteronomy 6:7, New American Standard Version.*

[2] *Matthew 7:9-11, New King James Version.*

[3] *Isaiah 49:15, author's paraphrase.*

We shall not cease from exploration, and the end of all our exploring will be to arrive where we started and know the place for the first time.

— **T. S. Eliot**

Chapter Eight

Living Free

Norma was out of town a few years back, and so for about a week it was just me and the girls. One morning as I pulled up to school to drop them off, I noticed that Callie had a big bubble gum "beard" on her face. You know, one of those situations wherein you blow a big bubble, it pops, and you have gum stuck all around your mouth? After a while, the gum gets dark from dirt, and presto, a bubblegum beard! Anyway, I stopped Callie on her way out of the car and said, "Wait, honey, you have dirty bubble gum all over your face. Let me get it off." She paused briefly but then exited the car, stating, "That's okay. Nobody has said anything about it so far this week."

I'm thinking this story will come as no surprise to you. By this point you have read my book and understand the caliber of my parenting. Presumably, like you, I had to have an escape plan from the "Perfect Parent Prison"—or else. Fortunately, as a young parent and a grad student, I discovered D. W. Winnicott and his notion of good enough parenting. Somehow, in a manner reminiscent of how God relates to us, he announced that the failures and missteps that we will inevitably commit in our parenting would not destroy our relationship with our children. That somehow love survives all of our failings. Winnicott discovered this through his love for his patients and their children. We discover it through the love of our Savior. There is grace to the humble, and those who have been forgiven much, love the best. Here, I believe, God incarnates his Gospel directly into our families. And we get to receive this gift of freedom.

When I was in the middle of the parenting years, I think I had this sort of underlying resentment for my friends who didn't have kids, or were empty nesters. I would be bleary-eyed from lack of sleep (why is it that kids only get stomach viruses in the middle of the night?). Then I would interact with my childless friends. "Oh my Gosh, I'm so tired," they would moan. "We were up 'til like, one o'clock last night at that Nickel Creek concert. And then that jazz brunch was at eight-thirty! I'm so sleep deprived!"

Now, we got rules about talkin' like that. I wanted to say, "I feel your pain! I was up until one in the morning as well—at the pharmacy, buying suppositories, in my pajamas!"

But though they get lots of sleep and Bellinis with brunch, individuals who do not live life with children miss a precious gift. A gift for which I hope you will all live grateful: The gift of being humbled by your failure. The gift of learning the insufficiency of your heart and mind to love well and to be always wise and giving. The gift of seeing your brokenness. Jesus comes to us and says that those who realize that they are thusly so "poor in spirit," live in a place that allows him to give them everything—even the Kingdom of God. Why? Because they know that they are not rich. They know that they need help. They are the humble. And to those people, he inclines his ear. And one of the richest couriers of this gift—the bringers of our constant humility—are our children. Full of need and ingratitude and anger and stupidity. And love and tenderness and wonder and the brightest simplicity.

This has been a book to set you free. I have wanted to teach you how to parent well. But I've also wanted to show you how your own limitations and brokenness can actually be gifts to you and your children. I have wanted to help you see that through God's grace, our screw ups with our kids aren't something to be afraid of. In fact, they can actually be part of what draws us together.

There is one more gift I would like to give you before we close. I've left it tucked under the tree until the end of Christmas. Here it is.

Let me remind you what I do all day at work. What I do is therapy with *adults*. Adults who are in situations in which life is requiring something of them that they cannot do. And that produces symptoms—depression, anxiety, marriage problems, addiction, etc. And here's our final Secret of the Universe. The struggling people I see in my office are not symptomatic because they are lazy or stupid or have a disease or a chemical imbalance. They're struggling with OCD, depression, or panic attacks because *life is requiring something from them that they cannot do.* They never developed the ability. No one ever taught them—or maybe they were wounded there.

So they get married. Can they be connected and understand intimacy and love? Did they learn the ability to be emotionally close? Or, after the honeymoon, is it sort of "me and my best friend the remote control"? Were they taught about mattering and connection?

Or they walk out into the freedom of adult life—can they make wise choices, or do they reach for destructive things? Can they say "No" to their own impulses? Can they manage difficult people in their lives? Were they taught to stand up to the contractor, or their boss, or their jerky spouse?

Can they apprehend what it means to be forgiven? Can they be humble? Were they taught to deal with failure and keep their poise, or are they judgmental and guilt ridden?

Over and over again the answer is "No."

God created us to need a whole software package of emotional, relational, and functional abilities in order to do life and to serve him. Things like the abilities to understand love or to be strong or to forgive or to manage my emotional world. And our lives will work well to the degree that we *have* these abilities. And we will struggle or develop symptoms to the degree that we are *lacking* or *injured* in one or more of these abilities. People don't get depressed because they "have depression." They get depressed because they are lacking some of these abilities or have injuries there. Help them restore the abilities, and the depression lifts.

So, now it's time to open your present. All these things we've been talking about teaching our children throughout this book are not just about parenting them well *today*. We have secretly been filling their inventory with the heart abilities that they will need in order to do *life*. We have been tucking their hearts with the software that adults need to thrive!

The goal of parenting is not to make our kids behave like good little soldiers. The goal is to prepare them to be whole, loving *adults*, in God's image. And as you have been learning and practicing the parenting principles we've discussed in this book, you've been doing more than just making bath time more manageable. *You've also been giving your kids the tools they need to live well as adults.*

Remember your child's first spend-the-night party? How you helped them pack all that they would need in their *Jurassic Park* backpack—just in case? Well, we've been learning about how to pack their hearts with the things that they will need for adulthood. And the best news is that once they get these things in their hearts, they cannot lose them, any more than you can un-learn how to read once you've been taught! These gifts become part of their character, and they will carry them always, even into eternity.

So now, when they develop an adult relationship (romantic or otherwise) and they realize that relationships only feel rich to the degree that we can open our hearts and be intimate and connected, they will think back to what you taught them from Chapter Two about *love and mattering*. They'll remember how it's safe and welcoming *to be them*. And they will reach in their toolbox and pull that out—and thrive.

And when they are tempted with all sorts of things in life that are pleasurable but destructive, they will reach inside and find the ability to say "No" to themselves, because you lovingly taught them from Chapter Three (and Three-and-Three-Quarters) about how to "hear no" and choose wisely.

And when their boss talks down to them at their job one day, it will feel wrong and it will hurt—and they will know that the right thing to do will be to respectfully push back on him. And they will reach inside to find that *strength and identity* that you taught them in Chapter Four—and they will pull them out and powerfully set limits.

And when they suffer, because they certainly will, their hearts will find refuge in that template you gave them for what it's like to hurt together. And they will reach for the *love and strength* we gave them. And they will have that blessed, rare ability to grieve.

And when someone talks about God's love, it will not feel to them like a doctrine or a creed. They will close their eyes and feel in their hearts the righteousness and the mercy and the long-suffering that they directly experienced in their years with you. And they will worship.

And last, but by far not least, when they screw it all up—and when they remember *your* screw-ups—perhaps they will smile and think of the tender, messed up group of broken humble people that your family was. And feel freedom and grace.

One downside to being a speaker or a writer is that you

begin your endeavor knowing that no matter how much you bring to your audience, you will still leave them with a hundred unanswered questions. I know that that will be the case with this book. As C. S. Lewis said in *The Problem of Pain*, "I am to give my readers not the best absolutely, but the best I have." I hope that I have done so.

However, as I have said, I have not intended this book to be a comprehensive parenting "manual." What I've wanted to do is to share with you what I've learned from working with parents and kids for way too many years—and create for you an atmosphere, a culture. I've wanted you to get a vibe for what it sounds like and feels like to parent out of your freedom. I encourage you not to look for a manual on child-rearing. Your kids need *You*! They need the ebb and flow of a relationship in which you are all learning together and failing together. Where your life together is good enough.

So, use the guidance I've offered you for teaching forgiveness, love, wisdom, resilience, the poise to walk into pain, and of course the gift of knowing and loving God and his way—but then throw the book away and *live it* with your kids. Even if you live it poorly! My hope and my prayer is that this heart I have wanted to help create for you will make your home a place that is blessed—and your children's lives rich. Live life with your children. Be people—and help them be people too. And thanks to our Savior, we are seen as better than good enough. We are his—immaculate and glorious and redeemed.

JLC

We are ghosts or we are ancestors in our children's lives. We either lay our mistakes and our burdens upon them— or we assist them in laying those old burdens down—and we free them from the chains of our own flawed behavior, and as ancestors, walk along beside them, and assist them in finding their own way—and some transcendence.

— **Bruce Springsteen**

THE END

Johncoxpsychology.com

Chapter Nine

Q&A Bonus Round

As I said earlier, some of my favorite interactions during a conference are the Q&A times. So I thought I would throw in a few more as a going away present.

Hey Doc—What are your thoughts on screen time—smartphones, television, etc?

I'm usually shaking my head and saying, *"Tsk Tsk"* with the rest of them as we bemoan how "addicted we all are to our phones." But then I need to check the status of my plane flight, or the weather in my child's current city, or take a photograph of something my grandson is doing—and I reach for this overwhelmingly helpful and convenient device. But just like the ocean—technology is beautiful, wonderful, and can cause you a world of hurt. So just like we don't throw our kids in the ocean and walk away, we need to be careful about their exposure to the Screens. Here are some thoughts for consideration.

When it comes to Littles, (ages newborn to four), minimize TV and pads as much as possible. For them, treat screens like you do candy. Every now and then you might give your little one some candy, but it's a rare occasion. And it's certainly not the foundation of their diet. By the time they are two years old, you can play some games together or watch a little *Baby Shark*—but avoid using the screen as a pacifier as much as possible. I love how Tina Fey calls TV, "The Neuralizer"!

My primary rationale for this with younger children has to do with brain development. The nature of most programming is a "flash-flash-flash" constant barrage of images. Turn on your TV right now and tell me I'm wrong. Rarely does five seconds go by that screen does not shift to a different image. I believe that this literally *trains* children's brains to be inattentive—and I think has some correlation with the rampant diagnosis of ADHD in our culture. I believe that screen time is a nasty impediment to our children's early brain development.

The second reason for minimizing screens for Littles (or for anyone for that matter) is relational. Your little one is developing their earliest templates for emotional connection. Let's help them bond with you, not Grumpy Cat.

As kids get older, watching a movie together or playing games on "the Pad" is lots of fun. I believe that both should be limited, however, especially during the school week. And until they are preteen, avoid getting them a phone.

By teenage years, welcome to the jungle. Continue to limit screen time entertainment as you see necessary for the sake of the child's school functioning and relational abilities. A junior high child can have a phone, but not a smart phone. Content should be supervised, filters installed, and feel free to check their texts. Even if you trust your child, don't trust the people who text them!

If you really want to dig into this topic read *iGen*, a book by Dr. Jean Twenge at UC San Diego. She's done admirable work researching all of the dynamics of screen time, smart phones, and their effect on the American Teenager.

Here's some of her data in a nutshell. The iPhone came out in 2007. In 2012, teenage ownership of smart phones passed the fifty-percent mark. *Correspondingly, between the years of 2010 and 2018, the number of adolescents who experienced at least one major depressive episode increased by sixty-percent in eight years.* (In 2010, six percent of teenagers struggled with significant depression. By 2018, that number was up to thirteen percent). Suicide deaths are also up sharply, currently at a forty-year high. (And that following a steady decline through the 1990s and 2000s.)

In Twenge's research, she found that these deficits in mental health were directly correlated to frequency of smart phone use. She found that kids who spent more than three hours a day on their smart phone (especially on social media) were thirty-four percent more likely to report increased feelings of hopelessness, depression, unhappiness, and even suicidal ideation—compared with kids who more rarely used their phones. Depression was forty-eight percent more likely with kids who were on screens for five or more hours a day.

And all of this has occurred across the board since 2012—the exact moment when the proportion of teens who owned smart phones surpassed the fifty-percent mark! And the increase in mental disturbance has increased at the same proportion as cell phone use (the graphs of each paralleling each other) ever since.

When she used research to rule out "correlation" or other stress factors (like rising student workloads or the stressful social/political climate) she found that those factors did not line up directly with the rise in teen suicide and depression. Teenage smart phone use did.

So why? Why are phones doing this? Well, number one, there's a sense in which we are making this way too complicated. If you do *anything* for more than three hours a day, it's bad for you! Working out, cleaning your house, eating chocolate chip cookies. Bad. For. You.

Secondly, the *relational dynamics* are huge. Though we are the most "connected" generation ever, it can come at the price of disconnection from other people relationally. Now kids sit together at lunch and text instead of interacting. (Don't we all?) This literal assault on human relational connection is enough to explain the depression data in my opinion.

Thirdly, thanks to social media, screens have become what I call "rejection machines." Teenagers already live defined by the acceptance of their peers. When I was a kid, that meant that for about forty-five minutes during lunch period, you knew whether you were cool or not. Now it's a 24/7 running "crawl line" of whether they are "In" or "Out." How many "Likes" did you get? FOMO! One of my teenage clients told me, "If you don't hear anything back within fifteen minutes, it means that you're rejected."

Another one of my teen clients was not invited to the beach with her friends. She then sobbed as she saw Instagram posts of the three of them without her. "OMG! We wrecked the golf cart! Can't have more fun than with friends!" And that's just hurt feelings. There's also the issue of online bullying. We could go on.

So what are we supposed to do with this? Screens are here to stay, and since schools have integrated the whole shebang into a child's schoolwork, it's impossible to just take them away.

Answer? As of this writing, we aren't sure. This question has never been asked before. No one on planet Earth has ever had this problem until now, so we're still trying to figure this problem out. Until then, let's retreat to our safe zone of "Protect and Prepare." In other words, let's walk that same balance we do with all teenage issues—doing all we can to protect them from the toxins out there, while being careful to not suffocate them with over-protective control.

So on the one hand, feel no compunction against setting some limits on your teenager's phone access. (And yes, this will start a war, but you just read a good book on parenting, so you will know how to deal with that.) Stand your ground!

On the other hand, the studies indicate that the risk of emotional disruption begins to increase after *two hours* of smart phone goof off time. Suggesting that moderation, not necessarily complete elimination of electronics, is a valid answer. In other words, under two hours of recreational phone-time shows few ill results.

I love this: In 2010, Steve Jobs was interviewed by *The New York Times* on the occasion of the introduction of the iPad. At one point, the interviewer asked Jobs if his kids liked the new iPad. "They haven't used it," Jobs replied. "We limit how much technology our kids use at home." Thanks Steve.

Like Mr. Jobs, we need to help structure our children's use of screens. A basic principle of human growth: if I can't limit my own behavior, I need someone outside of me to do it for me. Your kids need you to limit their screen time. Most of them can't do it on their own.

Some possible examples: No screens at the dinner table. No screens while doing homework. (Despite what your teenager says, the human brain is not good at multitasking.) No phone in their bedroom during sleeping hours. And keep up with their texts and content.

Kids may be more amenable to this than we think. Twenge describes some older kids who have started embracing what they call a "tech-light" lifestyle. When they all get together for lunch, screens go face-down in the middle of the table. Whoever picks up their phone first, pays the bill.

One of my adult clients told me her young son had approached her around the holidays. "I don't think I want an iPhone for Christmas after all, Mom. I've seen what it does to my brother. It scares me."

Stand for the Benediction.

(Again, read Twenge's book for more.)

Our kids won't stay in their beds at night. You've told us you were a total loser at this, John, but have you learned anything since?

Ah, you are generous! Here are a couple of thoughts. (At least future parents might get a good night's sleep.) One point is to reread the chapter on how to help your child manage their feelings and learn to be strong. Being able to stay in bed and put oneself to sleep is a skill, and requires your child to have some strength and autonomy. Your child's tacit message if they keep coming out of their room is, "I am weak and need you and other things in order to be okay." Now, that's not true. Requiring them to manage their feelings (with empathy thrown in) helps them develop the power and autonomy to sleep alone.

What about when you feel them standing next to your bed in the middle of the night (like those scary little girls in *The Shining*)? Say, "Hey man, remember, you are going to need to stay in your room tonight like we said. Let's go back." He will issue various protests at this point. Sweetly ignore them. When he comes out again, put an expressionless look on your face. Don't look him in the eye. And walk him back to his bed like a robot. Then close the door. When he comes back out, repeat the "Robot Responder" act. A lot of what he's getting by coming out is interaction with you. Maintaining a disconnected robot demeanor deprives him of that. You'll have to do this consistently. And yes, you'll have a few sleepless nights, but all things being equal this tends to teach kids to stay in their rooms.

I've seen other parents set up cool little token systems where kids pick treats and rewards for remaining in their beds. Lots of times that works. If not, go back to the "Robot Plan" above. Hope you have better luck than me!!

Any pointers for how divorced parents can best care for their kids?

Heartbreakingly, some families break apart. This is some of that "pain" that we said your children would endure in life. But as we said, pain itself will not harm children, though unresolved pain will. Wise parents, whether they are divorced or not, think about how best to continue to care for their kids, despite trouble in their marriage. This question deserves a book of its own, and such books have been written, but here are a few thoughts.

The best situations I've seen have been broken families in which the divorced parents are still willing to work together to think about how to best care for their children. After a divorce, there is no greater gift you can give your child than making a distinction between the ill feelings that you may have for your Ex, and your commitment to your child. I often look at divorced couples (Yes, the smart ones will still meet together with me regarding how to help their kids), and say, "I want you guys to essentially look at one another and say,

'Okay, I don't like you and you don't like me, but can we put that aside in order to love our kids well?'" To put it crassly, I'm essentially saying, "What is more important to you? Your dislike of one another, or your love for your kids?" To the degree that you can prioritize your kids and not your conflict, they will prosper.

Secondly, support and embrace your child's love for your Ex. A child's greatest fear after divorce is the feeling that they now no longer really have a family. (This can be exacerbated when spouses remarry.) Maintaining a welcoming heart that says your child can not only love you, but can love the other parent, helps maintain a sense of belonging for the child. They still belong to the two of you, regardless.

Thirdly, beware of "triangulation." One of the nastiest toxins you can throw into the life of a child from a divorce is for one parent to trash the other parent in front of the child. "I want to take you to the ballgame, but your mother won't let me." (That guy just created a "triangle," get it?)

If your child tells you that your Ex has said this kind of garbage, don't immediately respond to your child with a disagreement. "I did not! I just told him that I needed you home to do your homework!" That creates a situation in which the child is caught in the middle—they're hearing X from Mom, and Y and Dad. That's enough to make anyone pull their hair out.

Instead, enter into what this experience would be like for the *child*. Talk about what it was like for *them* to hear their father say that. "Well, that must've made you feel terrible!

You're out playing with your dad and he says all sorts of yucky stuff about me. What was that like? You have any questions for me?" Now the child has someone who is an advocate and an ally, rather than being a ping-pong ball tossed between two competitors.

Now, avoiding triangulation does not mean that you cannot engage with your child if your Ex has done something hurtful to them. It is legitimate to acknowledge with your child, "Yeah, that was a hurtful thing for your mother to say to you. Sometimes her anger can be yucky, huh? Wanna talk about it?" This is simply acknowledging the *truth* with your child. To do otherwise would be a bit crazy-making.

One way to determine whether you are acknowledging the truth or triangulating is to put a finger on your pulse and ask, "Am I working here to care for my child in the reality of this painful situation, or am I trying to 'win' them over against my Ex?"

Divorced families can still be "good enough," but you have to take seriously the added difficulty for your child, and make that difficulty part of your relationship with them. If your Ex doesn't want to play, then just commit yourself to relating to them and your child in the most loving, powerful way possible. This may mean strong limits and truth-telling to your Ex, and healing work with your child's pain. Don't despair—your child just having *one* sane person in their lives is more powerful than you realize.

Related to that last question. Any thoughts for single parents?

By now, we are all in agreement that parenting is demanding and difficult. But with two parents, you at least get to "split the check" when it come to the cost of attending to the constant childhood needs. Single parents have the same demands, but half the resources. In other words, they can't parent "man to man," they have to play "zone." Let's try to at least throw some pointers your way to make sense of dealing with the demands on a single parent.

Number one, feel very comfortable about pushing your kids to pull their own weight around the house. As a single parent, you can't afford to parent from that child-centered orientation that we've alluded to. Child-centered parenting says we need to work to meet a child's every need, never require chores, and basically live to be our child's servant. If a single parent lives that way they will burn out faster than a bottle rocket. Single parent are forced to require more of their kids—forced to push them to contribute. And good news for you, this is what your kids should be doing anyway. Get them to help. Make a list of "chores" and let the kids take turns picking their jobs for the week. Get them to help vacuum, clean, help you with the laundry. This is that preparation for adulthood that we have talked about, and it helps you out at the same time. A single parent needs to keep a tighter rein on maintaining structure and family roles around the house.

Secondly, don't worry about your kids getting "short

changed" by not having their other parent around. Certainly, there is a loss if the other parent is absent, but you can still significantly give them what they need. Another Secret of the Universe: technically kids don't actually need a "mother" or a "father". What they need is "Mothering" and "Fathering." A mother can teach the nurture and tenderness that "mothering" gives, but she can also teach the empowering and structure that a good dad provides. I've seen so many kids get both dynamics from one parent. When kids live in a loving home, they are incredibly malleable and will adapt to dad's "mothering," taking it in as the same tenderness than an actual mother would provide.

Thirdly, use your community. I've worked with so many single parents who make beautiful use of other family members or community friends who can swing into the lives of their kids, offering more of that "Mothering" or "Fathering" that their kids need. The notion of a "village" is a great asset to a single parent. Keep involved in your church or school or even extended family, and look for people who can give richly to your kids. They can be hard to find but persevere.

Finally, remember—good enough. Whether you are a single parent or not, you will let your kids down. The freedom I have wanted to offer is the good news that limitations, losses, and failures will not harm your kids as long as you are living those losses at their side.

We have a teen who argues and rages at us. What do we do?

Wow, teens are complicated! Trying to understand their brain is like burying your face in a box of Leggos! So much chaos is going on. And during this season, we parents have to make significant shifts in our parenting style as well. As mentioned in Chapter Two, we move from relating to them in *one way* (parent/child) to relating to them in *two ways*! (parent/child *and* person/person.) In other words, we are still *parenting*, but we are also folding in the element of relating to them like a *person* at the same time!

A second complication: they are *separating* from us, and therefore are more insistent on their own ideas, freedom, and opinions. The very thought of agreeing with us or being like us in any way makes them a powder keg on roller skates. Let's use the theme of Love and Limits to talk about some ways we can respond to that aggravated, rampaging teenager.

First, Limits for that raging teen. We don't make deals with terrorists, so regardless of the tantrum (and that is what it is), we are still going to stand by our limits. More on that in a moment.

But let's look at the Love side for a moment. Teenage Secret of the Cosmos: A major cause of teen tantrums is simply because they don't feel *heard*. It is vital for teen parenting that we at least let their ideas and opinions matter—be heard in some way. Even if we don't change our minds.

Let me put it this way. If a teen does not feel like you are hearing them, they'll be a jerk. If a teen does not feel like you are letting them matter in any way, they'll be a jerk. If a teen feels like you are just making rules with no room for flexibility, they'll be a jerk. Being heard and mattering is oxygen for a teen.

What teenagers tend to do if they don't feel heard is just crank the knob a little louder and try it again. And most of them get louder with *actions* as well as words, and since there are no rules in a knife fight, beware! So, even if you aren't going to give in and do what they say, at least remember the "talk with" part of parenting. Hear them. If we don't, it will feel the same way to them that it would feel to us if our spouse didn't listen to us! It would make us angry, belligerent, and say things we don't mean—just like them. So hear them first.

Now, back to Limits, we are also going to "Work With," not just Talk With. I see a lot of ornery teenagers who are angry because their parents basically continue to parent them in the same way they did when they were five-years-old. "That's what we say, and that's final!" You do that with a teen, and they will go "Compliant/Rebel/Sneak" jet plane quick. So, another way that we are going to hedge our bets against that teenager raging and arguing is to work *with them* regarding limits and discipline.

They want a midnight curfew, I'm not just going to say, "Your curfew is eleven o'clock, and I don't want to hear another word about it." We need to "work with" them. Say, "Are you embarrassed because all of your friends are getting to stay out later? I remember that. It's a terrible feeling. Tell you what. I'll work with you. As it stands, you are not even coming in on your current curfew. How 'bout you give me three weeks of coming in on time, and I will give you thirty more minutes, bumping you up to eleven-thirty? Then, you come in for a month at eleven-thirty sharp, and I'll boost you up to midnight. You scratch my back, I'll scratch yours."

You are letting them matter here. But you're also maintaining your authority. And better yet, you are beginning to relate to them more like the world relates to adults. Adults kindly negotiate and compromise. Our goal with teenagers is to send them off prepared to live in the adult world, remember. Stomping your foot and requiring obedience will never do that; it will just encourage conflict.

Related to this, I also recommend that with a teen, you *ask* them for what you want rather than *tell* them. At least at first. Remember how we are folding in that "person to person" dynamic into our relationship with our teenager? Well instead of just staying in that "parent" position and *telling* them to "go get the groceries," I like to *ask* them. Like you would a fellow adult. "Hey Stretch, would you be willing to help me get the groceries out of the car?" I find that if parents lay down their weapons first, most kids will respond in kind. (If your teen chronically refuses to help, no problem. We can always bring the consequences and limits a la Chapter Three. I just don't want to start there with a teen.)

Finally, even if you do everything right with a teenager, they are still going to be jerks at times. So we need to address the rage when it does happen—or more precisely, after it happens. Time for more Limits!

If they start raging and slamming doors—Step One—*do nothing*! Let them call you names and throw their phone. Don't do anything. Just wait. Nothing good is going to happen if you react too, so be cool. Otherwise everybody's acting like flying monkeys.

Don't react. But don't *forget* their behavior either! The next time you see them, when things are settled down, it's time to strike. Say, "I understand that you were really ticked last night, but it is not okay to talk to your mother and me like that. Here's the deal. You're welcome to talk to us about how unhappy you are or how unfair we feel, but if you are going to rage at us and call us names, your lifestyle is going to become very affected. So right now, I want your phone. After that, we'll graduate to your car. We're not going to fuss and fume. Just know that the cost for treating us that way might be extremely high to you. As always, you're free to discuss any of these problems with us when we are not having conflict."

If they refuse to give you the phone, be cool. Take their keys. You *own* all that they possess! No need for violence and stress.

By the way, there is one thing about parenting teenagers that gets easier. Once they have a phone and a car, it's like having a ring through their nose! You have a very powerful cattle prod that significantly gets their attention. But you have to use it! I see a ton of parents complaining about what a jerk their teenager is. All the while, their teen is driving a car that is nicer than mine! That makes *me* want to act like a jerk!

Regarding arguing. Teens love to argue! They've developed abstract reasoning and so they like using it! It's sort of like how once a toddler starts to toddle, what do they do? They toddle! Everywhere! It's their new thing! Well, a teenager's new thing is abstract reasoning, so given any opportunity, they'll argue. One of mine had an extensive impassioned interaction with me one night about how paintings were the only form of legitimate art. Not literature, not music, only paintings. Ya gotta love 'em!

Anyway, if given the opportunity to argue, they will. But it takes two to play. I would say to mine, "I don't think I am going to argue with you about this anymore." They, of course, would continue argumentatively citing all of the reasons that I should argue with them. It's like a Monty Python sketch. My response? Silence. It takes two to play. If they continue long enough, I would add, "You seem committed to creating an argument. I think if you don't contain that and stop, I'm going to take your phone." (An event.)

I also like anticipating and preventing the blooming of an argument. You tell them they can't go to that party this weekend. Their response of course is, "OMG, Why?" I would say, "Are you asking 'why' because you are wanting information, or because you want to start an argument? Because I will do the former, but not the latter. And I will know your answer by how you respond to what I say. If you're really wanting information, then after I tell you my reason, you will say, 'Thank you, Father. That is helpful. Now I understand your reasons'."

You can guess the rest.

We have one child who loves to tattle. Whenever her brothers do something wrong, she is quick to run to us with stories of the crime. Any thoughts?

Tattling is a fascinating little phenomenon. Of course, part of the question involves how to respond to her tattling testimony. But a more important problem involves asking how we should respond to *this role that she has claimed in the family.* The tattler establishes themselves as the "good child" in the family—and those guys upstairs are the "bad" ones. Essentially, the tattler is no longer functioning as just another one of the kids in the family, now they are taking on a role of authority—right alongside her parents. And that, we cannot abide.

Whether or not her brothers are building fires in the basement or not, we need to excuse her from this position. She needs to go back to being just one of the kids and let you be the parents. When one of ours became a chronic tattler, we ultimately told her, "From now on, any crimes you report will not be dealt with or disciplined in any way. Your sisters will get a "get out of jail free" card. In fact, if you continue this role, *you're* going to lose TV for the rest of the day for tattling." In other words, tattling is simply a "goody-goody" version of an inappropriate, out of control behavior, and needs to be stopped in the same manner.

I can't take my child to the grocery without them begging for treats the entire time. Usually it ends in a tantrum. Any thoughts regarding grocery store madness.

Here's one of my tricks for grocery store survival. I always told mine that they could get *one* thing at the grocery store. So they would see some cookies and ask, "Can I get these cookies, Daddy?"

My response? "Of course you can!"

Later, they would see the Popsicles and say, "Can I get Popsicles, Daddy?" My response again was, "Of course you can! But you they you will need to put the cookies back. You get to choose." Teaching Discipline is always working to get us out of the direct conflict with the child, and instead let them engage their own choices.

On one such trip to the store, I was working through this exact interaction with one of my kids. Suddenly, this strange lady passed us with her cart.

She interrupted our interaction and said, "Aw, come on, Daddy. Just let her get the Popsicles too!"

I replied, "Well, I'm actually trying to teach her to make choices on her own rather than living in conflict with me."

She rolled her eyes, pushing her cart away and said, "What are you, some kind of psychologist or something?"

We can't stand the way the grandparents relate to our children! What do we do?

Grandparents can be a blessing and a curse. Either way it's important to remember that the amount of impact that they actually have on a child's character development is minimal. I like to compare a grandparent's parenting footprint to what it's like to stay in a hotel. Think about it. Sometimes you stay at the St. Regis Hotel. You get big fluffy bathrobes and room service; walking through the marble lobby makes you feel like a king. But then what? You go home! Home is where you live. Home is what defines our life. Not a hotel.

On the other hand, some grandparents are like staying at the Hotel Sleaze. The squeaky beds vibrate when you put a quarter in the machine, and the guy next door brought his dog, and it's barking all night. Good news is that tomorrow, you get to go home! Whether wonderful or terrible, hotels don't define our souls. Home does. And though the grandparents may be wonderful or annoying, the core of your child's development comes from their relationship with you. So do not fear.

The other question, of course, is to what degree you feel you can push back on your own parents regarding how they relate to your children. This is where your own childhood junk might still creep into your adult life as a parent. Do some growth there and learn to relate to your parents as fellow adults, not a disappointed Mommy or Daddy.

What do you know about ADHD?

As you can tell, my specialty is the emotional/relational life of kids rather than their cognitive functioning, but I definitely have some thoughts. They may be "Weapons Grade Baloneyum," but I've come to believe they are true.

I'm intrigued at how the diagnosis of ADHD has become so overwhelmingly rampant. Rarely do I encounter a professional who tests for it who does *not* discover "ADHD" as a result of their testing. I've also seen a ton of adults who are obviously depressed or anxious, but they deny it. "I just have ADHD," they claim. It's as trendy as craft beer! Furthermore, I have seen a ton of kids with "ADHD" who actually had other things going on. Let's talk about that.

I look at it like this. Saying I have the *symptoms* of ADHD is sort of like telling you I have a runny nose. It's a symptom that could have many causes. I could have a runny nose because I have a cold. I could have a runny nose because I've been crying. I could have a runny nose because I just smelled pepper. I could have a runny nose because I have an allergy. Telling you I have a runny nose doesn't give you a lot of information.

Sure, there is a particular kind of ADHD that is directly connected to the brain's center of attention. It's like our brain has an orchestra conductor who is in charge of keeping us on task. When I start to stare out the window, he taps me on the shoulder and says, "John, come back to the book. You are writing, remember?"

With kids who have this classic form of ADHD, that orchestra conductor falls asleep. Consequently, the child can become distracted and there is no part of his brain reminding him to focus. That's why these kids are typically given a stimulant. Something to wake the conductor back up. That makes sense.

However, every problem that involves inattention is *not due* to this sleepy conductor. (There are other reasons for the "runny nose.") For instance, sometimes attention problems are really *emotional problems*. I've seen an enormous number of kids who have had attention problems because they were struggling emotionally. Perhaps they are in enough emotional turmoil that they become distracted. Haven't you gotten in a fight with your spouse, and then gone to work? Then you have trouble focusing on your job because your mind keeps turning over what "you wish you had said." The angry feelings from the fight are still rolling around in your head. Result? You are having an "ADHD" that is driven by emotional distress. Kids do this all the time. I have found that as we do some therapeutic work with these kids, and their parents learn to help address their child's emotional world more effectually, their attention can come back online. In other words, sometimes ADHD is not a brain issue but an emotional one.

Other kids have trouble with attention and hyperactivity because they have *impulse control problems*. In other words, they aren't able to control *any* of their impulses—not just the impulse to look away from their homework. These kids show marked improvement in their "ADHD" when they learn to manage their impulses at large. In other words, they don't have impulse control problems because they "have ADHD." They have "ADHD" because they have impulse control problems.

My point is that, though ADHD is a real phenomenon, I find professionals to be frequently limited in their exploration of the cause. Every child who has attention problems does not necessarily have the brain functioning issue of the sleepy conductor. A good therapist ought to help you tease out the difference.

Regardless of the cause, we can offer help to children who have difficulty staying on task. They often benefit from concrete structure, breaking their work down into steps. It helps them to have frequent breaks, and to receive short individual orders rather than long lists of tasks. Their minds struggle to break life down into manageable pieces. We can help do some of that for them. I believe that there should still be kind, loving consequences (not punishment) for their forgetfulness or distraction. Life will not give them a bye if they forget. Let's go ahead introduce them to that principle. Besides, we only learn through events, remember? Oh, and I'm cool with medication for ADHD—as long as you are also thinking about these other issues while you do it.

My teenager lives his life making stupid choices. He spends all of his allowance on the first day. He waits until the last minute to study for a test. We often find schoolwork sitting on the kitchen table after he's left the house. However, when we try to remind him or give him advice, he sneers, rolls his eyes and tells us to leave him alone. Would you like to take him home to live with you?

My answer is "No!" Next question.

Ha, ha, seriously—giving advice to teenagers is an art form. Their goal in life is to become independent and *not* to be looking to mom and dad to help them make choices. So they live in a little bit of a dilemma. Something sane in them knows that they are not equipped to deal with real life on their own yet. However, they wouldn't be caught dead looking like they actually need your opinion. What they need is a situation in which they can lean on us for help, while knowing that we won't rob them of their independence. Here are a couple of thoughts on how to help them with that.

Number one, learn to get comfortable with their making choices that create unpleasant cost for them. Let them spend all their allowance, even though you know that there is a ball game this weekend where they will need the money. Let the weekend come and let them be penniless because of their choices. As we said, the only way kids learn is through experience. So manage your own need for them to not suffer and fail from their lack of wisdom. These stupid choices now are gold! Remember, the consequences only get bigger.

However, when I *do* want to give advice to an adolescent, I always *ask* them first. This is a fun little psychological trick. You see them spending their money like Elvis during the Vegas years. Instead of just telling them "they'd better tune in!" I like to say, "I've got some thoughts about how you're managing your money. If you ever want to hear them, let me know"—and go back to reading my book. Half the time, their curiosity will get the best of them and they will mumble, "Okay, what?"

Now you've got the jump on them! Say to them, "Oh, okay. If you insist. I've just noticed that you are spending all of your money, and I was thinking that you might need some for the game this weekend. Given that I don't plan to give you more money, I just thought it might be smart for you to save some for later. But you can do what you want." (I don't have a shrimp on that Captain's Platter.) And since they've *asked* you for your sage wisdom, they can't roll their eyes and tell you to "get off their case."

Oh yes, we da best!

Mealtime is a war at our house. We have a child who is a picky eater and dinner becomes a war to try to get him to eat. Thoughts?

Short answer—don't make eating a power struggle. Many of us were raised by the generation that insisted that you "clean your plate." Pardon me, but that's just kooky. If they don't eat their dinner, don't fret, and certainly don't cook them something else, short-order-cook style; or give them their favorite foods: "Candy, candy canes, Kandy Korn, and syrup."

They need to take a "no thank you" bite of dinner, after which no one is going to require them to eat. But when they are hungry later, we set phasers to stun and kindly remind them that breakfast is just around the corner, and that ideally our family eats what Mom or Dad has put before us—at dinner time. That way we don't get hungry later. But you can do what you want. See you at the next meal.

I'm exhausted. Parenting takes everything from me. Any survival points?

Yeah, I'll tell ya that for nothin'! I was talking to a mom the other day who was thanking me for my parenting guidance. "However," she said, "even when I apply your principles, by the end of the day I'm completely exhausted. And even though I might have been a good mom all day, I end up screaming at my kids again by bedtime. (Classic parenting expert, James Dobson, called those late afternoon times, "The Arsenic Hour"—the times where you want to either *take* arsenic or *give* it!)

Children are overwhelmingly demanding creatures to raise. And, depending on their age, that gets easier or harder. The part of the question I want to speak to, however is the issue of *self-care*.

In previous generations, parents weren't as a child centered as we are now. They sent us out into the yard all day and told us to not come back 'til dinner time. We played sports because we loved them. Sometimes parents attended—usually they did not. The sport was *ours*, not some opportunity for more parental adulation and limelight. (Our current culture has stolen this from children.)

Now most parents live as if children are these empty little shells, unwanted and alone until we parents come and pour our adoration into them. And if we miss that recital, they will be consumed by how unloved they are. We've all been brainwashed to believe that our children's happiness and joy is *our* responsibility not *theirs*—that all of their well-being falls upon our shoulders. That kind of thinking is more of that "psychological legalism" we talked about in the first chapter. And it is hogwash! It has cost children and burdened parents enormously and unnecessarily. It is no wonder parents are constantly telling me how exhausted they are.

Your children need you to take care of yourself. Parenting is like a blood transfusion—one in which *you* are the one giving the blood! Therefore, part of good parenting involves remaining very conscious of the care *you* need. You are the big Exxon tanker truck, delivering gasoline to all the stations. Wouldn't it be ironic if that truck ran out of gas?

I was watching a nature show the other day. It was talking about how a mother octopus brings all of her little babies into a hole in the coral reef after they have hatched. She spends all of her time caring for them and feeding them. She never even leaves the nest to eat for herself. Finally, the baby octopi launch out to begin their new lives. And the mother octopus *dies*! She just lies there and *dies*!! Take away—*don't be a mommy octopus!*

This means that sometimes you need to prioritize *yourself*

over your *children*. (Yes, I said that. I never joke about my work, 007.) Even if "psychological legalism" starts guilt tripping you and telling you "but your kids *need* you!"—you have to matter too. So, if you are bone-tired after a killer day at work, I want you to bow out of attending that seventeenth soccer game. I promise you, your child is not going to need to process that one day in therapy.

Also prioritize your marriage! Feel free to put a lock on the door of your room—and use it. Keep a babysitter on your speed dial. Require them to pull their weight around the house. And start that early—not just for their sake, but for yours. Kids will treat you like a box of cookies, and if you don't limit how much of you they take, soon you will just be a crumpled box full of crumbs.

We used to vacation in Destin, Florida. One year I knew that we had become too consumed by our house full of diapers when someone asked Norma where we were going on vacation this year. She replied, "Oh, we're going back down to *"Desitin."*

Not only do I want to give you permission to take care of yourself, I believe it is your responsibility. Nurturing and taking care of other people is my job. And I have had to become an expert on making sure that my tank is full, even if that means disappointing some of those under my care. So let's get rid of the guilt. You are being good enough—and requiring your children to learn to deal with your own limitations is actually good parenting. Parenting is a give-and-take relationship like any other. It is not just a *give* relationship. And by all means, it is not some sort of performance that you have to excel at, or else. You are good enough.

By the way, I have a theory as to why the last two generations of parents have been so codependent on our children. Not to be critical, but the generation that parented our generations tended to parent from a somewhat shame-based model. "I can't believe that you would do such a thing." "Just wait 'til your father gets home." That is how they motivated—by saying in essence, "Don't upset Mommy and Daddy." In other words, instead of using consequences and wisdom to motivate children, they motivated us out of their own *disappointment*.

So our generation learn to obey, why? *To not upset the important people in our lives!* And what are we still trying to do? We're still trying to not upset the important people in our lives! Currently that just means our *children*. In other words, upsetting our children now creates the same feelings in us that upsetting our parents once did. We lived to please our parents. Now we live to please our children. Is there an Off switch?

Our preacher was talking the other day about how the father needs to be vigilant to step in and defend his wife when the children are being jerks. Any thoughts on that?

Ahh, the ole "Knight in Shining Armor" bit. Part of me sees the value of that kind of intervention, especially because I've seen what can happen if a father is absent from discipline. Even a very strong mom has trouble maintaining order if the dad is becoming "one of the boys." However, I've wondered about the father's role as a "defender" of the mom. I sort of want mom to be a force to be reckoned with *herself!* I want your family to be a world in which dad might say to the kids, "Let me get this straight—you are going to cross *her?* Can I watch?" A good mom can hold her own.

Let's try this variation on the knight in shining armor approach: What if we say that the best position is one in which *both parents* advocate for *each other!* Sure, I want dad stepping in if the teenage son is cussing his mom. But I also want mom to call out the children when they are jerks to their dad.

I encountered a situation a while back in which a teenage daughter would prance upstairs, saying, "Goodnight, Mom!" as her parents sat together downstairs. Once the mother realized that this was becoming a habit, she stopped her daughter halfway up, and said, "I think you have forgotten to say goodnight to your father as well." Parents who parent together like this are *better* than good enough.

This also touches on the issue of prioritizing your relationship with your spouse over your relationship with your kids. When our alien overlords seek to understand the puny conquered Earth one day, I believe what they will conclude is that "Humans seemed to procreate in order to create smaller humans, whom they then would worship."

Our child-obsessed culture has lots of downsides, but one

of the worse is that it has wreaked havoc on marriages. Just think what our marriages would be like if we cared as much about our spouse's unhappiness as we do our child's! We won't miss a school play because our kid might feel "left out." But we will blow off our spouse's needs without a second thought. And we wonder why divorce is rampant—more so during the empty nest years. You do the math.

Prioritizing the health of your marriage over your kids is not only the best thing for your marriage, it is the best thing for your children! Kids can read the vibe—they're smart. They know if they are the center of the universe, and they will exploit it. And they know if their parents' marriage is rocky, and it scares them. Get thee to a marriage counselor!

If my child needs therapy, do you have any tips for what to look for in a good therapist?

Certainly. First, look for a therapist who is going to talk to you and your child about the *heart*. Beware of interventions that just involve behavior modification. We are not empty bottles, and the fruit that we bear in our lives flows out of the root of our heart. It won't take long to determine whether a therapist cares about the heart. You will get a sense when they speak that they "get it" about your child. They will talk about your child's emotional motivation and character development—as opposed to filling your arms with notebooks, homework and boxes to check.

Also, be very guarded about your child seeing a therapist that does not meet regularly and strategically with *you the parents.* Parents are my treatment team and helping them is the background for helping a child. Early in my practice I did a good bit of play therapy with children. Later I started meeting with the parents during the last ten minutes of the session to bring them up to speed on the progress we were making. I quickly discovered that those ten minutes were having more of an effect on the child than the play therapy was!

Ultimately, I began working almost exclusively with parents—coaching and training *them* to intervene with their child. That way the child was getting 24/7 intervention from their own parents, rather than of fifty minutes of "me" once a week.

How can I learn to manage my anger at my kids? You talk about how much it can corrupt our relationship with them, but I blow my stack all the time. Help!

As I've told you, I struggled with my anger as a parent too. The parenting world is so full of helplessness, frustration and constant demand that all of us battle anger at some point. For the sake of our kids, we need to go to war against it.

I had a client once who was a big shot surgeon. He had been depressed, but was doing good work. One session he came in saying he really wanted me to help him with how much of a rageful jerk he could be with his kids. (That's half the battle right there, Cowpokes) He said he had tried and tried, but still found himself losing it with them. So we got to work.

Here's a principle for growth and change in your own life: The only way any of us can grow regarding an out of control behavior, is to receive *two things*: Number one, we need to have some understanding and healing of our *hearts*. What is driving this behavior? What is it that I am needing? Where might this part of me have been injured? Anger is the second thing we feel, remember? Work to understand what's driving yours. One of the best things that we parents can do for our children is to work through our own junk. Stop that legacy now. The line is drawn here! Do your own growth. In some ways, that's the most powerful gift you can ever give your children.

However, if that inner navel-gazing is all you do, what you'll end up with is a very nurtured and insightful rageaholic. So we need something else at the same time. And that something else is literal *limits* and *consequences* placed on our behavior when we act like a ponce. Here's why. The part of us that is out of control is like a child. And children are *concrete*. So they need *concrete learning*. Jerky parts of us only learn when they encounter a concrete cost.

Philosophizing about all the ways in which it is "damaging to my family" for me to shop too much or gamble too much or do porn, means about as much to the out of control parts of my heart as it would to tell an eight-year-old to go do his homework because "just think of all the people you will help one day as a neurosurgeon." He's like *"Whaaaaat?"*

You need to take his Xbox away! Concrete cost!

We will only get the attention of out of control parts of us by doing both *heart growth* and setting *literal experiential limits.*

So my client and I worked to understand some of the pain that was driving his anger (it was the same thing that was driving his depression, btw.) And we also created a *consequence* for him. Whenever he raged at his kids, he had to do their chores for two days. And he did it—pushing the garbage can to the street in his scrubs before he got in his Mercedes and headed to the hospital. His children were wide-eyed! And his anger began to soften. True repentance is everyone's love language.

> **Related to that last guy's question—so many of the things that you have invited us to help create for our children require our own hearts to be pretty full. I mean, teaching love and forgiveness, managing the pain and anxiety of watching our children struggle or hurt. I didn't get those things when I was growing up—how am I supposed to give those to my kids?**

Well, first let me say that if you are talking like that, you are "close to the Kingdom." What child would not want a dad like you—someone that humble and open to their own failings? Thank you. The first question God has when he meets someone is whether they are repentant or unrepentant. Do they think they are "righteous" or do they say, "have mercy on me the sinner"? Repentant people, he can work with. If you're beginning the story by asking those sorts of "humble parent" questions, I applaud you.

But our limitations also give us a chance to grow. How does that happen?

Growing and filling up the missing or injured places in our own hearts is possible—I do it for a living. God made us in such a way that we can learn and receive the kind of growth you are asking about, even as adults. That kind of growth takes place in what I call "developmental relationships." Developmental relationships are relationships in which one person is giving and the other is receiving. Parenting is obviously a developmental relationship—but it is not the only one. As Yoda says, "There is another."

One of the most wonderful developmental relationships we have as adults is the Body of Christ. The reason that there are so many "each other's" in the New Testament is because Paul is teaching us how to relate to one another in such a way that we can become more whole and Christlike, together. The Body of Christ, whether it be a safe wise friend, a pastor, a strong growth group, or a therapist—is a developmental relationship where our stifled growth can begin again. I've spent my life helping people fill up the empty places that you are asking about—and bear richer fruit. (All therapy is, is a systematic, strategic form of fellowship—a developmental relationship for adults.)

So, if you're serious about growing in the deficits you see, began finding safe people and telling them the truth about your heart. Find (and become) the kind of person who can listen to brokenness with grace and confidentiality—and respond with wisdom and truth. Then go to your growth places and say, "Guys, I'm clueless about this whole 'being emotionally connected' thing that Cox is talking about. Can you guys help me out?"

Wise friends will respond, "Yeah, you do pretty much 'live in your head,' Dude. We'll start pushing you some on that. Last week, for instance, you were talking about your kid being in the hospital, and it was like you were talking about the weather. What did that do to your *heart?* Dig in a little and let us know you!"

And as they push you, and call you out, and support you—what I see is that people grow. God uses the relational interactions between his people to help forge new strength in our hearts.

Love well and go be free.
JLC

Made in the USA
Columbia, SC
29 January 2020

87254817R10226